Pam Gems

PLAYS ONE

PIAF
CAMILLE
QUEEN CHRISTINA

OBERON BOOKS
LONDON

Piaf first published by Amber Lane Press in 1979. *Camille* first published by Penguin Books Ltd in 1985. *Queen Christina* first published by St Luke's Press in 1982.

First published in this collection in 2004 by Oberon Books Ltd
(incorporating Absolute Classics)
521 Caledonian Road, London N7 9RH
Tel: 020 7607 3637 / Fax: 020 7607 3629
e-mail: oberon.books@btinternet.com
www.oberonbooks.com

A catalogue record for this book is available from the British Library.

Cover photograph: Getty Images

ISBN: 1 84002 279 5

Printed in Great Britain by Antony Rowe Ltd, Chippenham.

Contents

PIAF

Foreword

In 1977 I was at the Almost-Free Theatre rehearsing a monologue about a girl who had a baby at a mainline station and stuffed it down the lavatory. The male director was about to resign when I was called for and asked to advise on a role for a Rumanian actress who had courageously been singing songs by Edith Piaf outside Oxford Street tube station. I suggested *The Rose Tattoo* but this was rejected in favour of my writing a piece about Piaf. I declined – if you wanted to know about Piaf you listened to the songs. However, the next day the actress and her son called on me and stayed for six months and I wrote the play. Alas, we never managed a production – the cast was large and my agent objected to the notion of a Cockney Edith, my solution to the argot.

And then, two years later, I read in the evening paper that *Piaf*, by Pam Gems, was to be produced at the Other Place by the RSC. (How they came by the script was never discovered.) Howard Davies came to see me and, after discovering that I was not Pam Gems' mother, said he would be directing. With Jane Lapotaire. But could Jane sing? On TV I heard her sing a lament for a dead son in a heart-breaking chest voice. So that was all right.

Nonetheless, *Piaf*, with its filthy language, seemed, to put it mildly, a chancy choice for the RSC. The first night audience was full of loyal club members, many ageing. Surely they would walk? At the interval a white-haired woman said, 'We must see this again,' and I was ashamed, remembering what these old birds were up to in the last war risking their lives, and having exciting times. We were a success and took the play to London and to New York, where Jane won a Tony. The play has been in production worldwide ever since.

What is it about Edith Piaf? You don't hear Vera Lynn or Gracie Fields when you switch on the radio nowadays. In France you hear Piaf – on radio, in cafés everywhere, those inimitable sonorous tones celebrating and keeping alive the French *chanson*. But it's more than that. In the world of popular ballad there are three giants and they are all female – Bessie

Smith, Billie Holiday and Edith Piaf. All supremely talented. And all authentic – what they sing you believe. You *believe* Edith. How else could a small, dumpy woman, looking like a concierge in a plain black dress, become the highest paid female singer in the world? Yes, she was musical – not always the case with singers – and she was an obsessive technician. But she was also a woman who never became inflated, never forgot her roots. A street singer from childhood, her attitude to materialism was always tangential. For her, singing was everything. It was her ecstasy. When she sang, she sang from herself, often as composer and lyricist. She sang about life. And she sang about love. Physical love. She sang of sexuality and, when love failed, of betrayal, rejection, of being deserted, of being alone, and you believed her. She lived her life in public and we, her public, shared her joys and miseries. She held nothing back. She had been there, she told us about it and we knew it was true. The accuracy and reality of her work is unique in a world characterised by the banal, by the contemptuously commercial. Miraculously, in a sentimental genre, Piaf found emotional truth. This was her genius.

Two anecdotes. We were worried about America. The mores are different: should we depilate the language? We decided to risk it. Out of town in Philadelphia I climbed up to the gods to listen for sound and found the usherettes, all middle-aged and elderly ladies in black dresses watching Jane, in *her* black dress, a tiny midget on stage way below. I mentioned it to the house manager. 'Yes,' he said, 'I never knew the girls do this before; usually they make for the rest room, pronto.'

On the other hand we were picketed on Broadway by The Friends of Edith Piaf for putting foul language into the mouth of their revered star and desecrating her memory. Little did they know how much we'd kept under wraps!

Edith was never tamed, and there is a wonderful triumph in that. There are those who feel that excess shortened her life. What is amazing is that, with her medical history from childhood, she lived so long. Her métier extended her life.

There will never be another Edith Piaf. In the world of the chanson she is unique and always will be.

Pam Gems

Characters

PIAF

MANAGER

LEPLEE

TOINE

PIANIST

EMIL

LEGIONNAIRE

JACQUES

EDDIE

LOUIS

INSPECTOR

AGENT

PAUL

TWO GERMAN SOLDIERS

GEORGES

BUTCHER

PIERRE

AMERICAN OFFICER

CHARLES

MARCEL

MARLENE

TWO AMERICAN SAILORS

BARMAN

LUCIEN

MADELEINE

WAITER

JEAN

NURSE

ANGELO

VOICE ON P/A

PHYSIOTHERAPIST

JACKO

DOPE PUSHER

YOUNG NURSE

THEO

Piaf was first produced at The Other Place, Stratford-upon-Avon on 5 October 1978, with the following cast:

PIAF, Jane Lapotaire

TOINE, Zoë Wanamaker

MADELEINE, Carmen du Sautoy

MARLENE, Darlene Johnson

NURSE, Susanna Bishop

INSPECTOR / GEORGES / BARMAN,
Conrad Asquith

LOUIS / BUTCHER / LUCIEN / DOPE PUSHER,
Bill Buffery

MAN AT REHEARSAL / PIERRE, Ian Charleson

MANAGER, Geoffrey Freshwater

LEPLEE / JEAN, James Griffiths

EMIL / JACKO / EDDIE, Allan Hendrick

GERMAN SOLDIER / ANGELO, Anthony Higgins

PAUL / AMERICAN SAILOR /
PHYSIOTHERAPIST, Ian Reddington

LEGIONNAIRE / JACQUES / GERMAN SOLDIER /
MARCEL / AMERICAN SAILOR / THEO,
Malcolm Storry

Director, Howard Davies

Designer, Douglas Heap

Music Director / Piano, Michael Tubbs

Accordion, Roy Stelling

ACT ONE

Scene 1

A bare stage. A middle-aged man in evening dress enters.

MANAGER: Ladies and gentlemen...I give you...your own ...Piaf!

(*He gestures to the wings and exits.*
Musical intro: 'La goualante du pauvre Jean'.
After a perceptible pause, PIAF appears. She comes to the microphone and announces the name of the song, and the names of the lyricist and music writer. She begins to sing but founders after the first few bars and sways at the audience, her stare unfocused. The music dies away and after a slight pause the MANAGER enters and tries to get her off. She resists, holding onto the microphone.)

PIAF: Get your fucking hands off me, I ain't *done* nothing yet.

(*Eventually the MANAGER manhandles her off. She does not go easily.*)

Scene 2

Outside the Cluny Club. The young PIAF appears, hunched with cold. She puts down a cloth, chucks a couple of coins onto it and starts to sing 'Les mômes de la cloche', moving slightly as though approaching people for money.

LOUIS LEPLEE, the owner of the club appears. He is middle-aged, with a long, smart overcoat, hat, silk scarf, gloves and cane, his hair well brilliantined. He makes to enter the club behind PIAF but pauses to listen. He lights up, tapping on a cigarette case thoughtfully, watching PIAF with a shrewd glance. PIAF sees LEPLEE and tries to dodge off but he grabs her with unexpected swiftness and expertise – obviously a man who knows his way around, despite the elegant clothes.

PIAF: (*Shrilly, unlike the growl of her first utterance.*) Get your fucking hands off me, I ain't done nothing.
(*LEPLEE grins. This arrests PIAF and she looks up at him cheekily. She watches avidly as he takes out his wallet and selects some notes. The sight of them galvanises her and she thrusts out a ready hand but he gestures his head into the club and goes inside. PIAF follows him, eager for the money.*)

Scene 3

PIAF bursts into her scruffy room. There is a sagging bed, not much else. TOINETTE, her mate, is sitting on the side of the bed, massaging her feet.

PIAF: (*Exultantly.*) Hey Toine, guess what!
TOINE: Fuck off.
PIAF: (*Injured.*) Wassa matter?
TOINE: Fucking pimp's had me on that corner, I thought my bleeding toes would burst. I haven't seen more than a couple of fellers all night. He's got to change my shift.
PIAF: Here…listen… (*Apologetically, her excitement evaporating before TOINE's cheerlessness.*) I've got me big chance, love.
TOINE: Bloody pimp with his favourites –
PIAF: You know, like on the pictures.
TOINE: – that fat Helene, does what she likes…in the fucking café half the time. I'm not standing for it.
(*PIAF tries again.*)
PIAF: This bloke…real toff…comes up to me – hey! Remember when we was doing the wheel of fortune last week and mine said –
TOINE: What!
PIAF: *You* remember! I was outside the Cluny Club… singing…
TOINE: Oh Christ. What?
PIAF: Singing! We-ell – look if you don't believe me –
(*She flashes the money. TOINE responds like a bloodhound on scent.*)
TOINE: How much?

PIAF: (*Flipping the notes tantalisingly at TOINE.*) I'm singin' away, all of a sudden, there he is! Real big bug – silver cane, silk scarf, the lot! 'Come in the Club,' he says, 'Take the weight off your feet.'

TOINE: Iyiy.

PIAF: Next thing I know, I'm sat on a gold chair, he's fetching me a drink.

TOINE: I get it. Another fucking funny. He must have been hard up – here, can you see any crabs?

PIAF: No, listen! He says to me, he says, 'You've got a really good voice' – don't laugh – (*She laughs herself at this idea.*) 'Get on,' I say. 'No,' he says, 'You've really got something, kid.'

TOINE: (*In disbelief.*) Huh!

PIAF: 'I want you… (*She fixes TOINE with a compelling stare.*) I want you…to star in my Club!' (*Slight pause. She has awed herself.*) What do you think of that?

TOINE: Christ, she's away.

PIAF: Naow, I mean it! He looks at me with these deep-set eyes – he ain't young or anything but he's ever so good-looking…hey, you should of seen the furniture – blue velvet chairs, little gold lights everywhere – hey, are you listening?

TOINE: Look, Ede, what the fuck are you talking about? Have you gone off your head or something?

PIAF: (*Enraged.*) I keep trying to *tell* you! He wants me to sing in his *show*!

(*TOINE considers this. She frowns and chews her lip in thought. This takes time. At last she shakes her head slowly. There is something wrong with the deal.*)

TOINE: Nah. Nah, sounds funny to me. I wouldn't have nothing to do wiv it, kid. Look, he's got a little business going, he's short of goods – hah, must be!

PIAF: Speak for your bloody self.

(*TOINE rises, threateningly. PIAF backs off prudently.*)

We-ell.

(*TOINE ignores her, picks up a comic and starts to read.*)

Hey, what am I going to wear?

(*No response. PIAF approaches TOINE'S working dress, now on the floor. She puts out a tentative hand.*)

TOINE: (*Without taking her eyes from the page.*) It's too big for yuh. (*She turns a page.*)

(*PIAF is at a loss. She mooches, her enthusiasm waning.*)

PIAF: I know!

(*TOINE looks up.*) What about that dress you was knitting – to visit your Mum in?

TOINE: (*She is thick.*) Which one was that?

PIAF: You know – *you* know…for her funeral.

TOINE: (*Going back to her comic.*) Never finished it.

(*PIAF sighs, defeated. She scuffs around, dejected. TOINE puts down the comic with a martyred air.*)

All right. Here you are. (*She offers PIAF her mauve shiny rayon scarf.*)

PIAF: (*Overwhelmed.*) Thanks! (*She puts it on, then laughs, reminded.*) Hey, he told me to have a bath, wash me hair!

TOINE: Christ! (*They both laugh at this.*)

Hang on.

(*TOINE searches in her bag and finds an old comb. PIAF at once sits on the floor before TOINE to have her hair done – an apparently loved and familiar ritual to judge by the response. TOINE mucks about with PIAF's hair, then turns her round and spits, making a spitcurl for her forehead. She murmurs, absorbed in her art.*)

There, that's better. Well, you wanna look decent.

PIAF: Thanks! (*She jumps up, then dawdles irritatingly near TOINE.*)

TOINE: What is it now? (*She is tired.*)

PIAF: Could I…could I lend your handbag?

(*TOINE glares up at her. This is unacceptable cheek. However, to get PIAF off her back, she nods, grimacing viciously. PIAF grabs the large, black, sateen poche and shoves it under her arm proudly. It is much too big for her.*)

Right, I'm off then. Thanks ever so much. (*She preens, trying the handbag.*) Hey, I'm late! (*She dashes off without ceremony.*)

TOINE: (*Calling after her.*) Take it easy, squirt. Well, can't be for the fucking singing, can it? He can hear that for nothing in the street. She'll end up in Tangier, silly bugger.

Scene 4

The Cluny Club. Chairs on tables – the Club is closed. PAPA LEPLEE strolls, waiting. A PIANIST strums 'Les mômes de la cloche'. LEPLEE looks at his watch. The PIANIST pulls a face. PIAF is late. She rushes on.

PIAF: Sorry!

LEPLEE: All right, all right…

(*He nods. PIAF begins to sing 'Les mômes de la cloche'. Responding to her surroundings, she tries a more up-market style, with delicate gestures. LEPLEE looks puzzled, then grins. He waves an arm and stops her in mid-phrase.*)

LEPLEE: No, no…no, no, no.

PIAF: What?

LEPLEE: Not like that –

PIAF: (*Humbly.*) Sorry. Only I haven't done much –

LEPLEE: No, you don't understand. I want you to sing it in your own way…like you did on the street. I want it rougher – it's a rough song, Edith.

PIAF: Oh. (*She belts into it.*)

LEPLEE: (*To the PIANIST.*) Edith! We'll have to do better than that.

PIAF: What?

(*She hums away at the song. The PIANIST strums with one hand, giving her the melody. They repeat a phrase, and again, and again.*)

LEPLEE: Eeedith… (*He shakes his head.*)

PIANIST: (*Banging down a note repetitively for PIAF.*) What about the one you said yesterday?

LEPLEE: Ye-es. Tich…Nipper…what was it…the little Nipper?

PIANIST: Tich Sparrow. (*He concentrates on the song. PIAF sings. She has perched herself up on the piano and sprawls, watching his hands on the keys. At the sound of 'Tich Sparrow' she pulls a face in horror.*)

LEPLEE: What do you think?

(*The PIANIST breaks off and thinks for a moment.*)

PIANIST: S'all right. No good going for anything glamorous.

PIAF: Whaddya mean?

(*The PIANIST tinkles. LEPLEE muses.*)

LEPLEE: The Little Sparrow...la Môme Piaf...the Kid Sparrow...Piaf...

(*PIAF mimes being sick all over the keys.*)

PIANIST: (*Testing it out.*) Piaf...Piaf...

PIAF: Piaf? What sort of name's that?

LEPLEE: Well, it's a damn sight better than Edith Gassion.

(*Insulted, PIAF grabs her bag, leaps off the piano and makes to go.*)

LEPLEE: Nothing wrong with it, it's just not a stage name, kid.

PIAF: Oh. Oh well...what about Huguette del Sol?

PIANIST: Piaf...yeah, that's OK.

LEPLEE: Not bad. Not bad at all.

PIAF: I know – Zozine Heliotrope!

LEPLEE: Piaf. Piaf...Piaf...Piaf...Piaf? (*With increasing conviction.*) Piaf! Piaf!

PIAF: (*Getting desperate.*) No, look! Hey...hey, I know! Desiree de la Renta! Desiree!

LEPLEE: (*Slapping himself, making the decision.*) Piaf!

PIAF: Piaf? Piaf? I'm not calling meself Piaf! Where'm I going to get with a name like that?

(*PIAF sings 'Les mômes de la cloche'. At the end of the song she stands, blinking uncertainly in the lights. LEPLEE smiles invitingly, and gestures her to a table set for dinner, with EMIL, the waiter, in attendance. PIAF crosses and sits, awed by her surroundings. The others smile at this and, while they are distracted, quick as a flash, PIAF slips the contents of the bread basket into her bag. Then, uncertain, she picks up the finger bowl and sips delicately. EMIL guffaws.*)

PIAF: (*Lifting her head ominously.*) What's the matter?

EMIL: That's the finger bowl, scruff. For washing your 'ands.

(*PIAF rises, evading LEPLEE's restraining arm. EMIL ducks out of the way, grinning malignantly to see the new favourite make a fool of herself.*)

PIAF: All right, clever cock. You seen me drink – now you can watch me piss. (*And she does so, and stamps off huffily as LEPLEE laughs uproariously.*)

(*Light change. LEPLEE, alone, is locking up. He places a last chair on the table. He notices PIAF at a distance. He jumps slightly.*)

LEPLEE: Oh, it's you! I thought you'd pushed off. What do you want?

PIAF: I thought you'd want to see me.

LEPLEE: What for? Come on, I'm tired, I've had a long day.

PIAF: Up to you, innit?

LEPLEE: What do you mean?

PIAF: I thought you might want – you know...well, you give me my big break...I mean, it's OK by me.

LEPLEE: What?

PIAF: Well, you must have done it for something. If you want sucking off or anything, just say the word. No skin off my nose.

LEPLEE: (*Dryly.*) Oh, I see.

(*He laughs a little. EMIL now appears. LEPLEE puts out his arm for his things. EMIL robes him reverently – the hat, scarf, coat, cane and gloves. LEPLEE puts his arm on the boy's shoulder. EMIL smiles malevolently at PIAF.*)

LEPLEE: As you see, little fish.

PIAF: Oh. Oh! Why din't you *say*! (*She gives LEPLEE an affectionate and familiar dig in the ribs.*)

LEPLEE: (*To EMIL, over her head.*) What do you think, baby?

EMIL: Well, they seemed to like her. At least you can hear her over the cutlery!

Scene 5

The street. Music of 'Un sale petit brouillard'. PIAF, up against a wall, is getting it from a SOLDIER.

SOLDIER: And sun and sand and sea and sand and sand and sand and sea and sea and... (*PIAF is noisy with it.*) Flies, flies, flies, flies, flies!
(*TOINE enters.*)

TOINE: Ede! Ede, is that you? We can hear you half way down the street...hey, you're supposed to be down the Club, Papa's screaming blue murder!

PIAF: Oh Christ. Hey, cop on to this, will you Toine? (*She divests herself of the soldier.*)

TOINE: What, for nothing?

PIAF: Do us a favour. I'm pegged out.

TOINE: Oh, all right. (*She takes over.*)

PIAF: (*Going.*) He's a legionnaire.

TOINE: Oh...why didn't you say? (*She livens it up a bit.*) What's he on about?

PIAF: He's a fucking Algerian!
(*PIAF goes.*)

TOINE: (*Calling after her.*) You ain't half late...hang on, hang on... (*To the SOLDIER.*) holdee on a bittee, matey...here, you wouldn't like to lie down, would you...only I got bad feet, see?
(*Blackout. Music of 'Un sale petit brouillard', up, then down.*)

Scene 6

The Cluny Club. PAPA LEPLEE sits, smoking, with a glass of something for his stomach. He looks at his watch. PIAF rushes on and embraces him, kissing him noisily.

LEPLEE: You're late. Now steady on, my head's not too good.

PIAF: You know your trouble – too much of the other.
(*LEPLEE laughs, then leans back, assessing her shrewdly through the smoke of his cigarette.*)

LEPLEE: You're a familiar little devil. You'll have to settle down a bit if you want to make anything of yourself. You won't always have me, you know.

PIAF: (*Cheekily.*) Why, where you going?

LEPLEE: Well, I shan't last forever.

PIAF: Get on.

LEPLEE: Funny thing, I had a nightmare last night. Never happened to me before. D'you know, I saw my old mother clear as daylight. 'Oh, it won't be long now, son,' she said. (*He draws thoughtfully on his cigarette.*) Gave me a turn, I can tell you. We were very close, mother and me.

PIAF: Lucky you. Mine took one look, she was off.

LEPLEE: All on your own, are you?

PIAF: Yeah. (*As a casual afterthought.*) I did have a little girl once.

LEPLEE: (*Surprised.*) You?

PIAF: Cunts. They only never told me, the people looking after her. Somebody said – 'Hey, d'you know your kid's ill?' I was straight round there. 'Oh no, you can't come in, it's not convenient, anyway she's dead, died six o'clock this morning.' I wasn't having that. (*She laughs, reminiscent.*) Real old punch-up. She was sliding all over the parquet in the end – hey, did you know people go stiff when they're dead? We had a real old fracas, I can tell you.

(*LEPLEE gets up abruptly and walks away.*)

What's the matter? I only wanted a bit of her hair, it's not unreasonable.

(*Music of 'Un sale petit brouillard, up, then down.*
PIAF turns to her three friends, who enter and sit down – JACQUES and EDDIE, who look tough and are immediately deep in talk, and LOUIS, who greets PIAF. PIAF throws her arm about JACQUES. He throws her off, irritably.)

JACQUES: You said you'd get him over when you'd done singing.

PIAF: Sure, sure.

JACQUES: (*Twisting her arm.*) Well, get him over!

PIAF: Ow! Hey, Papa, come and have a drink.

(*LEPLEE approaches, genially.*)

Jacques…Eddie…and little Louis.

(*JACQUES gives her a dig.*)

Hey, what do you think of little Louis? Look at his eyelashes…cor!

LEPLEE: Some other time perhaps. Emil will give you a drink.

JACQUES: Got to count the takings, eh, Papa?

LEPLEE: (*Jovially.*) Never you mind about that.

EDDIE: Go on, you must be rolling in it.

LEPLEE: That's what they all think.

(*He takes another glimpse at LOUIS. LOUIS smiles. LEPLEE dallies. The others begin to move away discreetly but PIAF blows it.*)

PIAF: (*Wrecking the moment in a seeming spasm of panic.*) Hey…hey, d'you hear the story about the man with cock trouble?

(*They turn on her murderously. But LEPLEE sits, pouring himself a last noggin.*)

JACQUES: (*To PIAF.*) Shut up.

PIAF: (*Unable to stop.*) He goes to the chemist and says, 'Look, there's something wrong with my cock.' No listen…and the chemist says, 'For fuck's sake, man, can't you see I got a shop full of ladies, you'll do me out of business.' Ah…what was it? 'Take these three times a day and if you have to come back, for Christ's sake call it your elbow.' So he comes back the next week and the chemist says, 'Tablets any good? How's your elbow?' And he says, 'Oh, much better…but I still can't pee out of it!'

(*PIAF shrieks with laughter. LEPLEE laughs heartily and get up to go. LOUIS half rises but LEPLEE puts a restraining hand on his shoulder. The moment has been lost. LEPLEE goes.*

Music of 'Un sale petit brouillard'.)

JACQUES: (*Twisting PIAF's arm.*) You pissed it up, didn't you!

PIAF: No I never.

JACQUES: What's your fucking game? (*He wrenches her bag off her, turns it out and takes the money and the lighter.*) Ten bloody francs. All right, where'd you say he kept it?

PIAF: What?

JACQUES: His money, you twat, the cash box!

(*EDDIE shakes his head at JACQUES, pulls him off PIAF and gets close to her.*)

EDDIE: Look, Piaf…hey, look (*Feeling her up.*) why don't me and you get together…

PIAF: Yeah…

EDDIE: Great…great. Yeah, but what about little Louis?

JACQUES: Where's the safe, you bitch?

EDDIE: Poor little Louis's got no billet. I know! Where's Papa's room? Little Louis could go up there and proposition him. You never know, might work out for them. Then you and me can enjoy ourselves.

PIAF: (*Stupefied.*) Yeah.

(*The music starts to get very loud.*)

JACQUES: Does he keep it in his room?

(*The music is very loud. The lights are low. The boys slip away. PIAF, white-faced and tense, drinks and collapses over the table. There is the sound of a shot, loud and frightening. Music of 'La ville inconnue.' PIAF sings.*)

Scene 7

PIAF is alone. A POLICE INSPECTOR enters and gestures her to a seat.

INSPECTOR: Come and sit down.

(*PIAF crosses.*)

Let me see…ah…Edith.

(*He gives her a dazzling fatherly smile and uncaps his pen and writes for a perceptible moment. PIAF fidgets.*)

(*Without looking up.*) Name?

PIAF: You've got it written down there.

INSPECTOR: (*Glares, then remembers to be foxy.*) That's right. Edith…Gassion. Known as… La Môme Piaf.

PIAF: What am I supposed to have done? I haven't done nothing, what am I supposed to have done wrong?
INSPECTOR: Address?
PIAF: Haven't got one.
INSPECTOR: (*Writing.*) No fixed address.
PIAF: It's not fair, I haven't done nothing.
INSPECTOR: Let us proceed with your involvement –
PIAF: Eh?
INSPECTOR: (*With a sudden frontal bark.*) What was your involvement in the Leplee affair?
PIAF: What?
INSPECTOR: Name?
PIAF: Oh Christ!
INSPECTOR: I advise you to cooperate.
PIAF: I ain't done nothing!
INSPECTOR: That is what we are here to find out. (*Pause.*) Father's occupation?
PIAF: Street acrobat. (*And as an afterthought.*) And businessman.
INSPECTOR: What was your relationship with the deceased?
PIAF: Who?
INSPECTOR: With Louis Leplee?
PIAF: Oh, no relation. He was a big shot.
INSPECTOR: You were with Leplee the night he was murdered.
PIAF: And all the others.
INSPECTOR: Including friends of yours.
PIAF: People I know, yes.
INSPECTOR: (*Showing her a paper.*) These names. You were seen together.
PIAF: Just having a laugh.
INSPECTOR: Planning to rob your patron, Louis Leplee.
PIAF: No!
INSPECTOR: You told them where he kept his money.
PIAF: No.
INSPECTOR: Where did he keep his money?
PIAF: In his room.

INSPECTOR: You told them!

PIAF: They *asked* me! (*And could bite her tongue out.*)

INSPECTOR: Edith Gassion, I ask you formally, what was your implication in the Leplee affair? (*He stands over her, slapping his leg lightly with his right hand.*)

PIAF: (*With an eye on his right hand.*) I never had nothing to do with it...leave me alone!

(*The INSPECTOR slaps her in the face.*)

He was the guvnor, he give me my big chance...

(*He hits her again. She doesn't break.*)

...I'm not going to do him in, am I?

(*He hits her again. She sobs noisily.*)

I keep seeing him with his brains all over his chops! (*She sobs, then, with an effort, pulls herself together. She glares up at him defiantly.*)

I never had nothing to do with it.

(*The INSPECTOR goes. PIAF sticks out her feet and hums, as if whiling away time in a cell. She sings to herself. It cheers her up.*)

Ah, what a shame. What a shame, I was doing so well.

(*TOINE bursts in.*)

TOINE: Hey, Ede, you're famous.

(*She is carrying newspapers and reading them feverishly. She is followed by an AGENT.*)

PIAF: What the fuck's going on?

AGENT: Piaf, you'll be doing a guest appearance tonight at the Pickup Club. Give her the piece to read over...can she read? Your life with Papa, *ménage à trois*, that sort of thing...geddit?

PIAF: What's it all about?

TOINE: Ede, it's the big time!

AGENT: You're famous, girl!

TOINE: (*Cheerfully.*) Yeah, they think you done him in!

AGENT: (*Quickly.*) But they can't prove it, you're in the clear. Sign this.

PIAF: What?

TOINE: Go on, Ede!

PIAF: What the fuck's he talking about? Push off.

(*The AGENT hits her in the face, the same as the INSPECTOR.*)

AGENT: Now listen squirt. *You* – are money. And while you're money you'll do as I say. Here's five hundred. Get yourself toffed up. I want you soignée, sophisticated and elegant. Oh, and get rid of that. (*He points at TOINE.*)

TOINE: What do you mean? I'm her partner – any way, where's that fifty you promised me? (*He goes.*)
How much?
(*PIAF and TOINE both look down at the money, flabbergasted. PIAF counts it and has to start again, she is so unnerved. She holds a note up to the light to see if it is genuine.*)

PIAF: (*Awed.*) Hey…hey! (*They look at each other in wonder.*) Hey! (*She suddenly smacks herself in the face with the money and lets it fall into the air.*)

TOINE: What you doing? (*She falls on the money, grabbing at it in a frenzy before someone comes.*)
What you want to do that for?

PIAF: OK, come on, let's push off before he sobers up –

TOINE: No look…!

PIAF: You nuts? He's gonna be back here, bloody cops on his –

TOINE: Neow! He's working for *you.* Didn't you get it? He's your *agent*! Well, he says he is.

PIAF: What for?

TOINE: He's gonna get you bookings. Once he knows you can't sing…but while it lasts!

PIAF: (*Warming.*) Yeah!

TOINE: We could *buy* things.

PIAF: Yeah…new clothes…

TOINE: We could put down for a room…with a bath…

PIAF: Steady on.

TOINE: No, honest, he…

PIAF: He's probably gone daft, pinched out the till. He'll be in the wagon by now.

TOINE: No, they all knew him! He bought me a brandy!

PIAF: For nothing?

TOINE: I said I knew you.

PIAF: Yeah? Right. OK, then…right… (*She splits the money and gives half to TOINE.*)

TOINE: Thanks!

PIAF: We gotta think this out. (*Fast.*) I'm gonna get one of those little black skirts with the diamond panel down the front. Yeah. Nice little blouse…couple of blouses…

TOINE: What about shoes?

PIAF: Yeah! Three inch courts…snakeskin!

TOINE: Christ!

PIAF: We'll have to entertain, you know…got to do it properly. Ashtrays…a proper cigarette box – I know – cocktail snacks!

TOINE: Where'd you get those?

PIAF: Christ knows, buy 'em, I suppose. Fresh flowers…soap…proper toilet roll…Christ, we're really into…

TOINE: Can I come?

PIAF: What d'you mean? Sure!

TOINE: Only I didn't know if you'd want me –

PIAF: You found him, mate! We're in this together! (*For a moment they glow with mutual regard.*)

TOINE: What about gloves?

PIAF: Gloves?

TOINE: Yeah, what about gloves? You must have gloves!

PIAF: Gloves! What you want gloves for?

TOINE: (*Hard and bright with excitement, as always, a beat behind.*) Dunno!

PIAF: Waste of money, innit…don't tell me you want to start using gloves…oh, I get it…you're getting classy ideas…it'll be fancy fun and games…

TOINE: All I need's the gear…

PIAF: Yeah, you could – hang on, hang on – you're working for me now.

TOINE: Yeah!

PIAF: Fuck the gloves!

TOINE: Yeah!

PIAF: We'll have proper furniture, three-piece suite, fridge, telephone…

TOINE: Telephone…

PIAF: Some bar stools…

TOINE: Bar stools…

PIAF: With squashy seats…

TOINE: Made out of elephants' testicles…

PIAF: Eh?

TOINE: Well, it's what I heard.

PIAF: Oh, well, if it's the fashion. Christ, kid, have you realised, we can have all the fellers we want – the ones *we want*!

TOINE: (*Not at all turned on.*) So what?

PIAF: There's that little guy down the garage.

TOINE: Which one?

PIAF: The little one – you know, with the walk. Always keeps hisself clean. I'll get him a lovely blue suit, cuff-links, camel coat…you could find him a couple of girls so's he could make a living, feel independent…

TOINE: Yeah… (*She ponders, frowning with thought.*) There is Big Louie.

PIAF: (*Waggishly; this hasn't come up before.*) Oh… is there? (*TOINE looks foolish.*)
I *thought* you were holding out on me. Big Louie! (*She starts to laugh.*) Oh Christ!

TOINE: (*Getting nasty.*) What's wrong with him?

PIAF: Nothing, only his two asses.

TOINE: Shuddup.

PIAF: And both his feet pointing the same way. We're going to look a right foursome, me with the squirt from the garage, all neck and knees, and you with King Kong, they'll see us coming. We could have a party! Eow! (*She throws her share of the money in the air.*)

TOINE: Ee-dith!
(*She scrabbles, picking up the money feverishly while PIAF prances about humming and singing 'Tu me fais tourner la tête'.*)
I suppose if we had a room we could invite them round. We could have 'em round for a meal.
(*But PIAF isn't listening. PAUL has entered. He is handsome and well-dressed. He crosses, kisses PIAF's hand and presents his card with impeccable style.*)

TOINE: (*Kneeling up and swaying from the bending and the excitement.*) Ooh, I do feel funny.

PIAF: (*Murmuring.*) Shut up.

(*She has fallen in love. She gazes up into PAUL's eyes, dazzled. With confident sexiness he strokes one finger down her face, kisses her hand again – on the palm this time – bows, and walks off.*)

PAUL: (*Turning back.*) The Restaurant Lamartine…ten o'clock. I shall be waiting with impatience.

(*PIAF steps towards PAUL as he takes the carnation out of his buttonhole and tosses it at her. Instinctively she ducks. He goes and she bends and gropes for the flower, smelling it soppily.*)

PIAF: Ooh! Oooh! Ah! Hey, Toine, Toine where are you?

(*She sings a few bars of 'Tu me fais tourner la tête', turning to the rhythms.*)

TOINE: Christ, my stomach feels like a box of budgies.

(*She staggers off.*)

PIAF: Where you going?

TOINE: (*Groaning.*) Oh Ede! (*She lurches off and urges, having a crap through PIAF's transports.*)

PIAF: He's tall, good-looking – ever so good-looking – hey, where the hell are you?

TOINE: Oh, for Chrissakes, Ede.

PIAF: Wait till you see him, I've never *seen* such blue eyes, they're like…they're like – irises…! God, whatever must he have thought of this place, look at it! You're supposed to be the bloody hostess…

TOINE: Edith –

PIAF: I *gave* you the money for the shaker…what *is* it?

TOINE: (*Humbly.*) Can't find any paper.

PIAF: No, well, there you are…(*She looks about her, irritably, then picks up a newspaper.*) Use *this.*

TOINE: Thanks, Ede.

PIAF: You're gonna have to pull your fucking socks up, mate…fine bloody hostess, all you do is let down the whole feel of it –

TOINE: Sorry, Ede.

PIAF: No, well.

(*PIAF picks up a wandering microphone and breaks into a reprise of 'Si tu partais', the music coming in behind her softly. She directs the song at PAUL, who is sitting at a club table.*)

Scene 8

A classy club. PIAF, after singing her song, crosses to PAUL, visibly awed by her surroundings. Nonetheless, she slips her hand in his crotch. With a quick glance to see if they are observed, he removes it firmly.

PIAF: What's the matter?

PAUL: Nothing. (*Slight pause.*) You know how I hate to be touched.

PIAF: (*After a short, sullen silence.*) Well, what about it? Was I OK?

PAUL: I thought you were over the top a bit.

PIAF: Never!

PAUL: Your private life is your private life, Piaf. Don't mix it.

PIAF: Bollocks...! They love me singing to you – everybody knows! (*She manages to grasp his hand and kisses it before he withdraws it.*) Oh, I used to think of you every single night when I was away on tour, love. All I needed to see meself off was to think of you in that blue dressing-gown.

PAUL: Piaf, your voice.

PIAF: Oh Christ, nothing's right. I wish I was back with Toine and the boys.

PAUL: You don't have to stay in the gutter just because you were born there.

PIAF: I don't know about that. Well, I feel out of place! I'm doing like what you said.
(*Absently, she hawks and spits on the floor. PAUL is horrified.*)
You know, trying to be a lady, what's the matter? Oh...
(*She realises what she has done and shrinks down into her seat. Silence.*) Sorry, love.

PAUL: After all… (*He takes his time, sipping his drink fastidiously.*) After all, they don't want rubbish at the ABC.

(*PIAF's face is transformed. She jumps up and hugs him, knocking over the flowers and the glasses.*)

PIAF: (*Screaming.*) The ABC? The ABC! You rogue…you devil! He never said! He's bloody gone and done it and you never said! Is it true? Have I got it, the ABC? No, I don't believe it!

(*But he leads her to the microphone. She stands for a second, taking deep breaths. Then, announcing the names of the lyricist and music writer, she sings 'L'accordéoniste', ending the song with the spoken words:.*)

Arrêtez…stop the music!

(*The MANAGER enters and takes the microphone.*)

MANAGER: Ladies and gentlemen…countrymen… countrywomen…I have to tell you…it is war…*war*!

(*He breaks momentarily into a large, white handkerchief. PIAF, excited, grabs the microphone.*)

PIAF: Bloody Boche – give 'em the old Maginot Line! Not a good prick among 'em and I should know! (*She laughs raucously.*)

MANAGER: Piaf – Piaf, please…ladies and gentlemen, in this solemn moment in the history of our –

PIAF: (*Crowding the mike.*) They do it all by numbers, you know!

MANAGER: Let go of the mike – Piaf! The National Anthem, ladies and gentlemen, if you please.

PIAF: (*Singing to the tune of King Farouk.*) 'Make them squit, make them puke, hang their bollocks on a hook…'

MANAGER: (*To PIAF, losing his cool.*) Look, will you shut your fucking mouth, I've got the fucking King of Rumania over there!

(*Blackout.*)

Scene 9

PIAF's apartment. Sumptuous whorehouse furniture. TOINE enters, wearing the style of the forties – huge hat, sling bag, square-shouldered suit and platform shoes. PIAF, likewise dressed, follows her on.

TOINE: No, he said he couldn't get it up on account of me not having fat thighs.

PIAF: No shit? (*She puts out a bottle of whisky and two glasses.*)

TOINE: He said if I had fat thighs he could come whenever he wanted but seeing as how I hadn't, he couldn't.

PIAF: Give him the push!

TOINE: Yeah. It's funny, I like him, I don't usually like men with big conks and hairy arms…funny, innit?

PIAF: Face up to it…you two ain't meant for each other.

TOINE: Hey, that's real whisky, where'd you get it? What you doing all this for, is it somebody's birthday upstairs?

PIAF: Look, it's got nothing to do with Madame and the girls, so keep your trap shut and no messing about.

(*A knock. Two GERMANS enter and click their heels. TOINE flips.*)

Help yourselves… (*She gestures the whisky.*) Make yourselves comfortable.

(*Delighted, the GERMANS help themselves to the whisky.*)

This is me mate, Antoinette.

TOINE: (*Crossly.*) I wondered what you wanted me for.

(*The GERMANS are pleased with the real whisky and toast PIAF.*)

FIRST GERMAN: Mademozzelle Piaf…you are…gut singer!

SECOND GERMAN: Huzzah! (*He makes PIAF and TOINE jump.*)

FIRST GERMAN: I was seeing you in Amsterdam in '37!

PIAF: (*Politely.*) No shit?

FIRST GERMAN: You are first with me. My friend also likes very much your songs.

(*The SECOND GERMAN, hampered by having no French, murders a few bars of a PIAF song. The GIRLS grimace puzzlement. The SECOND GERMAN breaks into a eulogy about PIAF in German. PIAF interrupts.*)

PIAF: I wish we could offer you some grub, I mean, something to eat. Only we ain't got nothing. Nothing to *eat*...skint...hungry.

(*She makes chewing motions. TOINE opens her mouth and points in graphically.*)

FIRST GERMAN: Ach Himmel, supplies very short. We too are cut in the ration.

(*TOINE sniggers. PIAF shoves in an elbow to shut her up.*)

PIAF: Aren't you in the catering corps, then? I thought you two were in the catering corps! (*She snatches back the glass from the GERMAN's hand and gives it to TOINE, who knocks it back in one.*)

Share and share alike, that's our motto, mates.

(*The SECOND GERMAN says something in German to the FIRST GERMAN.*)

FIRST GERMAN: Ah, I am the small gift forgetting.

(*He lumbers off nimbly and staggers back with a huge crate of tins and bottled fruit. TOINE reacts like a dog with rabies. PIAF flicks an eyelid. She walks about mayorally, casting a casual eye on the food.*)

SECOND GERMAN: (*Plunging in and bringing out tins.*) Gut? Gut?

PIAF: Gut.

(*They all smile and say 'gut'. The SECOND GERMAN kneels down with TOINE who is already at the fruit, and starts to touch her up.*)

Hey, tell you what, why don't you two boys nip upstairs...Madame and the girls are dying to give you a good time.

FIRST GERMAN: (*His jacket is already unbuttoned.*) Oh, but we was thinking –

PIAF: Oh no. Me and my friend nottee whorees. We just live here because the old girl gets fuel and grub off the Boche, I mean, our German allies.

TOINE: We're freezing to death!

(*The disappointed GERMANS are thrust out. They go, talking in ruffled German as they leave. The GIRLS fall on the fruit.*)

(*With her mouthful.*) I've never seen so much grub in all me life...tinned peaches! (*She is eating with her fingers, half a peach in each hand.*)

PIAF: Don't be so fucking greedy...what about me?

TOINE: I've only had two bits!

PIAF: You've had three!

(*They pull the jar between them. A man – GEORGES – runs on, holding up his trousers.*)

GEORGES: (*Furiously.*) Did you send those bloody Boche upstairs?

PIAF: Oh Christ, I forgot it was Monday.

TOINE: What?

PIAF: She lets 'em in for nothing.

TOINE: What – *all* the Resistance?

GEORGES: Shut up!

PIAF: Where's the others?

GEORGES: Went out the window. I hope that bloody glass roof holds –

(*There is a sound of smashing glass.*)

TOINE: (*As the last tinkle dies away.*) They've fallen through.

GEORGES: Sharp as ever, Einstein. (*To PIAF.*) Got the photos?

(*PIAF has trouble finding them. GEORGES snatches them, riffles through the pictures and throws them back at her, fed up.*)

These are no fucking good, they're all smiling! How can we use them for workcards, you'll have to go again.

PIAF: Oh Christ.

GEORGES: Get your agent to fix another tour...there won't be any trouble, you're clean as far as Jerry is concerned. We want plenty of pictures with the boys but steady face shots, and for Christ's sake tell them not to smile, we can't get 'em out without pictures.

PIAF: All right, all right.

GEORGES: Well, don't fuck about. It's people's lives!

PIAF: (*Humpily.*) I know, I know.

GEORGES: Fine bloody way to win a war.

TOINE: We got to eat.

(*PIAF gives GEORGES some of the tins. He goes.*)

Christ, Ede, how many you give him?

(*A MAN tries to enter.*)

MAN: Hello, lovely ladies...you going to give me a good time?

PIAF: (*Laconically.*) Piss off.

MAN: Come on...

TOINE: (*Laconically.*) You heard.

MAN: I'm in the meat business. Now, you're not going to turn down a nice boy in the meat business, are you?

TOINE: (*Helping herself liberally to tins.*) It's time I got back, anyway, Ede. You know...the kids...

PIAF: Honest, what you'll do for a bit of offal.

(*TOINE goes off with the BUTCHER.*
A knock.)

The answer's no.

(*GEORGES sticks his head round the door.*)

Oh, it's you again.

GEORGES: I thought, seeing as how I was here...one for the road?

PIAF: (*Beginning to get undressed.*) I thought I was supposed to be rotten at the war effort.

GEORGES: (*Taking off his trousers.*) Oh, I didn't say that.

(*Music of 'Hamburg'. PIAF comes downstage and sings.*
Blackout. Sounds of bombing – distant – and ack-ack guns, closer. Light flashes. Several people run this way and that, caught momentarily in the lights.
Blackout.)

Scene 10

A street. PIAF is in outdoor clothes, her hair in a snood. PIERRE rides by on a bicycle. He nearly falls off when he sees PIAF.

PIERRE: Hey, aren't you Edith Piaf?

PIAF: D'you know, ever so many people have told me that.

PIERRE: (*Beginning to ride off.*) You really look like her, you know.

(*PIAF laughs. PIERRE wheels round and comes back, skidding to a halt by her side.*)

You *are* Piaf, aren't you?

PIAF: How d'you know?

PIERRE: The laugh.

PIAF: (*Worried.*) Here, what are you doing on the streets?

PIERRE: Ah.

PIAF: You wanna be careful, kid. They'll pick you up.

PIERRE: I'm OK. (*He gets on his bike.*) Listen, Piaf, after the war, can I be your agent?

PIAF: (*Laughing.*) What a nerve. Had any experience?

PIERRE: No, I've never worked, couldn't get a job. Does that rule me out?

PIAF: From being an agent? No!

PIERRE: (*Going.*) Right then…see you after the war!

PIAF: Mind you…I got me own conditions.

PIERRE: Good! (*He goes.*)

PIAF: Bloody nerve…bicycle clips and all.

(*There is a sound of distant guns.*)

Scene 11

PIAF's apartment. PIAF is on the phone.

Sitting close by is an AMERICAN ARMY OFFICER. He is very good-looking but seems crest-fallen. He plays with his hat nervously.

PIAF: (*Into the phone.*) Look, I'm not touring with a bunch of hopheads… (*Aside, to the AMERICAN.*) You should have said you couldn't get it up, if you'd said you couldn't get it up… (*Into the phone.*) That's not my worry, I said, that's not my worry… (*To the AMERICAN.*) I mean, it's no skin off my nose, all I'm saying is, thank Christ your public doesn't know, if they knew you couldn't get it up… (*Into the phone.*) No, not you…sure…sure…all right… (*Irritably to TOINE, who appears, very excited and waving her arms to attract PIAF's attention.*) What's the matter? (*Into the phone.*) Hold on…

TOINE: Hey, guess what!

PIAF: What?

TOINE: Guess!

PIAF: Oh, fuck off…

TOINE: The war's over!

AMERICAN: What? What!

PIAF: No shit. (*Into the phone.*) And listen, I'm getting those pains in my wrist again, I want a fire in my dressing room…

(*TOINE gestures at the AMERICAN in excitement, then agitates in front of PIAF again.*)

Well, it's bad enough having to sit up all night in freezing cold trains… (*To the AMERICAN, with a brooding look.*) As for all those bloody beef pictures of yours, talk about misleading…

TOINE: (*Glowing, to the AMERICAN.*) Are you the one that plays the cowboy? Where you went into that river to get the girl out, with all them cows coming at us?

PIAF: For fuck's sake! (*Into the phone.*) No, not you!

(*TOINE gestures violently.*)

What's the matter now?

(*The AMERICAN gestures also, trying to attract her from the phone.*)

AMERICAN: Darling! (*He tries to embrace PIAF.*)

PIAF: Get off! (*Into the phone.*) No! Not you! They've all gone nuts! Here, Henry, the war's over – so *she* says…(*To TOINE.*) Satisfied?

TOINE: Aren't you going to say nothing?

PIAF: (*Into the phone.*) Yeah…yeah…well, so she says… (*She holds the phone away from her ear.*) He's gone mad! (*To the AMERICAN.*) And what the fuck are you grinning about? I don't see what the fuck you've got to grin about…I mean, all you had to say was you couldn't get it up, I'm not spreading it round the clubs, ruin your image, wouldn't it… (*She jiggles the phone.*) Henry…Henry? He's rung off! Fuck me, what's the matter with you all?

TOINE: We keep trying to tell you –

AMERICAN: Piaf, the *war's* over!

PIAF: All right! I'm trying to get a bloody *tour* together.

AMERICAN: Honey, does it matter? (*He and TOINE clutch each other in excitement. PIAF is outraged.*)

PIAF: (*To the AMERICAN.*) Look, why don't you just piss off!

AMERICAN: Piaf!

PIAF: It's no good beating about the bush, the whole thing's been a waste of time. Perhaps when you get home, local air…

(*She gives him his hat. He tries to kiss her, à la silver screen, but she shoves him off. He retrieves his dignity, manages a slight bow, and goes.*)

TOINE: Edith!

PIAF: And what are you hanging about for – did you get my fags?

TOINE: I tried, but I couldn't get through the crowds, they're all yelling and singing.

PIAF: (*Puzzled.*) Singing? Oh, honest, least bloody thing, she sits on her ass, bloody useless washed-up whore.

TOINE: (*Going.*) You ain't half rude sometimes, Ede.

PIAF: (*Shouting.*) And get my bleeding fags…now she's got the hump, all they do is sit and cadge off you. (*Shouting.*) What crowds?

TOINE: (*Sticking her head in.*) I keep trying to tell you. (*Quietly.*) The war's over.

PIAF: (*Patiently.*) Why didn't you say?

(*They embrace and run off, laughing and screaming.*
Sounds on the P/A – 'La Marseillaise', bells, rifle shots, crowd noises, singing and cheering.
PIAF and TOINE enter with a sailor. PIAF wears the sailor's hat. They are singing 'Milord', arms linked. They circle the stage, exit, and return, singing 'Auprès de ma blonde'. They exit singing. Their voices die away.
Fade to Blackout.)

Scene 12

Nightclub. CHARLES TRENET sings 'La Mer'. He joins PIAF, they embrace and kiss in greeting, she pours him a drink.

CHARLES: How was I?

PIAF: *Comme toujours* – perfection.

CHARLES: And yet you know at midday I couldn't get above an E.

PIAF: You shouldn't keep your throat covered Charlot – it weakens your voice!

CHARLES: Can't say I've noticed.

PIAF: (*Laughs her low laugh.*) I can always make a sou foghailing, eh?

CHARLES: (*They laugh.*) Congratulations.

PIAF: On what?

CHARLES: I heard about your fee for the American tour – good for us all, Edith.

(*She seems depressed.*)

You'll love the States – they'll adore you – wonderful steaks – plenty of – what's the matter?

PIAF: Nothing.

CHARLES: So? (*Looks round.*) Where's Gerard tonight?

PIAF: I've given him the elbow.

CHARLES: You two broke up? Edith! Gerard's a great guy.

PIAF: Great at spending money, you mean.

CHARLES: Sure, but attentive, good suits, nice hair-style –

PIAF: Seen his feet?

CHARLES: Actually, no.

PIAF: Webbed. Makes you think.

CHARLES: *Alors.*

(*They drink.*)

So – you're alone.

(*They drink.*)

PIAF: What I –

CHARLES: (*Together.*) You should –

(*They both stop. She gestures for him to go on.*)

You need a companion, cherie.

PIAF: Too right. It's no good on your own.

CHARLES: *Absolument.*

PIAF: Unnatural.

CHARLES: We agree.

PIAF: So?

CHARLES: So why don't I introduce you to a man of class – about the feet I'm not sure but for the rest – trust me.

PIAF: Who? (*Flat.*) I probably know him already.
CHARLES: I don't think so.
PIAF: What's his name?
CHARLES: Marcel.
PIAF: Marcel? Marcel who? Not Marcel – you don't mean you know him – you know him? You know the Champ? (*CHARLES takes her glass from her, throws a kiss and goes. Light change. PIAF, downstage, is on her feet like a boxer.*) (*Screeching.*) Go on, Marcel…kill him, kill him…give it to him, let him have it…oh no…oh no…stop him, Marcel…come on, come on, love…let him have it…go on…go on! Ah! You're on the way…that's it…that's it…that's it…the Champ! The Champ! (*She screams with excitement.*)

Scene 13

The music of 'Mon dieu', soft. MARCEL and PIAF are smoking, in post-coital mood, slow and mellow.

PIAF: I wish you could have seen me when I was a kid, I had lovely little tits.
MARCEL: (*His speech is affected by boxing.*) They look all right to me.
PIAF: (*Touching her jawline.*) I'm getting bad here, too. Let's see yours. (*She inspects his mouth.*) Christ, Aladdin's cave…ain't you got none of your own, Marce?
MARCEL: They get loosened, rot off at the neck. At least, take 'em out, you don't get your cheeks cut.
PIAF: Yeah, like the little daft kids…when I was in the home. They pull out all their teeth, you know…so's they won't bite each other. They can't enjoy an apple.
(*She cuddles up, punching him lightly on the arms and chest with pride.*)
Champ.
MARCEL: I'm just a guy with a fist, Edith.
PIAF: Go on! You're Cerdan! The Champion! You don't have to go round with an old loose-bum like me, you could have anybody! You don't need me – oh, I've

helped fighters spend it before now…not you, though, eh? When we go out shopping it's for your old lady and the kids…I don't know why I stand for it.

MARCEL: You know I'd marry you if I could, Edie.

PIAF: No. You're the faithful sort.

MARCEL: Well, she don't get much of a life, stuck at home.

PIAF: Better than any woman in the world. Except me. I've got this, haven't I? You know, I think I will have these lifted – all the stars are doing it.

MARCEL: You don't want to get yourself cut about…why take the risk?

PIAF: Well, you do.

MARCEL: That's different, it's part of the job. Mind you, they think you don't give a bugger. I had a guvnor once, put me in for anything…anything for a bout, I was only a lad. Somebody down the gym said, 'His face'll be all over his shoulders.' 'Oh, we don't care what we look like,' he says… 'Just so long as the money's right.' He was right about the money. You don't go in the ring except for that, no way. (*Slight pause.*) No, you're on your own in there.

PIAF: Oh, I know what you mean. (*He looks at her.*) Well, same for me in a way, innit? I mean, I'm not going to get me head bashed in – not unless I'm dead unlucky. Still… (*She plays with his hand.*) What I mean is…just before I go on…it's the same every time. Never mind what they've said to you in the dressing room…your mates – that walk to the mike after the intro… it's from here to Mars, I'm telling you. (*Slight pause.*) Sometimes you fuck it. You can't say, hang on, I'll…well, I have been known to. (*She laughs.*) Even worse if it's gone well. Fucking anguish. Well, what is there to come off for? You're only on your own again.

(*They have both expressed more than is usual between them.*
They exchange a baffled look and both start to speak together.
They smile at this and embrace.
The music of 'Mon dieu', becoming louder.)

Don't go.

MARCEL: I must, love.

PIAF: Get an earlier plane back. For me.

MARCEL: (*Kissing her.*) All right. (*He kisses her again – a long embrace. He extricates himself gently from her arms and goes.*)

(*The music of 'Mon dieu', becoming louder, the drumroll at the end turning into the loud and increasing roar of aero-engines, ending in a deafening crash.*)

PIAF: Marcel!

(*PIAF sings 'La belle histoire d'amour'.*)

(*End of Act One.*)

ACT TWO

Scene 1

A stage dressing room. It is empty. PIAF enters, fast, a whisky in hand. She throws herself down.

PIAF: Fuck me. (*She jumps up and refills her glass.*) Fuck me. (*There is a rap on the door.*) Stay out! (*She drinks and kicks off her shoes, muttering in fury.*) Bloody believe it…like singing to a box of eggs…OUT!

(*PIERRE, the young man with the bicycle, now PIAF's agent, enters.*)

Oh, it's you.

(*She gestures the bottle. PIERRE helps himself and makes to speak.*)

Don't say anything.

PIERRE: Piaf, there's nothing we can't fix – a change of repertoire, that's all.

PIAF: OK, so they play off the beat, that's all they can fucking do, we begin where they leave off as far as – they're all like *kids.*

PIERRE: Perhaps you could –

PIAF: I'm going home. I must have been daft. Why the fuck d'you put me up for it? I should have listened to Maurice, I should have done that film. We're gonna be right down the sluice, you know that?

PIERRE: Not necessarily.

PIAF: Don't be so daft.

PIERRE: Now, don't forget, we've got signed contracts, coast to coast…and a return spot here.

PIAF: Bollocks.

PIERRE: We're contracted, Piaf!

PIAF: When were you born, kid?

PIERRE: I'm telling you, there's –

PIAF: (*Shaking her head.*) No…no, no. Listen…look…look, love…it's not worth – asspaper!

PIERRE: (*Toughly.*) If the Yanks think they can renege on their contractual obligations, it's going to cost them a great deal of money.

(*PIAF shakes her head.*)

They're legally contracted to us.

PIAF: (*With a short laugh.*) You got a lot to learn. Look, Pierrot, what do you think the law is? Who do you think it's for? Not for people like us, I can tell you that. People who make laws do it for their own use. Listen, the contract that can't be split up the middle doesn't exist. If they don't want us, we don't play. Believe me. Fact of life.

(*There is a knock at the door.*)

Look, I told you, I don't want to see no-one.

(*It is MARLENE. PIAF embraces her needfully. PIERRE offers MARLENE a drink, which she declines.*)

MARLENE: Don't worry...don't worry...

PIAF: Are you kidding? I just died out there!

MARLENE: Sure, we have to go to work, make some changes.

PIAF: No, I'm going home. Book the flights, love.

PIERRE: Piaf, I think you should listen.

MARLENE: We'll talk about it.

(*She smiles at PIERRE over PIAF's head. He nods at her understandingly and goes.*)

PIAF: (*Drinking.*) I don't know what I'm supposed to be celebrating.

MARLENE: There's nothing that can't be fixed.

PIAF: It's a long time since I got the bloody bird.

MARLENE: I'm going to make a few telephone calls...

PIAF: I'll shave under me arms next time.

(*MARLENE laughs.*)

MARLENE: Stick with it, Piaf. You'll make it here – OK, a diffewent appwoach –

PIAF: They don't know what I'm singing about half the time – anyway, who wants to see some little cunt looking like a war widow when they can have Doris Day?

MARLENE: Don't put yourself down.

PIAF: It's what they want, good clean fun. Maybe I should sex it up a bit.

MARLENE: Over my dead body.

PIAF: No, well, we don't exactly have the same problems. Let's face it, love, it has to be easy for you.

MARLENE: You think so?

PIAF: Yeah, well, I didn't start out with what you've got.

MARLENE: Neither did I. Piaf, don't tell me you fall for all that stuff. Women as factowy pwoducts, courtesy of Pawamount, MGM? Till the cwunch comes. You don't need to envy them, believe me.

PIAF: You seem to manage OK.

MARLENE: I look after myself.

PIAF: Well, there again, that has to be easier for you… I mean, you've got discipline.

MARLENE: You mean because I'm a Kwaut…a junker's daughter? It has to come from within, fwom yourself. You don't need so much of that for a start. (*She indicates the bottle.*)

PIAF: It helps.

MARLENE: Not for long.

PIAF: Ah, it all goes onstage. Nothing left nowadays.

MARLENE: Learn to conserve a little. That way you stay on top.

PIAF: Sure, sure. I know. I just haven't got it. Anyway, what's the point? If only I hadn't asked him, if I hadn't said that. That one sentence.

MARLENE: Piaf, you've got to get over it. You know you have.

PIAF: Yeah. (*She turns away.*)

MARLENE: Don't cwy, you'll wuin your eyes.

PIAF: Well, I'm all on me own, aren't I?

MARLENE: Nonsense, you're suwwounded with love. You've got good fwiends…

PIAF: I know, I know. (*She sniffs and blows her nose on a tissue.*) Did I ever tell you about my little girl?

MARLENE: Oh yes.

PIAF: Poor little thing.

MARLENE: I know.

PIAF: Died in my arms!

MARLENE: Oh, but –

PIAF: Her father was a marquis. Racing driver. Fantastic connoisseur. And good-looking.

(*MARLENE nods. PIAF is in one of her more fanciful moods.*)

I nursed that kiddie for over a year. Longer. Lovely little curls she had…just like Shirley Temple…but pretty, you know. I was only a slip of a thing meself…I was barely out of convent, still in plaits. (*She slips a look at MARLENE, who is nodding with infinite kindness.*)

MARLENE: Uh-huh…uh-huh…

PIAF: Never left her side, day or night…! Except to go to the lav, of course.

(*They both nod at the appropriateness of this dereliction.*)

I only just made it back when she snuffed it.

(*A short, reverent silence is observed.*)

MARLENE: (*Wickedly.*) What was the twouble, Piaf?

PIAF: Oh…ah…TB…consumption…galloping!

(*She starts to break up and then roars with laughter. MARLENE smiles broadly.*)

Well, what did they expect? I know what they *wanted*…some crap with a feather up its ass. Like hell. I'm Piaf!

MARLENE: That's better.

PIAF: When I do a song it's *me* that comes on. They get the lot.

MARLENE: Sure!

PIAF: They *see* what they're getting…everything I've got.

MARLENE: Sure. But learn to save it.

PIAF: Nah.

MARLENE: Piaf, you can't have an orgasm every single time you walk on a stage.

PIAF: *I* can.

MARLENE: Darling, nobody can peak all the time. Technique, Piaf! Twust it. That way you don't exhaust yourself. You're going to be a big success here. Forget tonight – OK, some changes, you can do that. Please stay. Stay and fight.

PIAF: I'm flat broke.

MARLENE: Good, then you'll have to stay. We need you. You're the best. Highest paid woman singer in the world! You should be pwoud.

PIAF: Nah. It's not the money. It's not the money.

MARLENE: Oh sure...we do it because we need to be loved. Like all the other myths by people who never gave one ounce of themselves.

PIAF: Well, whatever it is, it certainly ain't the money. They couldn't *print* enough for the way you feel just before going on – I've seen *you* shaking away enough times. Nah, it's got to be more than money. Singing ditties? Yelling your lungs out night after night? Nah. Got to be more than the fucking tourist trade. No...when I'm out there...it's got to happen. If it doesn't happen...terrible.

MARLENE: I know. I know what you mean. (*They smile at each other.*)

PIAF: All there is, really. The rest – well, once the novelty's worn off...(*Slight pause.*) I've tried, you know...bought meself a house...even ordered some furniture. But what are you? Fucking caretaker. Till the rogues get in and nick it off you...good luck to them if they want to take the risk...well, all you got's the maintenance, I've never heard a table tell a joke. No, I'll stick to the singing. You know, the trouble is, I'm off me patch here, that's why I'm going wrong.

MARLENE: You see? You're beginning to work alweady.

PIAF: OK. Give it a whirl. (*They embrace and kiss.*)

MARLENE: Good. But pwomise me one thing.

PIAF: For you, anything.

MARLENE: I'm sewious. This is a big country. Take care of yourself.

PIAF: OK.

MARLENE: I mean it.

PIAF: Sure...Mutti! (*They laugh and embrace.*)

MARLENE: Listen, we'll have a gweat time. We'll do the town. Do you want to meet Hawwy Twuman? He's about your size and he tells vewy good stowies, I think you'd get along together.

PIAF: Yeah, sure, why not, bring on the natives.

Scene 2

A bar. Two American SAILORS and a BARMAN. PIAF enters and joins them at the bar. She is wearing a short, silver fox jacket over her dress.

PIAF: Hi boys!
FIRST SAILOR: Say!
SECOND SAILOR: Well, hello!
PIAF: What are you drinking?
FIRST SAILOR: (*Leaning over her drunkenly.*) Hi, shorty, where've you been all my life?
PIAF: (*Smelling the whisky on his breath.*) Better make it three double whiskies.
BOTH SAILORS: Thanks Ma'am.
SECOND SAILOR: So, what's a fancy little lady like you doing in a joint like this?
PIAF: You'd be amazed to know.
(*The BARMAN brings the drinks.*)
Thanks.
FIRST SAILOR: Here's looking at you.
PIAF: (*To the BARMAN.*) Got a room upstairs?
(*The BARMAN nods. PIAF throws a note onto his tray.*)
So, what are you doing, boys?
SECOND SAILOR: Anything you say, little lady…anything you say.
FIRST SAILOR: Got any ideas?
(*PIAF takes his arm. The SECOND SAILOR lags, rejected.*)
PIAF: (*Turning back.*) What are you waiting for?
SECOND SAILOR: You mean me too, Ma'am?
PIAF: If I'm giving lessons I may as well take the whole class.
(*The BARMAN puts down his cloth and follows.*)

Scene 3

PIAF's apartment in Paris. If furnished, the furniture is still partly crated, unpacked. There is a usable sofa. PIAF enters in travelling clothes, followed by LUCIEN. He is much younger than PIAF and is wearing clothes 'au courant' for the fifties. He is wire-tight. MADELEINE, PIAF's secretary, enters from within.

MADELEINE: Piaf…you're back! We were coming to meet you!

PIAF: Caught an earlier plane.

(*She takes off her coat and drops it on the floor unheedingly. MADELEINE automatically picks it up.*)

Nice drum, I like it.

MADELEINE: It was jolly difficult finding an apartment with seven bedrooms…you *did* say seven?

PIAF: Knew you could do it…Lucien here likes a change of view every night.

MARLENE: (*Looking at LUCIEN.*) I see.

PIAF: Nah, it's for his group. There's seven of them …eight including me, we're working together… I'm gonna put these boys on the map. Did you get that big fridge?

(*MADELEINE nods.*)

MADELEINE: (*Faintly.*) Will you all be dining at home?

PIAF: Nah, it's just for snacks…cheese, ham, steaks, they're growing lads. Oh, and don't forget cornflakes, they're very into cornflakes.

(*MADELEINE takes frantic notes. PIAF throws herself down.*)

Read me the notices, then, Lucien…ah, look at his dear little bum.

(*MADELEINE goes. PIAF clicks her fingers and LUCIEN gets her a drink. He picks up the notices.*)

LUCIEN: (*Reading.*) 'At first sight you wonder…this dumpy little woman with the big forehead…'

PIAF: (*Groans.*) It's not *that* big.

LUCIEN: '…black dress, pale, agitated hands…'

PIAF: Christ.

LUCIEN: '…then she opens her mouth…sound like you never heard…a cat mewing on the tiles…the ecstasy of morning…they are all here.'

PIAF: Do you want to touch me up?

LUCIEN: (*Reading a new notice.*) 'How is it possible to listen to one woman singing twenty numbers in a foreign language and find one's face wet with tears at the end? There is only one word for it – genius. And that genius is Piaf.'

PIAF: Bet that's Alan, the bugger owes me money. Go on.

LUCIEN: (*Reading a new notice.*) 'The voice, rising like the slanting sun from the floating bric-a-brac of the Seine on a warm spring morning fuses your backbone. She sings of love. She sings of being depressed...alone...of being made helpless by love. She sings of sexual treachery...of unhappiness. She feels bad, and we believe her. We can't bear it for her.'

PIAF: (*Abruptly.*) Who wrote that? (*She jerks round, slopping her drink. LUCIEN turns the page, trying to find out.*) Christ, can't you read! Bloody kids, can't even get myself a decent man.

LUCIEN: (*Muttering without conviction.*) Piaf, you know how I feel about you.

PIAF: Sure, I'm your fucking meal ticket, well where would you be without me?

LUCIEN: Nowhere.

PIAF: You're damn right. You're damn right and don't you forget it.

LUCIEN: Piaf, don't let's get in a fight –

PIAF: And who said you could call me Piaf? Who said you could call me Piaf?

LUCIEN: (*Sullen and frightened.*) Oh, come on, what do you want me to call you?

PIAF: It's Madame to you and don't you forget it.

LUCIEN: Even when we're fucking?

PIAF: *Especially* when we're fucking. Madeleine! Madeleine! Where is that middle-class bitch? Oh –

(*MADELEINE enters.*)

MADELEINE: Piaf, I wish you wouldn't speak to me like that.

(*Behind PIAF's back LUCIEN grimaces and makes his escape, taking the suitcases. PIAF, at the bottle, catches the tail-end of his exit.*)

PIAF: And don't forget to give the dog his enema. What do you think of him?

MADELEINE: The young man?

PIAF: Yeah, Lucien...my new feller.

MADELEINE: He's very good-looking.

PIAF: You can say that again. We really get it on together. Cold little prick. I said, cold little prick.

MADELEINE: I heard you, Piaf.

PIAF: Well he'll do till I trade him up.

MADELEINE: You look tired.

PIAF: Always set up your next trick before you shove in the ice pick. There was a guy on the plane I fancied but he was Australian – you gotta draw the line.

(*PIAF lets MADELEINE tuck her up on the sofa.*)

MADELEINE: You'd be much more comfortable in bed.

PIAF: No, I'll kip here...I can't sleep if I try. Got any tablets?

(*MADELEINE already has the bottle in her hand. She tips out two tablets. PIAF reaches up, takes the bottle of tablets, tips it into her mouth and takes a swig of whisky.*)

MADELEINE: Piaf, that's too many!

(*But it is too late. MADELEINE tucks PIAF up and makes to go.*)

PIAF: Madeleine?

MADELEINE: Yes?

PIAF: I want full coverage for this opening...no messing about – I'm gonna put these boys on the map!

MADELEINE: It's all taken care of. (*She makes to go.*)

PIAF: Rub the back of my neck for me.

MADELEINE: Do you want Gordon?

PIAF: No, you do it. I don't want to listen to how many times he's been raped this month.

(*MADELEINE returns and rubs PIAF's neck.*)

It's worse on the right.

MADELEINE: Mmm, I can feel the fibrositis. Try to relax.

(*She massages.*)

PIAF: I still miss him, you know.

MADELEINE: I beg your pardon?

PIAF: (*Rearing up like an angry sealion.*) I said I still miss him – Marcel!

MADELEINE: I know, Piaf. I know.

PIAF: I wish you could have seen him. Oh, we'd have packed up in the end...he'd have gone back to his wife. We got on so well. (*Pause.*) I hate being without a feller. It's no good on your own. (*Pause.*) What do you do?

MADELEINE: Sorry?

PIAF: You're on your own...what do you do? Do you see yourself off?

MADELEINE: Do I have to answer that?

PIAF: (*Rapping.*) Yes.

(*MADELEINE sighs. Pause.*)

MADELEINE: Well, actually, I have a little dog.

(*Slight pause. PIAF's laugh rings out.*)

A chihuaha.

(*PIAF laughs, heartily tickled.*)

PIAF: Ah, you old fucking middle-class put-down...serves me right, eh?

MADELEINE: Come and lie down.

PIAF: (*Crossing.*) No, I asked for that. I mean, you got a right to your own life.

MADELEINE: I'll tuck you up.

PIAF: Sure, you got a lot to do.

(*MADELEINE goes.*)

Patronising bitch. (*Calling.*) Madeleine!

(*MADELEINE enters.*)

MADELEINE: What's the matter?

PIAF: I'm lonely!

(*MADELEINE sits with PIAF. She tries to creep off when she thinks PIAF has dropped off but PIAF hauls her back with a snatch of the arm. Same again. Eventually PIAF begins to snore. MADELEINE rises very carefully, not making a noise with her chair. She almost makes it but the arm snakes out again.*)

Hey! Caught you...where you going?

MADELEINE: I must get some sleep!

PIAF: You must? What about me? Get somebody on the phone...get Eddie...

MADELEINE: It's five o'clock in the morning.

PIAF: So what? They'll just be coming out the clubs. Get Jean-Claude.

MADELEINE: He's on tour.

PIAF: Well, what about Guy...? Get Eddie, get Lucille... I must have somebody!

MADELEINE: I could try Helene.

PIAF: That fat bitch, what do I want to see her for? I know! Get old Toine, she's good for a laugh. My old mate from Belleville, she's good for a laugh, get Toine.

MADELEINE: Before my time, I think.

PIAF: Right...haven't seen her lately. Fucking friends, never here when you want them. Find her for me, she can take the strain for a bit. Only real friend I ever had...from Belleville...big-looking cow...

(*She is confused with drowsiness. MADELEINE exits quietly. Light change. PIAF mutters, groans in her sleep. TOINE enters in coat and headscarf, followed by MADELEINE.*)

TOINE: She's asleep. (*She approaches the sofa.*)

MADELEINE: Oh, don't wake her please! She has such trouble sleeping. (*She gestures TOINE away.*)

TOINE: Who, Ede? Sleeps like a horse.

MADELEINE: (*In a lowered voice.*) Would you like to wait? She's dying to see you. I mean, it seems a shame after all the trouble we had finding you –

TOINE: Yeah, well, I had to finish my shift.

MADELEINE: Of course, I understand.

TOINE: Took me ages to get a train. I missed me lunch.

MADELEINE: I'll get you something. (*She goes.*)

(*TOINE crosses to PIAF, bends over her, sniffs, and flinches at the smell.*)

TOINE: Ede? Ede? Christ, we know what you been on. (*She sits and waits.*)

(*MADELEINE enters with a tray of food and a glass of wine. TOINE falls on the wine at once.*)

MADELEINE: Would you care for coffee?

TOINE: No thanks, upsets my liver...well, if it's going.
(*MADELEINE goes, then returns with coffee. TOINE eats heartily. Her appetite appeased, she looks up from her plate.*)
Who are you, then?

MADELEINE: I'm Madame's secretary.

TOINE: Oh.
(*MADELEINE refills TOINE's glass.*)
Not the hostess?

MADELEINE: Er... No.

TOINE: Don't she have a hostess now, then?

MADELEINE: (*At sea.*) I... I really don't know. I don't think so.

TOINE: Oh. How many rooms she got?

MADELEINE: The whole floor.

TOINE: The whole floor? Christ.
(*MADELEINE pours her more coffee. She knocks it back.*)
Thanks.

MADELEINE: You...you and she are old friends, I believe?

TOINE: Yeah. We was on the road together. I'm a... performer.

MADELEINE: I see. What do you –

TOINE: (*Quickly.*) Well, I was. Retired now.

MADELEINE: I see.

TOINE: (*Quickly.*) So you wouldn't have heard of me. (*She belches, suppressing it a bit, and undoes her coat for comfort. She expands a bit.*) So you're the secretary?

MADELEINE: Ah...yes.

TOINE: (*Expanding with the wine.*) You mean typing, that sort of thing?

MADELEINE: I look after Madame's affairs.

TOINE: Christ. (*She appraises MADELEINE.*) Been here long?
(*Slight pause.*)

MADELEINE: Not very long.
(*Slight pause.*)

TOINE: Get on with her all right, do you?

MADELEINE: Oh yes.

TOINE: Hmm.

(*PIAF moans and stirs. They turn towards her. She coughs, hawks, and spits on the floor, then sees TOINE.*)

PIAF: Christ, what the fuck are you doing here? (*She turns to MADELEINE glowering.*) Madeleine? Look, for Christ's sake, there is a limit. I've got to have *some* privacy. (*She glares at TOINE and exits, coughing. There is the sound of a lavatory flushing.*)

MADELEINE: Oh dear. I'm so sorry.

TOINE: Don't worry, she can be ever so rude sometimes.

MADELEINE: Perhaps when she's –

TOINE: I wouldn't bank on it. D'you think you could pay my fare?

MADELEINE: Of course.

PIAF: (*Off.*) Where's the fucking gargle?

Scene 4

A Parisian cafe. TOINE staggers on in her old coat, a string bag of shopping in each hand, a long loaf under her arm, and a newspaper. She passes a cafe table, wavers and sits down. She flops, and watches the traffic, this way and that. A WAITER approaches, cloth on shoulder.

TOINE: *Crème.*

(*The WAITER wipes the table automatically.*)

Oh, and I'll have a cognac chaser. (*She pulls a face at her own extravagance and opens the newspaper. She is looking for something.*)

(*The WAITER brings her order. She adds some of the spirits to the coffee and sips it with pleasure. Then, fortified, she finds the pictures she is looking for on the front page – and the continuation of the article inside. GEORGES, the Resistance man, on his way home from work, sees her and comes over.*)

GEORGES: He-llo! If it isn't Einstein!

(*They shake hands, French style.*)

How's it going then? Haven't seen you about lately.

TOINE: I'm on the other shift.

GEORGES: Oh yeah. How's the family?

TOINE: Short of money.

(*The WAITER brings GEORGES a beer. GEORGES jerks his head and the WAITER brings TOINE another cognac.*)
Oh! Thanks! (*She knocks it back.*)

GEORGES: (*Nodding at the newspaper.*) You've seen it, then?

TOINE: (*Brightening up visibly with the cognac.*) Yeah!

GEORGES: Bit sudden, wasn't it?

TOINE: She looks ever so young!

GEORGES: Hah-ha, which one you looking at?
(*They pore over the pictures.*)
What's he like?
(*TOINE shrugs.*)
Have you met him?

TOINE: Nah. I don't have much to do with her now.

GEORGES: What's it say?

TOINE: Hang on. (*She dives into her bag, fetches out her glasses and puts them on, giving GEORGES a dirty look when he grins.*) 'The bride was radiant in a powder-blue two-piece suit in raw silk with rouleau belt, single-breasted jacket and assisted shoulders...' (*She pauses, gazing into space, imagining the suit expressionlessly.*)

GEORGES: What's his name?

TOINE: Shut up. '...over a cream silk blouse with simple open collar...' Hah, that's not simple, you can't do that sort of satin stich with a machine, that's all hand-done... Hold on. '...an off-the-face Breton-brimmed hat in peach-bloom velour, trimmed with silk taffeta carnations and over-the-face self-veiling in Parma violet.'
(*TOINE blows out her cheeks and again gazes into space, conjuring up the details, her lips pursing in pure enjoyment of the finery. She reads on.*)
'...our reporter asked the new Madam Durssac if a family was planned. Laughed Edith...' What...? Oh... 'Laughed Edith, "Jean and I will be touring together when we return from our honeymoon in Tahiti. However, we plan to start a family next year," with a silvery laugh.'
(*TOINE guffaws.*)

GEORGES: Hah! Silvery laugh?

(*They laugh.*)

TOINE: I bet. ' "We would like two boys and a girl. I think three is a nice number." ' Christ.

GEORGES: I see the poor bugger doesn't get a word in. Still, nice young lad, should keep her happy for a bit. Can I have a look at the football? (*He takes a piece of the newspaper.*)

TOINE: Fancy her going off and getting married. What for? Can you see her with kids? I can't.

(*GEORGES throws down a note and TOINE tucks it under her coffee cup to anchor it. They get up and GEORGES picks up TOINE's shopping and carries it for her.*)

GEORGES: Well, you never know, love. Look at you.

TOINE: (*Suspiciously.*) What you mean?

GEORGES: Nothing. She'll probably make a lovely little mother.

(*They go.*)

Scene 5

A hospital waiting room. A young man – JEAN – walks up and down with a bunch of flowers and a large box of chocolates. PIAF enters, her head swathed in bandages. She has two sticks and is assisted by a NURSE.

NURSE: Steady…steady Madame…

JEAN: Edith! Darling…!

PIAF: Look who's here! Only the pisser who tried to finish me off! (*She lashes out at him with a stick.*) Christ, my head!

NURSE: Gently, Madame! No, no, no, no, no…you mustn't disturb yourself. (*She shakes her head firmly at JEAN.*) Please, Monsieur…

JEAN: Piaf, it wasn't *my* fault. It wasn't my fault, it was an accident!

PIAF: Get him out!

NURSE: Of course, Madame. Please go, you're upsetting the patient.

PIAF: Out!

JEAN: But you were the one who was yelling at me to go faster…it was *you* made us late…Piaf!

PIAF: (*To the NURSE.*) You'll have to give me something for the pain, love.

NURSE: (*Soothingly.*) Of course, Madame, of course.

PIAF: You'll speak to the doctor?

NURSE: Oh yes, he'll see that you're comfortable – that's what we're here for.

(*PIAF and the NURSE go.*)

JEAN: But what about our tour together? Piaf! I'm your husband!

Scene 6

A rehearsal studio. A PIANIST enters and sits at the piano. The MANAGER enters, pauses at the piano, then crosses to meet PIERRE, PIAF's agent, who arrives with hat, coat and briefcase. They shake hands.

MANAGER: Good to see you.

PIERRE: Long time…

MANAGER: Sit down, take the weight off your feet. Any idea of…ah…?

(*PIERRE purses his lips non-committally.*)

Only I said ten-thirty because naturally I didn't expect to see you until…well, about now.

PIERRE: She'll be along.

MANAGER: Oh yes. (*Slight pause.*) So, how's it going?

PIERRE: Very well, very well.

MANAGER: Plenty of money coming in?

PIERRE: Oh yes.

MANAGER: I should think you earn your screw, son. You've stayed the distance. How do you manage it?

PIERRE: We get on all right.

MANAGER: She does what she wants, you mean.

PIERRE: No, no, there's give and take. (*He looks at his watch.*) She was up when I left. Car's probably on its way.

MANAGER: Well, it wouldn't do for me. There's only one thing to do with a woman who makes trouble.
PIERRE: What? Make love to her, you mean?
MANAGER: No. Hit her in the face. They don't like that.
PIERRE: (*Dryly.*) I'll remember.
MANAGER: No...clip round the kisser, you'd have no trouble at all. (*Pause.*) What about songs... anything new?
PIERRE: A couple of good 'uns. Really good.
MANAGER: Hmm. Now, look...about the other.
PIERRE: Oh, come on...you know how she is! It's worked before! She *is* a professional – where the work's concerned she's the best in the bloody world, now you know that. Where else can you fill this bloody barn without back-up artists? She's always been a good thing from that point of view.
MANAGER: ...pay for it...
PIERRE: Sure, sure. We can come to an arrangement. Look, if it keeps her happy, that's all that matters. Believe me.
(*The MANAGER digests this without agreeing.*)
MANAGER: How's she looking, has she recovered?
PIERRE: She's looking fine!
MANAGER: No scars?
PIERRE: No, no, she looks great. She's in love...younger than ever, believe me!
MANAGER: I must have sophistication, my audience expects it –
(*PIAF enters, at a rush, a bulging handbag under her arm. She is wearing an untidy, very dirty bandage around her head, askew, from under which her hair pokes, greasy and ludicrous. She is slightly pot-bellied in a seedy pink jumper – appallingly dressed. The MANAGER blanches.*)
PIAF: (*Embracing him.*) Hello, Henry, me old fruit, how's it going? Still the stiffest prick in Paris?
MANAGER: (*Muttering.*) Christ Almighty...
PIAF: Go on, say it...I look like an old ratbag, eh? Never mind, we're on the way...wait and see what I've got for you...where is he? Fuck me, where's he gone?

Angelo…Angelo…oh, there you are…the audition's in here, love, not in the bloody lav. He's a bit nervous.

(*ANGELO has entered. He is tall and handsome, despite his Italian bumfreezer and little hat with a feather. He wears cowboy boots. The MANAGER and the PIANIST look at him, and at each other. PIERRE gazes into space. PIAF throws herself down by PIERRE's side, leaving ANGELO cruelly stranded, centre-stage.*)

What about that, then?

(*The MANAGER, lost for words, turns his back and walks away.*)

How about that, eh? (*To ANGELO.*) Go on, love! Go on!

ANGELO: You want I should sing?

PIAF: Yeah!

ANGELO: Sing now?

PIAF: Well, that's the fucking idea.

(*ANGELO takes a creased brown paper bag from his pocket, removes a battered piece of sheet music, crosses and hands it to the PIANIST who looks down his nose at it.*)

PIERRE: Take it easy, son. When you're ready.

(*With a look of anguish, ANGELO bends down to the PIANIST and confers in whispers, using his hands a lot. The PIANIST shrugs, unresponsively. ANGELO takes the centre of the stage. He takes his stance, in Italianate fashion, and takes another anguished look about him, then gives a formal nod to the PIANIST. He launches into 'Deep in the Heart of Texas', with an attempted American accent, and gestures. PIERRE bends low as if he has a stomach ache, trying to stifle hysteria. The MANAGER looks grim. PIAF claps noisily.*)

PIAF: Yeah! Yeah! What did you think of that, Henry?

(*The MANAGER looks to PIERRE for support but PIERRE has turned away, his hand over his face. He looks towards the PIANIST, who grins and gestures. The MANAGER is not pleased with this frivolous response and turns back, grimacing. PIAF looks up at him eagerly as he tries to find words.*)

MANAGER: Piaf…Piaf…he's…he's…ah…he's a nice looking boy.

PIAF: Yeah, right, didn't I tell you?

MANAGER: Piaf...have him... God knows you deserve him. But... (*He gestures towards the boy.*) Please!

PIAF: (*Dashed.*) What do you think, Pierrot?

(*PIERRE, unable to contain himself, rolls with laughter.*)

PIERRE: He...he...he stinks!

(*The PIANIST joins in the laughter. PIAF, her face full of rage, rises.*)

PIAF: What's so funny?

MANAGER: Now, come on...

PIAF: (*Beginning to attack the PIANIST physically.*) And what's the matter with you?

PIERRE: (*As a reminder that she has promised not to do this.*) Piaf.

PIAF: All *right*! (*She makes an effort to be judicious.*) Look, you're wrong...all of you.

PIERRE: He can't sing, love.

MANAGER: Piaf, we're not talking about his cock.

PIAF: Aren't you? Aren't you? Then you bloody well should be.

ANGELO: (*Now totally embarrassed.*) Pleasa...darling...we should go.

PIAF: (*To ANGELO.*) Shut up. Look at him. Six foot tall, good hairline, nose...look at his thighs! All right, the suit's a joke, even I can see that. But put him in something decent, give him some decent material to sing,the girls'll go mad! He needs *ballads* – he's a fucking Eyetie, for God's sake! Here...here, sing them *'O Sole Mio'*, pet...

ANGELO: No, no...

PIAF: Come on, some of the old *buon giorno...*

ANGELO: No, no...izza too square, Piaf.

PIAF: Nah, come on, come on...you do what I say...

(*She starts to sing 'O Sole Mio', gazing up at him, holding his hand. A true Italian, ANGELO breaks into 'O Sole Mio'. PIAF stops singing and he continues solo until he reaches up to the first glorious high bit – where she cuts him off.*)

PIAF: There you are...OK, OK, Angelo...there you are...! See what I mean? When he forgets to perform he's lovely! Oh, fucking men, no wonder we can come ten times to their one... Look, when have I been wrong? What do I have to do? He's a winner! They'll come in their seats, believe me!

(*No response.*)

OK. OK. If it's down to me...how about if I whack in for thirty per cent? Fifty...

PIERRE: Piaf!

PIAF: Shut up, whose side are you on?

(*Pause.*)

PIERRE: All right. OK.

(*The MANAGER nods and goes, assessing ANGELO's body shrewdly. PIERRE goes, separately.*

PIAF helps ANGELO to change. She gives him a new tie she has bought for him. He accepts it with a tortured smile and puts it on shakily. He fidgets.)

PIAF: What's the matter?

ANGELO: Nothing, nothing.

PIAF: What is it?

ANGELO: I donta know.

PIAF: I do. (*She watches him, restless in the new suit.*) You feel a pansy, don't you? No, it's all right, love, of course you do.

ANGELO: I always worked with my hands.

PIAF: I know what you mean! (*She laughs.*) Look Angelo, there's nothing wrong with this...this is work too. We've worked hard, haven't we? (*He shrugs, unconvinced.*)

I bet your stomach never felt like that when you was doing the labouring.

(*ANGELO grins and shakes his head. She pursues her advantage.*)

Look, all those bloody union meetings you go to...make a name, you'll find people will listen to yuh. Only you got to make a name first.

ANGELO: As a singer?

PIAF: Yeah, I know it's daft, but that's the way it works.

ANGELO: I don't belong here.

PIAF: Neither does anybody else, love. Performing's what you make it. It's a job, same as anything else – only amateurs believe in the glamour. Wait till you've seen as many cold, damp rehearsal rooms as I have, as many shitty dressing rooms with no hot water...your bloody unions would never put up with it.

ANGELO: I miss my mates.

PIAF: Sure. Me too. Know what? Sometimes I nip out and do a bit of street singing. Just to keep me hand in...well, you never know. I was down Raspail once, not long ago...two women went by, I heard one say, 'She sounds like Piaf...' The other one said, 'Trying to.'

(*This makes ANGELO laugh. He kisses her.*)

ANGELO: I owe you everything.

PIAF: Stand still. (*She adjusts his tie.*)

P/A: Your call please, Madame Piaf and Monsieur Angelo, your call, please. Thank you.

PIAF: Don't forget the plot on number three. (*He nods.*) And the double intro...second pause...bam-bam, you come in.

ANGELO: Thanks.

PIAF: And remember not to waggle your head. Keep still, make them come to you...make *them* talented. Let's have a look at you...no, over here...

(*He crosses and stands before her. She grasps him about the hips, looking up at him with fierce physical admiration.*)

...wah, they'll come in their knickers. But don't forget the men, they've got to like you too...they've got to want to *be* you. And stick to the gestures we worked out...don't drift into things of your own.

ANGELO: OK.

PIAF: And come off cleanly, big strides, but slower, like we rehearsed. Oh, and don't keep lifting your chin up, it makes you look ugly. And don't hunch. What are you looking like that for?

ANGELO: Darling, could you shut up a leetle bit?

PIAF: Bloody nerve! (*But she gets the message. ANGELO has stage-fright.*) Don't worry, love, I'll be there. It's together from now on. Here... (*She dives into her bag.*) I was going to give it to you after. (*She drops a key into his hand after jingling it in his face provocatively.*)

ANGELO: What is it?

PIAF: What do you think...? Vrmmm...vrmmmm!

ANGELO: Edith! (*His face is pure happiness. He embraces her.*) But you shouldn't spend like this!

PIAF: Just this once.

P/A: Your call, Madame Piaf...your call, Monsieur Angelo. (*PIAF moves away from ANGELO.*)

ANGELO: What you doing?

PIAF: Oh, just something for the rheumatism, love. (*ANGELO goes. PIAF injects herself.*
On the P/A, the sound of a fast car, topped by the sounds of a horrendous crash.)

Scene 7

PIAF's apartment. PIERRE and a PHYSIOTHERAPIST.

PIERRE: (*Writing out a cheque for the fee.*) So, you'll be coming to do the treatments daily?

PHYSIO: Yes. Though I entirely agree with the hospital, it's madness for Madame to discharge herself.

PIERRE: I know. However, she insists.

PHYSIO: Her forehead is still full of glass! How did she lose the three ribs, by the way?

PIERRE: A previous car accident.

PHYSIO: Obviously she should give up driving.

PIERRE: No, no, she doesn't drive. She tends to be driven by young men.

PHYSIO: I see.

PIERRE: Look, we fully accept the risk, but we need to get Madame working again. When can she sing?

PHYSIO: I beg your pardon?

PIERRE: She has a big concert coming up.

PHYSIO: But the mouth is badly torn – ripped! I can't start on that sort of scar tissue for months – she mustn't even speak!

PIERRE: No, no, that's impossible, the concert's in six weeks.

PHYSIO: I don't think you understand! This patient is lucky to be alive! Most women of her age would have been dead from shock on arrival. There's been severe internal injury, laceration, bruising...she's probably alive because she's a singer...we got good response from the diaphragm. I can't seem to make you understand, you've got an invalid on your hands!

PIERRE: She wants to try. She's determined.

PHYSIO: She'll need to be more than that. I'm afraid there'll be a lot of pain for some time. Of course, she can be helped with that.

PIERRE: You mean morphine?

PHYSIO: Yes. (*He catches PIERRE's anxious look.*) Why, has she been on – ?

PIERRE: (*Giving him the cheque.*) No, no, no, it's nothing. Just...there was a lot of pain last time, that's all.

(*PIERRE goes. The PHYSIOTHERAPIST prepares for the treatment. PIAF enters, looking the worse for wear.*)

PHYSIO: Good morning, Madame Piaf.

PIAF: (*Evilly.*) Oh Christ, here it comes. (*Then she manages a winning smile.*) Are you going to give me a shot?

PHYSIO: I'm sorry, Madame, you've had the prescribed dose.

(*PIAF stands, her face changing – becoming a glare. But he will not budge. So, heavily, she slumps into the chair. He bends, to start the treatment. But she postpones the moment.*)

PIAF: Look, is this going to do any good? It doesn't seem to –

PHYSIO: Just lie back. Try to relax. (*She tries. He begins pulling at the scar tissue around her mouth, working at it gently but firmly. She moans and jerks out of his hands.*)

PIAF: Christ Almighty!

PHYSIO: (*Formally.*) I'm sorry. Doctor's orders.

PIAF: Madeleine...Madeleine!

(*She catches the PHYSIOTHERAPIST's eye. Obviously something is up. They both glance off.*)

Oh fuck, I forgot. Oh, all right, bloody get on with it. Take it slower...something, for Christ's sake.

(*The PHYSIOTHERAPIST begins again.*)

Ow! Ow!

PHYSIO: *Madame*, please. You say you want to sing in six weeks. It's impossible, but at least I'm trying.

(*PIAF submits, grasping the arms of the chair in agony. MADELEINE enters, with a large suitcase and a small travelling bag. She is dressed for travelling. She stands, a little apart. PIAF ignores her.*)

MADELEINE: Piaf...

(*PIAF cannot or will not reply. MADELEINE comes closer. She tries to take PIAF's hand.*)

I've come to say goodbye.

PIAF: (*Snatching her hand away.*) Piss off.

(*MADELEINE stands, humiliated and miserable.*)

MADELEINE: (*In a low voice.*) Please, Piaf.

PIAF: (*In a high, prissy voice, exaggerated by the distortion of her scars.*) 'After all you done' – well, fuck off.

(*She thrusts her scarred, squinting face up at MADELEINE.*)

That's my answer to you, cock. Stone cold sober.

MADELEINE: (*Very upset.*) Very well. (*She fishes into her handbag and holds out an envelope.*)

You've given me too much. I can't accept it.

(*PIAF turns her head and spits on the envelope. The PHYSIOTHERAPIST and MADELEINE exchange a glance over her head. MADELEINE gently puts the envelope on the floor at PIAF's feet. She picks up her case and looks again to PIAF.*)

Goodbye, then.

(*With a sudden witchlike viciousness, PIAF picks up the envelope, wipes it on her ass, and throws it in MADELEINE's face. MADELEINE flinches.*)

(*Quietly, her voice breaking slightly.*) The very best of luck.

(*She goes, turning at the exit, but there is no change of heart from PIAF. The PHYSIOTHERAPIST, embarrassed by the scene, has ceased working.*

Slight pause.)

PIAF: All right! We know what you think! Why don't you piss off after her...you've really got something to tell them now. Go on, piss off if you want to.

PHYSIO: (*Feigning ignorance.*) I beg your pardon, Madame?

PIAF: You know who she thinks she is...St Bernadette! 'Ew, I'll never leave you, Piaf, I'll do anything for you...just lean on me.' Like hell. They're like Dracula. D'you know...d'you know... (*She turns and looks up into the PHYSIOTHERAPIST's unresponsive face.*) They're after your balls, the lot of them! 'Yew don't appreciate me!' Then it's the bloody waterworks, as if you could do with that on top of everything.

(*The PHYSIOTHERAPIST pushes her down and sets her head straight. She makes as if to submit, but her rage is too great.*)

Who do they think you *are*? (*She turns to the PHYSIOTHERAPIST, wincing.*) Listen, I'll tell you something... What goes on here is the rest of me...and it's not worth knowing, I can tell you. (*She settles back in her seat, muttering.*) Come here looking for glamour – they want glamour, they can pay to see me down at the Olympia, and I don't mean shoved-up tits neither.

PHYSIO: Could you put your head straight, please?

PIAF: No, they all want a slice. Even the bloody managers. Will they take the rough with the smooth? Will they hell! They want the bloody product – they want that all right, all wrapped up with a feather up its ass – but *songs*? They don't want *songs*! Sing the fucking telephone directory, they wouldn't know the difference, who wants to break in new stuff, well, it's all trouble innit? Then it's...*I* know...why don't we book Charlie, or old Jean...no trouble there...quiet drink at the bar, split the divvi. Do you know what? D'you know how Charlie writes his songs? By committee! They all sit round a bloody table! 'What rhymes with June, lads?' 'It's not professional behaviour, Piaf!' Nah, they've all got lodgings up each other's assholes, these *professionals*. They can shove their glamour up there and all, they don't get the goods on show from me, I've always put that where I want.

(*Slight pause. The PHYSIOTHERAPIST lifts his hands to begin work again, but PIAF has not finished.*)

No, pretty soon they're not going to want my stuff. My sort's dying out. Going extinct. What they want now is discs, they don't really want performance – well, they think they do, but what they really want is something canned. In the can. The real thing…well, dodgy innit? Trouble. Nah. I mean, look at it this way, it stands to reason…you can *count* discs…stack 'em…put 'em in containers. They don't bloody answer back. (*Again it seems as if she will settle, but she continues.*) I said to him, I said, 'No, I'm sorry, love, I don't reckon it.' 'Oh, I thought you'd like it, it's a love song, Piaf.' Love! Fucking love. I'll tell them about love. I was sitting with a little brass once…

PHYSIO: Sorry?

PIAF: Whore…a tart…!

PHYSIO: Oh.

PIAF: She was dropping a kid, back of a club…Christ, there was blood everywhere. Anyway, get an old nurse to her in the end…dear little baby girl. She starts mopping her up – 'Hello,' she says. 'Where is it?' 'Where's what?' says my friend. 'All your bits and pieces,' says the old biddy. 'Your thingme!' 'Oh,' says my friend, 'Chewed off years ago.' That's bloody love for you. (*She turns and gives the PHYSIOTHERAPIST a look.*)

PHYSIO: It's not uncommon.

PIAF: Well, you'd know, working in hospitals. Hey… (*She is all ready for some juicy stories.*) I bet *you've* seen a few things, eh?

PHYSIO: (*Formally.*) Just keep the head still, please. (*She subsides with a rancid face. A knock reprieves her. The PHYSIOTHERAPIST turns.*)

PIAF: Come in!

(*It is a nicely dressed pageboy – JACKO – from an expensive flower shop, bearing a tribute for PIAF. She half sees the flowers and subsides, uninterested.*)

JACKO: Hi, Piaf.

(*The PHYSIOTHERAPIST begins to work on her face.*)

PIAF: Cheeky with it. How d'you like to be in pictures?

JACKO: Knock it off, I'm a singer.

(*PIAF turns and clocks him in his blue and gold suit.*)

PIAF: Are you now?

JACKO: Well, trying to be.

PIAF: Pity about your nose.

JACKO: What's wrong with it?

PIAF: Has to go, dunnit?

JACKO: What d'you mean? It's not a tyre, you know… I ain't got a spare.

(*PIAF laughs. She rises and crosses to him.*)

PIAF: What's your name, love?

JACKO: Jacko. Here… (*He proffers the flowers. PIAF throws them aside and gives him a kiss.*)

(*Light change. The PHYSIOTHERAPIST leaves. PIAF crosses. She applies make-up to her face.*)

P/A: Your call, Madame Piaf…Madame Piaf, your call, please.

PIAF: That you Jacko?

(*JACKO enters wearing a blue 'Piaf' suit. He kisses her.*)

What's it like out front?

JACKO: Sizzling.

PIAF: Buggers think I can't make it.

JACKO: No, no, they love you…same as ever.

PIAF: Well, I don't give 'em no shit, that's for sure. Remember that, kid. Give 'em the real thing. (*He bends and kisses her.*)

Ah, you're good for me…we're good for each other, Jackie – tell you what, I'll give you a nose job for your birthday.

JACKO: You don't have to give me anything. I'm here because I like you.

PIAF: I'll believe you. No...you're all right, kid...you can sing, too.

JACKO: I don't know about –

PIAF: (*Sharply.*) Don't piss on yourself, plenty do that for you – here, how do I look?

JACKO: Bloody good. Will that stuff stay on?

PIAF: Don't worry.

P/A: Madame Piaf...your call, please...your call, Madame Piaf...thank you.

JACKO: It's OK, darling.

PIAF: Sure. You go on...I'll just have a minute to meself...get it together.

(*JACKO gives her a sharp look but leaves. PIAF injects herself. PIAF sings 'Droit d'aimer'. If there is applause from the audience, she accepts it with radiant charm, then, looking up, with a murderous face.*)

Kill the fucking lights! And where the hell were you?

(*Indistinguishable excuses from above.*)

No, well, I'm not that bloody small. (*More explanations.*)

Look son, just do what you're paid for – right?

(*The MANAGER enters, genially, and embraces her.*)

MANAGER: Marvellous, Piaf, marvellous. We can't get them out of the building. I've got a little proposition.

PIAF: It'll have to wait, I'm tired.

MANAGER: It's important. I wouldn't bother you otherwise...

PIAF: Can I have a sub?

MANAGER: (*Gently remonstrating.*) Piaf...

PIAF: Only till tomorrow.

MANAGER: They've cashed up. You know what we agreed.

PIAF: Look –

MANAGER: You ready?

PIAF: Look, Henry...

(*The MANAGER goes. PIAF, alone, seems agitated. A SMALL MAN appears. PIAF crosses to him.*)

I thought you weren't coming. Have you got it?

(*The MAN nods. She opens her hand but he delays.*)

PIAF: Look, I haven't got any money on me, I'll see you tomorrow.

PUSHER: Sorry, Piaf, it's more than I dare do, you know that.

PIAF: But I can fix it tomorrow, no trouble.

PUSHER: Can't you get it from the Box Office?

PIAF: No, he won't have it.

(*The PUSHER begins to move off. PIAF becomes agitated.*)

Look, I must have a delivery.

PUSHER: I'll be round in the afternoon.

PIAF: No…no…

(*She hangs on to him. He extricates himself sadly.*)

PUSHER: Piaf, you know better than that. Look, I'd do anything for you, you know that – I've got all your records. We're in the same boat, remember? (*Pulling away from her.*) I'll see you tomorrow.

(*He goes. Alone, PIAF becomes more and more agitated. She begins to shake.*)

PIAF: Oh God…oh God…dear God…

(*JACKO enters.*)

Get out…get out!

(*Frightened, JACKO goes. Alone, PIAF's mania increases. She pulls off her clothes, plunges about, shivers, heaves as if wanting to be sick, and whimpers. She crouches, picking at herself. She goes into a fit. An ATTENDANT enters. She fights him savagely, screaming. He cuffs her and carries her out.*)

Scene 8

A room at the Ritz. Pieces of appropriate furniture. JACKO enters, trim. He looks around to make sure everything is comfortable. He turns – PIAF is there. She is wearing a new outfit.

PIAF: How do I rate?

(*JACKO crosses, picks her up and swings her round.*)

JACKO: Fan-bloody-tastic.

PIAF: Pay for an all-nighter, would you?

JACKO: (*Laughing.*) You can have one now if you like.

(*PIAF nods, taking off her clothes.*)

PIAF: Nah, we'll keep the hey diddle diddle till after ...unless...have you got an erection?

JACKO: It'll keep.

PIAF: It better, after six weeks in St Mortiz and all that *après-ski* stuff I bought you. Like me new dress?

(*JACKO begins to fondle her. PIERRE enters.*)

PIERRE: I like it, keep it in.

(*PIAF turns, screams a welcome and leaps on PIERRE, who nods cordially to JACKO.*)

PIERRE: Has she been a good girl?

PIAF: Cross me heart!

JACKO: Oh yes.

PIAF: Where's the vino, love...? (*To PIERRE.*) I'm allowed wine.

JACKO: Two a day if you're good.

(*JACKO serves the drinks.*)

PIERRE: What the hell are you doing here? I went to the apartment.

PIAF: They turned off all the gas and light.

JACKO: Slight problem with the bills.

PIERRE: I see, so you moved into the Ritz?

PIAF: Oh, it's only for now, love, just while we're broke. Everything's going to be different from now on. Like me engagement ring? (*She lifts her head to JACKO for a kiss.*)

PIERRE: Very nice.

(*They drink.*)

PIAF: Right. Down to work.

(*PIERRE fusses with his briefcase.*)

What have you come up with? I can't wait to get started.

(*PIERRE looks at her, then at JACKO. Pause.*)

PIERRE: (*At last.*) Piaf, I have to know. Is it finished?

PIAF: Yes, love. It's finished. All I want – (*She thrusts out a hand to JACKO.*) I've got all I want. Hey, how d'you like his new nose?

(*PIERRE smiles and nods.*)

Just the work now.

JACKO: Edith can't wait.

PIAF: When do we start, boss?

PIERRE: Piaf, it's bound to take time.

PIAF: What do you mean? I'm off the shit.

PIERRE: Well, we know that but...ah... (*Slight pause.*) I can't get any bookings. They don't want to know.

PIAF: But I've told you, I'm cured.

PIERRE: We've tried everything. Nobody's playing.

(*Silence. PIAF swears under her breath. She lifts her glass but it is empty.*)

JACKO: Some more?

(*But in a moment of decision PIAF waves the bottle away.*)

PIAF: No, love. Right. If that's the way they want it. If we have to prove it, we'll prove it. We'll do the provinces... fleapits, cinemas, holiday camps – I feel like a tour. Kill the bottle, Jacko.

JACKO: Sure, love.

PIAF: Better give Michel a ring, I'll need some songs...

JACKO: Right.

PIAF: ...and ring Eddie – we'll start rehearsing tonight. OK, Pierrot?

(*JACKO pauses for ratification.*)

PIERRE: (*After a pause.*) I don't know. It may be difficult.

PIAF: Oh come on, I'll be a draw! They'll come to see if I can stay on my feet!

(*PIERRE does not respond.*)

The press are on my side, we'll have all the publicity we want and more.

(*PIERRE still does not reply.*)

Pierrot! Come on! I've done it before, I can do it again!

PIERRE: One-night stands, fit-ups, travelling overnight ...that was a long time ago. We're all older.

(*Silence – held.*)

If we do it...

PIAF: Thanks, boss!

PIERRE: (*Bleakly.*) I said 'if'...I hold the purse. No running up debts, no freeloaders, no private shows, parties, subbing everybody in sight. You've got to start hanging on to something. It won't last forever.

PIAF: I know, love. I'm an ignorant cunt who'll end up skint.

PIERRE: If you know so much, why don't you do something about it? You've got to start putting a few things together.

PIAF: Like stocks and shares, you mean?

PIERRE: Well, you could do a lot worse.

PIAF: Ah, don't insult me.

PIERRE: I wasn't.

PIAF: (*Quietly.*) Yes you were. All right, I made a mess of it with the shit –

PIERRE: It's just common sense, Edith!

PIAF: Ah, you're all the same, even you. (*She sounds tired.*)

JACKO: All right, love?

PIAF: Can't get me the bookings, eh? Been trying? Or is to second thoughts time?

PIERRE: What do you mean?

PIAF: Where were you when I was in the bloody bin?

PIERRE: Look, I told you –

PIAF: That's right, you got a lot on. What with your place in the Dordogne, your new apartment, your portfolio...the little bit of land near Bordeaux. Not to mention your new clients. I hear you're collecting glass now.

PIERRE: What's wrong with that?

PIAF: (*To JACKO, in a semi-jocular tone.*) Never asks me to his little dinner parties.

PIERRE: Only because I know you wouldn't come.

PIAF: Damn right I wouldn't. Think I don't know what it's all about? You're all the same – (*To JACKO.*) Don't you get into money, you'll end up in the soup, I'm telling you, not that you'll listen. I'm not sitting at table for your old lady to show off the Sèvres to a couple of accountants, no sir. You got another thing coming. Oh no. I'm not bloody joining and there's an end to it.

PIERRE: Nobody says you should.

PIAF: Come off it, you never let up! Night after night, out the corner of their eye...what's she wearing, how much they got…who's on first, what's on second, I wouldn't insult meself. You can't understand, can you? You think we all want to get ahead. Like you. Pile it up for tomorrow. When's tomorrow? Nah, I was born lucky. Never had it, don't want it, never had the bother. OK, a bit draughty, but I know all I need to know. You got nothing to bribe me with…well… (*She grins up at JACKO.*) Perhaps a couple of things. (*Slight pause.*) You're a chancer, love. You think being born working class is like having a disease.

PIERRE: Look, Piaf, I'm just an ordinary –

PIAF: Oh, we all know what you were. I know what you *were*…and I know what you *want.* Think those two little girls want *you* down at the school gates? You've made such fucking little ladies of them, they're ashamed of you already.

(*Slight pause.*)

PIERRE: Who told you that?

JACKO: Come on, love…leave it.

PIAF: Yeah. OK. I'm sorry. Only just leave out all the buying and selling.

PIERRE: Piaf, there's nothing wrong with honest trade. After all, you sell your voice.

PIAF: That's a laugh.

PIERRE: Only because you fuck about. You've had the rate for the job, you just haven't hung onto it.

PIAF: No, well, I'm just a bit of old Belleville rubbish, inni?

JACKO: (*Kissing her hand.*) Don't worry about it, love… you're never going to be a lady.

PIAF: Too right I'm not. I've seen them, the ladies – if they get a buzz for a feller, somebody touches them up, are they going to give it away? Not on your nelly – might give their old man a chance for a bit on the side. Get a damp spot on their knicks, they take it out on a day's shopping. Look in *Printemps* any afternoon, you'll see 'em mooching round the handbag counters, put themselves to better use, there wouldn't be so many wars, not that they'd be any good at it. They really think they can take it with 'em, like the fucking tourists so busy taking pictures they never see anything, it's like that man…remember the joke…the one who goes to see his mate and his wife comes to the door and says, 'Ew, new, yew cawn't see him, he's dead.' 'Dead?' says the man, 'He can't be…he's got my big chisel!'

(*They laugh.*)

Nah. We'll get on as we are. Just get me the bookings.

(*PIERRE gets up, comes close to her, takes her hands and looks into her eyes.*)

PIERRE: Edith, I have to know. Is it over?

(*PIAF looks him straight in the eye.*)

PIAF: Yes, love. It's finished.

(*PIERRE embraces her. They kiss. He rises and JACKO sees him out. Alone, PIAF takes out her syringe.*)

Scene 9

An empty stage. The MANAGER enters and crosses to the microphone.

MANAGER: (*Testing the mike.*) One, two, three… (*He raises his head.*) Ladies and gentlemen…I give you…your own…Piaf!!

(*There follows a reprise of the first scene of the play: musical intro – 'La goualante du pauve Jean', as before.*

After a perceptible pause PIAF enters. She comes to the microphone and announces the name of the song, and the names of the lyricist and music writer. She begins to sing but, exactly as before, founders after the first few bars and sways at the audience, her stare unfocused. The music dies away and after a slight pause the MANAGER enters and tries to get her off. She resists, holding onto the microphone.)

PIAF: Get your fucking hands off me, I ain't *done* nothing yet.

(*They go off. Empty stage. The MANAGER enters.*)

MANAGER: Ladies and gentlemen…I give you…your own…Piaf!

(PIAF enters. Even the walk to the microphone is an obvious effort for her. Musical intro. But PIAF does not come in. The music begins again but she does not seem to be aware. The MANAGER enters and quietly leads her off.

Empty stage. The MANAGER enters.)

MANAGER: Ladies and gentlemen...I give you...your own...Piaf!

(PIAF enters, visibly weaker. She exudes fear and flinches at the lights. She approaches the microphone. Musical intro – but she is not even close enough to the microphone. She puts out a hand to the audience, but there is nothing. JACKO runs on, followed by the MANAGER. JACKO manages to catch her as she hits the floor. He bends over her inert form, his face full of alarm. After a slight pause she moves, lifts her head, looks up and is slowly aware that it is him.)

PIAF: *(In an exhausted voice.)* It's all right, love...it's all right...I'm still here...

(She tries to get up but he carries her off.)

Scene 10

PIAF's private room in a nursing home. JACKO, spruce in a blue suit, enters with flowers and presents. A YOUNG NURSE, pretty and lively, enters, wheeling PIAF in a wheelchair.

NURSE: Good morning, good morning...oh, what lovely flowers! Shall I take them?

(But PIAF puts out a restraining hand. JACKO is looking at her, shocked by her appearance. PIAF is aware of this. He recovers himself swiftly, crossing to kiss her, and shows her the presents.)

JACKO: A few little... *(He gives the stuff to the NURSE, who smiles at him. But he only has eyes for PIAF. The NURSE is making sure that her patient is comfortable.)*

NURSE: All right, dear...sure you're all right?

(She goes at last. Silence.)

PIAF: Nice girl.

JACKO: What? Oh…yes. (*Silence. He doesn't know what to say. He can't stop looking at her. She looks so old.*)

PIAF: (*At last.*) They let you in, then.

JACKO: (*With a sickly attempt at jollity.*) Try keeping me out.

PIAF: I told them you were working nights.

(*The awful silence falls again.*)

How's it going?

JACKO: OK. OK.

PIAF: Good houses?

JACKO: More than break point. Seventy percent last night.

PIAF: Really! That's good!

JACKO: Well, Friday of course.

PIAF: Still, good though.

(*Short silence.*)

JACKO: How, ah…how've you been?

PIAF: Not so grand.

JACKO: Did you get any sleep?

PIAF: I had to ask them for something.

JACKO: I'll have a word with him.

PIAF: I wish you would, I can't get any sense out of them.

(*She turns her head away and we see JACKO's look of alarm at her. We see the gravity of her condition in his submerged alarm.*)

So, it's going all right?

JACKO: Yeah, very nice. New company, and they're good guvnors.

PIAF: Well, I told you. You're all right there, just the right spot. Funny you never heard any more about the tour. (*She catches his eye.*) *Did* you hear any more?

JACKO: Yeah, but…nothing came of it.

PIAF: What do you mean?

JACKO: The terms weren't right.

PIAF: What do you mean? It's a number one tour…are you nuts or something?

JACKO: I'm not going.

PIAF: You bloody are. You bloody are if I say so.

JACKO: I'm not leaving you.

PIAF: Oh! Oh! Like that is it? And who'll be the first to throw it in my face when the time comes? Don't be a fool, they won't ask you twice, cockie.

JACKO: Piaf, I'm not leaving you in here.

PIAF: Why, what's the matter, have they told you I'm going to fucking die or something? Well, have they?

JACKO: No, of course not.

PIAF: Well, what *did* he say?

JACKO: That you need a rest.

PIAF: (*Muttering.*) I'm rigid with rest.

JACKO: Edith, why won't you let me marry you...if we got married I could take care of you properly... *I* can take care of you.

PIAF: Look...it's a number one tour...d'you think that's *nothing*? I don't understand you, I really don't.

(*There is a muddled silence between them.*)

All the bloody work I put into you! They don't care...! They don't give a toss.

JACKO: Well, I'm not leaving you. When you're ready, we'll tour together. I am not leaving you in the shit and you can shout as much as you like, Edith, I shan't change me mind.

(*He looks down at his hands, embarrassed. She looks at him. She smiles, then figures a way to make him go.*)

PIAF: (*At last.*) We-ll, as far as that goes, I suppose it'll have to come out in the open.

JACKO: What do you mean?

PIAF: It's the elbow, old son, haven't you seen it coming? That's why... (*She searches.*) That's why they haven't been letting you in! (*She laughs her throaty laugh.*) Oh, there's been some real fun and games.

JACKO: (*Failing to catch her eye.*) No, I don't believe it.

PIAF: Hard luck on you, then. (*He tries to take her hand. She withdraws it.*) Get the message, son. You've had a good run for it.

(*JACKO is stunned with shock. He turns away, to control himself, then looks at her again, blinking and frowning with shock.*)

PIAF: Now, listen…don't forget…you've got to lift the voice. Lift…lift. It's a lovely tone, but keep it light. And don't forget diction – it never hurts them to hear what you're on about, never mind the A and R wizards. My God, those eyes of yours, you'll knock 'em cold. Here, something for luck.

(*She takes off her cross of St Theresa and gives it to him. He starts to cry.*)

Come on…come on. Here, give us a kiss.

(*He leans over her, but she proffers only her cheek.*)

Now piss off, I want to kip.

JACKO: If ever –

(*But she shakes an irritable hand. He kisses her hand fervently and goes, confused and crying.*)

PIAF: (*Clutching his flowers and muttering fiercely to herself.*) You bloody old martyr.

(*The NURSE enters.*)

NURSE: Oh, he's gone! That was a love-you-and-leave-you! I'll put them in water with the others.

(*She takes the flowers and bustles about, humming – young and shining. PIAF regards her for a moment, then looks away.*)

Oh, by the way…he's here again.

PIAF: What?

NURSE: (*Coyly.*) You know…

PIAF: Who?

NURSE: The foreign boy!

PIAF: (*Uninterested.*) What's he want?

NURSE: (*Giggly.*) We've been trying to find out but honestly, he's so shy! I think he wants to see you.

PIAF: Are you kidding?

NURSE: I said I'd ask you.

PIAF: Oh, tell him my fanny's dropped off, I'm having a transplant.

NURSE: I shan't tell him anything of the sort. There, that's better. (*She finishes tidying PIAF and turns to go.*)

PIAF: What's he look like?

NURSE: The foreign boy? I keep telling you…tall, dark and handsome! You could just thank him – he's called every day.

PIAF: Oh, well, just for a minute. But only if he's good-looking, mind.

(*The NURSE goes.*)

Probably frighten him for life.

(*She scratches at her hair. THEO enters. He stands shyly, with a small posy of flowers, unlike JACKO'S big offering. He inclines his head in shy greeting.*)

THEO: Hello.

PIAF: Well… (*She laughs.*) Now you've seen me!

(*He crosses, stands over her and proffers the flowers. She takes them.*)

Thanks, kid. What's the matter, died of shock?

(*She laughs, and starts to cough. At once he has a handkerchief, and wipes her mouth gently. He gives her a drink.*)

Thanks. Thanks, kid…you a male nurse or something?

(*He shakes his head.*)

What's your name?

THEO: Theo.

PIAF: Theo what?

THEO: Theophanis Lambouskas.

PIAF: (*Laughs.*) That'll have to go for a start. Tell me about yourself, Theo.

THEO: I have seen all your concerts…Olympia, Lyons, Bordeaux.

PIAF: Oh, Bordeaux…not so hot.

THEO: I wanted to come in America but that was not possible for me.

PIAF: They applauded for fifteen minutes in Carnegie Hall. That's a long time. (*Slight pause.*) You're a nice-looking boy, Theo. (*She pats and pulls at her hair, conscious of her appearance.*)

THEO: You want I should do your hair? (*He takes out a comb. He moves swiftly behind her and beings to comb her hair gently.*)

PIAF: Ah…you're a hairdresser.

(She smiles up at him, and he smiles down, absorbed in his task. The moment is held. He combs deftly and with concentration, lifting up the hair, improving her. Then he helps her out of the chair – she lifts her hand to tell him she is OK – and she walks to the microphone. She lifts her crippled hands, her eyes shining like lamps.)

(Into the mike.) Ladies and gentlemen…ladies and gentlemen…I don't deserve such happiness… Ladies and gentlemen…I would like to present my husband…Theo Sarapo! *(She calls off, throaty and commanding.)* Theo!

(THEO enters, a gold medallion over his black sweater. They sing, in duet, 'A quoi ça sert, l'amour'.

THEO goes.

PIAF sings 'Non, je ne regrette rien'.)

Scene 11

PIAF's room in the South of France. A piece of Provençal furniture. PIAF is in her wheelchair. THEO is tucking her up. He looks up, as at a sound.

PIAF: What was it?

THEO: A visitor, darling. The nurse will see to it.

PIAF: Who was it?

THEO: An old friend, from Belleville, she says… Toinette…

PIAF: Toine? Old Toine? Never! Where is she? *(Calling.)* Toine!

(TOINE enters.)

TOINE: Ede?

PIAF: Where are you?

TOINE: Is it you?

PIAF: Who the fuck d'you think it is? I'm not dead yet. Christ, you've put on weight. Let's have a look at you. How d'you find me?

TOINE: I took a train.

(PIAF lifts her head at TOINE's unchanging style.)

PIAF: Here, Theo… (*She takes his hand.*) Well, what do you think of him?

(*TOINE smiles, embarrassed.*)

TOINE: I heard you was married.

PIAF: Come on, no farting about, what do you think of him?

TOINE: He's a bit young.

(*PIAF laughs.*)

PIAF: Oyoy! (*She lifts a clenched fist suggestively.*) Haha, never think she was an old Belleville streetwalker, would you?

TOINE: Edith!

PIAF: Oh Christ, you never could take a joke – here, have a drink – you still drink, don't you?

TOINE: Only wine now.

PIAF: (*Ignoring her.*) Theo, fetch in the whisky.

THEO: Darling, you should sleep soon.

PIAF: Never mind that, where's the whisky? That's what she's after.

(*THEO goes.*)

What do you think of him? Best bloody looker I ever had, better than anything you ever got.

TOINE: How old *is* he?

PIAF: Old enough, don't you worry yourself about that.

(*She plucks the rig with her crippled hands.*)

TOINE: You don't *do* nothing, do you?

(*PIAF looks at her.*)

PIAF: Nah. Nah. Still…never know. (*Pause.*) Anyway, thanks for coming. See your daft face, cheer anybody up. What your old man say?

TOINE: Never told him.

PIAF: Just as well.

TOINE: You know what he's like. He thinks you ought to have set us up.

PIAF: Ah, you know me…never could hang on to nothing…still, we had some good times, eh? Remember running in and out of Coco Chanel's buying two of everything…I never did pay that bill.

(*Pause.*)

TOINE: (*Getting out the Gitanes.*) Mind if I smoke?

PIAF: It's bad for you, you know. I read it in the paper.

TOINE: Oh well, you can only die once. (*And could bite her tongue off PIAF, her head back on the high pillow, like a little old cardinal, smiles sardonically.*)

PIAF: Trust you.

(*THEO returns with wine for TOINE.*)

TOINE: Aren't you having nothing, Ede?

THEO: Edith's on a diet just now.

TOINE: Oh, I brought you some apples. (*She gives them to THEO, getting in a flurry with her drink, the fag and her bag as he bends over her.*)

PIAF: Hey, you two, no getting off. (*She laughs.*) We could tell him a thing or two, eh Toine? D'you know, we had our own band at one time, her and me. She spent more time seeing fellers off at the back than we ever copped in fees.

TOINE: We had to eat.

(*Pause. TOINE tries to think of something, to keep things going.*)

Hey – hey, remember that time in Milan?

PIAF: You never came to Milan.

TOINE: Yes I did.

PIAF: No you didn't.

TOINE: I did!

PIAF: You never!

THEO: Darling –

PIAF: (*Lying back, her eyes closed.*) All right, love. Yeah, I remember. Go on, tell him.

TOINE: (*Starting to laugh.*) We brought these…these Chinese acrobats back to the hotel where we was staying…they was sharing the bill…

PIAF: Go on…

TOINE: There was ever so many of 'em…

PIAF: Tell him about the goldfish…

TOINE: I was going to! Anyway, there was this pond…they had this ornamental pond, you know, in the foyer…so we got them all paddling…catching the fish in their little shoes …then we…

(*TOINE and PIAF are laughing, TOINE noisily.*)
We...oh, ho ho...we got them all in the kitchens making breakfast...and had 'em on toast...d'you remember, Ede? Little bit of garnish...

PIAF: And noodles!

TOINE: (*Shrieking with laughter.*) Oh Christ, I forgot about the noodles.
(*They both bend over with laughter at some private joke, TOINE wiping her eyes.*)
(*Subsiding.*) I can't remember what we did after that. Oh yeah...that's right...you tried to slash your wrists. (*She smiles in fond reminiscence.*)

PIAF: Did I?

TOINE: I bloody nearly let you and all, she was always playing that game on us.

PIAF: (*Momentarily bleak.*) Pity you didn't.
(*It's an awkward moment.*)

THEO: (*Murmuring.*) Darling, no –

PIAF: No, you're right, love. I wouldn't of met you.

TOINE: We got thrown out.

PIAF: He's lovely. I don't deserve him. (*Pause. One hand plucks the rug.*) Go on...go on, Toine.
(*TOINE looks helplessly at THEO. She is not much of a talker.*)

TOINE: Ede, you know my youngest kid...the little one, Simone...hey, she's ever such a good dancer! We're paying for classes...I mean, I don't know if it'll come to anything. Be nice, though.

THEO: Do you want to sleep now, darling?

PIAF: No...go on...go on...

TOINE: (*Searching about and eventually coming up with something.*) Oh...yeah...remember the Boche, Edith? One of them looked me up after the war...I never told you! (*To THEO.*) They locked us up once, during the war – well, Ede was passing messages to our chaps in the prison camps, I really thought our number was up, I can tell you –
(*PIAF seems to be drifting off. TOINE whispers to THEO.*)

Is she all right?

(*THEO drops on his knees by PIAF's side. He is concerned.*)

THEO: Edith?

(*But PIAF has collapsed – indeed, may be dead. THEO puts his arms about her, cradling her head.*)

TOINE: Ede?

(*Lights slowly down.*)

The End.

CAMILLE

based on
La Dame aux camélias
by Alexandre Dumas *fils*

Foreword

Sometime in the early '80s I received a telephone call from set designer Hugh Durrant. Would I go to lunch?

We ate at a quiet French restaurant. Hugh asked me if I would be interested in doing a new version of *The Lady of the Camellias*. This was surprising. Romantic plays were totally out of fashion – we were still in the days of 'committed' theatre.

Re-reading *The Lady of the Camellias*, written in the 1840s by Alexandre Dumas *fils*, was a reminder that, by modern standards, the book is a romantic old boiler. An impoverished young man falls in love with a Parisian courtesan. His dear old father persuades her to give him up. She does. And she dies. The book didn't inspire.

Some time later, one morning, a piercing memory from childhood surfaced. We lived, my mother, brothers and I, in a gardener's bothy, in the grounds of a large estate. The tap was across the yard and we lived in a tiny kitchen where the range kept us warm and mottled our legs. The owner of the beautiful Georgian house (Lady L) charged us 12/6 a week rent – out of my mother's income of 22/6d. (She also, occasionally, gave us vegetables from a trug.) Lady L had three grandsons. Two were often away at boarding school, but we played together, bunking over the high wall and escaping down to the marsh and the river. We swam, fished, took birds' eggs, played Cowboys and Indians and jumped from the dredged gravel heaps onto New Forest ponies, sent down to brackish water to strengthen their legs. It was, I know now, Arcadia.

One day I asked my mother why the boys, especially the older two, were so stiff and cold. Was it because they were posh? She said no – it was because they were orphans. I didn't understand. How could they be orphans when they had parents? Much later I realised what she meant. That the parents orphaned their children by sending them away to boarding school. And that their coldness was due to emotional trauma.

Suddenly, there he was. Armand – my Armand. Not a poor boy who couldn't afford a mistress, but an aristocrat, reared by servants and sent away to school. Armand would stand for Imperialism – the old Aristotelian notion that the gentleman stained his hands only with blood, never with work or trade. Armand – unloved and unable to love. And Camille, the low-born girl who had only one asset for sale – herself. Camille – Marguerite Gautier – would stand for the new – the replacing of the medieval 'conquer and possess' by the laws of contract and the market-place.

But there is a problem with the market-place. You can't give things away – it messes up the system.

In the original Dumas, the kindly father persuades Marguerite to renounce Armand in order not to ruin him. In my version she would be blackmailed. The lovers would be parted, and both Marguerite and Armand destroyed. Love in modern society has become a commodity. Marguerite would die and Armand become a husk again – even more cold and revengeful than before. Commerce would destroy them both.

The production was a success – in great part due to an astonishing performance by Frances Barber.

Pam Gems

Characters

MARGUERITE GAUTIER

ARMAND DUVAL

PRUDENCE DE MARSAN DE TALBEC

SOPHIE DE LYONNE

CLEMENCE DE VILLENEUVE

JANINE

OLYMPE

YVETTE

GASTON DE MAURIEUX

MONSIEUR LE DUC

COUNT DRUFTHEIM

HONORÉ DE SANCERRE

PRINCE BELA MIRKASSIAN

JEAN

THE UPHOLSTERER

JEAN-PAUL

THE GRAVEDIGGER

THE INSPECTOR

PIERRE

MARQUIS DE SAINT-BRIEUC

SERGEI, THE RUSSIAN PRINCE

ERNESTINE DE MARSEILLE

Camille was first performed at The Other Place, Stratford-upon-Avon, by the Royal Shakespeare Company on 4 April 1984, with the following cast:

MARGUERITE GAUTIER, Frances Barber

ARMAND DUVAL, Nicholas Farrell

PRUDENCE DE MARSAN DE TALBEC, Polly James

SOPHIE DE LYONNE, Alphonsia Emmanuel

CLEMENCE DE VILLENEUVE, Rowena Roberts

JANINE/OLYMPE, Katharine Rogers

YVETTE, Sarah Woodward

GASTON DE MAURIEUX, Paul Gregory

MONSIEUR LE DUC, Norman Henry

COUNT DRUFTHEIM, Charles Millham

HONORÉ DE SANCERRE, Arthur Kohn

PRINCE BELA MIRKASSIAN, Andrew Hall

JEAN, Peter Theedom

THE UPHOLSTERER, Andrew Jarvis

JEAN-PAUL, Brian McGinley or Richard Parry

THE GRAVEDIGGER, Peter Theedom

THE INSPECTOR, Norman Henry

PIERRE, Andrew Jarvis

MARQUIS DE SAINT-BRIEUC, Bernard Horsfall

SERGEI, THE RUSSIAN PRINCE, Arthur Kohn

ERNESTINE DE ARSEILLE, Sarah Woodward

Director, Ron Daniels

Designer, Maria Bjornson

Lighting, John Waterhouse

ACT ONE

Scene 1

MARGUERITE's bedroom. White, with a white draped bed, and white silk damask cover. A few touches of blue. A dressing table, with crystal and silver appointments. A beautiful mirror in an ornate silver frame. Everything is labelled.

AUCTIONEER: (*Offstage.*) Lot one hundred and twenty-four...one steel fender, fire irons en suite, ditto firedogs – may I have your bids for this handsome lot, please? Note the chasing on the handles, ladies and gentlemen. Fifty francs? Fifty francs, *Monsieur.* Fifty-five...sixty – hold them up, boy, let them see the lot – there, fit for a gentleman's residence... (*Laughter.*) ...sixty? I'm bid sixty. Yes, sir – sixty-five?

(*A PORTER wearing a green baize apron lets a YOUNG MAN through. He erupts into the room, brushing past the PORTER, who closes the door, cutting down the sound. The YOUNG MAN comes to a halt. He seems in a daze. He looks pale, but sweating, as though ill. The sight of the room seems to affect him. He looks about, at first confused, then, recognising the room he moves about, touching pieces of furniture with a locked, neutral expression. This goes on and he prowls, with increasing signs of agitation. He does not notice the PORTER at the door receiving a tip from another, slightly OLDER MAN, who enters and strolls, curious to see the room. At a sound ARMAND turns abruptly.*)

ARMAND: Who are you?

GASTON: *Monsieur?*

ARMAND: What do you want?

GASTON: Forgive me, I am intruding. I was enjoying the spring sunshine – a shower drove me in, the crowd intrigued me. Mere curiosity... I beg your pardon. (*He makes to go but ARMAND's urgent sigh halts him.*) *Cher Monsieur*, you're ill! Allow me to fetch a doctor.

ARMAND: It's nothing. A fever. I was in Egypt.
GASTON: Ah indeed. I am well acquainted with the rigours of foreign infection. I have been abroad myself... Persia...the Levant...for over a year. (*Slight pause.*) I lost my dear wife.
ARMAND: (*Voice thick.*) Lost?
GASTON: In childbirth.
AUCTIONEER: (*Offstage.*) *Chère Madame*, don't resist!
(*Laughter, off.*)
ARMAND: And the child?
GASTON: My son? In the coffin, with his mother.
AUCTIONEER: (*Offstage.*) Fifteen bonnets, all trimmed! Thank you...thank you! (*He bangs the gavel.*) Sold to the enchanting Mam'selle by the window. Adieu the bonnets...or, may we hope...*au revoir*?
(*Laughter, off.*)
GASTON: You are not here to buy?
(*ARMAND looks up at him uncomprehendingly.*)
A remembrance, perhaps? The house is full of the most beautiful things. Quite lovely...alas, all going at a price.
AUCTIONEER: (*Offstage, bangs gavel.*) And now, *messieurs, 'dames*...lot one hundred and thirty. A fine looking-glass, silver-gilt frame as described. One thousand francs for this fine mirror – may I say twelve hundred? And fifteen. Going at fifteen hundred –
(*ARMAND crosses rapidly to the door.*)
ARMAND: (*At the doorway.*) Two thousand!
AUCTIONEER: (*Offstage.*) Two thousand behind me. And one? And two.
ARMAND: Three thousand.
GASTON: No, enough!
AUCTIONEER: (*Offstage.*) Three thousand. And two-fifty. Three thousand five...and seven-fifty –
ARMAND: Five thousand!
AUCTIONEER: (*Offstage.*) *Monsieur*?
ARMAND: Five thousand francs!
AUCTIONEER: (*Offstage.*) At five thousand then, to the gentleman by the door! (*He bangs the gavel, to applause.*) And now...the lot you've all been waiting for. Lot one

hundred and thirty. The bed. As sketched in the journals, you've all read about it...decorated with – what are they, boy?

BOY: Camellias, sir!

AUCTIONEER: (*Offstage.*) To be sure. Camellias. Twenty-three days of the month she wore white camellias, the other five days she wore red... (*Laughter.*)...

ARMAND: (*Low.*) No.

AUCTIONEER: (*Offstage.*) Truth of it, sir. You've all viewed this lot, ladies and gentlemen. A unique piece of carving...cherubs, swans, *pointe de Venise* trimmed sheets and pillows in situ as shown. What am I bid for this beautiful bed?

ARMAND: No.

AUCTIONEER: (*Offstage.*) You bidding, sir?

GASTON: The gentleman is ill.

(*He assists ARMAND away from the door.*)

VOICE: Two hundred thousand for the bed!

ANOTHER VOICE: And fifty!

VOICE: Three hundred thousand –

AUCTIONEER: (*Offstage.*) Thank you, sir – three hundred thousand I'm bid, three hundred thousand –

ARMAND: No! No! No!

(*He leaps off.*
Sounds of a tussle.
GASTON wrestles him back into the room.
The auction continues in the background.
ARMAND puts his hand on a piece of furniture, as if to prevent its being sold.
The bang of the gavel.
Applause.
The noise rouses ARMAND.
He jumps up.)

GASTON: You are too late. The bed is sold. The auction is over.

(*ARMAND staggers.*
GASTON helps him to sit.
ARMAND seems in a daze.)

GASTON: (*After a pause, gently.*) Who was she?
ARMAND: I wasn't here.
GASTON: May I know the lady's name?
ARMAND: (*In a dream.*) Marguerite...Marguerite...
(*He rises suddenly, knocking a chair over. He seems dazed, then leaves swiftly.*
GASTON, alarmed, follows him.)

Scene 2

The foyer of the Paris opera house. Two WAITERS prepare for the entr'acte. Music, then applause. PRUDENCE enters, followed by SOPHIE and CLEMENCE. They promenade, nodding and smiling at acquaintances.

PRUDENCE: (*Behind a bright smile and a wave.*) Thank God for intervals.
CLEMENCE: Prudence! Aren't you enjoying it? I'm very affected.
SOPHIE: That's true.
CLEMENCE: Sophie, you're so hard. What's wrong with being moved?
PRUDENCE: Rubbish. The diva's a shrimp! Not my idea of a prima donna – well, apart from the singing.
SOPHIE: The baritone's cross-eyed –
PRUDENCE: And we all know what that means – (*As CLEMENCE tries to ask.*) – never mind, dear, it's medical.
CLEMENCE: Well I don't care what you say, I'm transported – I believe in love.
SOPHIE: Hah!
(*PRUDENCE notices a YOUNG MAN who enters shyly. She gives CLEMENCE a shove.*
CLEMENCE crosses obediently and accosts him.)
CLEMENCE: Count? Remember me? (*He is dazzled but backs away bashfully.*) We met in Ostend – or was it Baden-Baden?
COUNT: (*Retreating.*) Excuse me please (*Shy bow.*) – I am in the opera losing my hat.

(*He makes his escape.*)

PRUDENCE: His hat!

SOPHIE: A serious matter.

CLEMENCE: What, losing your hat?

SOPHIE: Known to cause impotence –

CLEMENCE: What?

SOPHIE: (*Reassuring.*) – but only in men. (*She and PRUDENCE snigger, irritating CLEMENCE.*)

CLEMENCE: Well I like him, I'm good with shy boys.

PRUDENCE: Hands off…he's Marguerite's…ah, Monsieur le Duc!

(*An ELDERLY MAN is steered on by ERNESTINE, a young girl. He swerves towards them genially, ALL THREE WOMEN drop deep curtsies.*)

DUKE: Ah, Prudence…fat as ever, eh?

PRUDENCE: Ah, Duke, always the wit!

CLEMENCE: (*The DUKE kisses her hand.*) Ooh, lovely cold hand… (*To herself, puzzled.*) …like a snake.

DUKE: Fine soprano! What did you think of her execution?

SOPHIE: I'm all for it.

CLEMENCE: (*Copying PRUDENCE.*) Yes, not a bit like a prima donna…apart from the singing. (*Turns, lofty, to ERNESTINE.*) You enjoying it?

(*ERNESTINE, who lacks rank in the métier, is surprised at being favoured by being addressed. Her manner is rough and timid at once.*)

ERNESTINE: What? Oh, yes.

CLEMENCE: Didn't you like the horses, and the waterfall?

ERNESTINE: Never saw them.

CLEMENCE: Eh? You couldn't miss them!

(*But ERNESTINE steers the DUKE off firmly.*)

DUKE: Must be off!

PRUDENCE: I'll bet he must.

SOPHIE: (*Laughs.*) She won't have sat up once.

PRUDENCE: The old bastard.

CLEMENCE: He's not bad. For a duke.

(*PRUDENCE screeches as a TALL YOUNG MAN, exotically dressed, lifts her from her feet and whirls her round. She stumbles to her feet in a fury, righting her headdress.*

Another YOUNG MAN enters and regards her with a slight smile. She glares at him.)

BELA: Seven on the black! (*He capers.*)

PRUDENCE: (*To ARMAND.*) Where have you been?

BELA: Seven on the black!

ARMAND: (*To PRUDENCE.*) I had seven on the black.

CLEMENCE: Have you been at the tables, Armand?

BELA: *Pénétrante, Mam'selle.*

SOPHIE: (*Disbelieving.*) You're saying he won?

CLEMENCE: Aren't you clever, isn't he clever?

PRUDENCE: Waiter, champagne...we must celebrate! A party – I'll arrange everything...a trip on the river – we'll hire boats –

SOPHIE: I don't believe it –

PRUDENCE: Rude girl, disbelieving the word of a gentleman.

(*BELA laughs loudly.*)

PRUDENCE: What?

SOPHIE: Put them out of their misery.

ARMAND: The eighth was red.

BELA: He lost.

PRUDENCE: All of it? Ohh! You never know when to leave off.

ARMAND: (*Moves away to CLEMENCE.*) Ah, *la belle Clemence*!

PRUDENCE: And you can stop that. She hasn't forgiven you – have you?

CLEMENCE: What?

PRUDENCE: You've broken that poor girl's heart, I had to prise the laudanum from her hand, she was going to finish it all – weren't you?

CLEMENCE: What? Yes.

PRUDENCE: (*To BELA.*) She'd even made out her will, Prince – chosen the anthem, and the flowers for her catafalque.

CLEMENCE: I'm having white violets.

PRUDENCE: And tuberoses. For the smell. And her body's to be shipped to Lisbon.

SOPHIE: Lisbon?

BELA: Why Lisbon?

CLEMENCE: Because I've never been there, silly.

ARMAND: (*Accosts SOPHIE with a deep bow.*) *Mademoiselle de Lyonne.*

SOPHIE: *Monsieur Duval?*

ARMAND: I thought we'd seen the last of you.

SOPHIE: You're surprised?

ARMAND: By you?

PRUDENCE: Armand, that's enough.

ARMAND: (*To SOPHIE.*) Where have you been?

SOPHIE: Where? I've been at the opera.

ARMAND: No doubt an – elevating experience?

SOPHIE: (*Shakes her head.*) The bass was disappointing.

ARMAND: I see. In what way?

SOPHIE: Insufficient.

(*She stares at him insolently.*

He leans across and grabs CLEMENCE by the wrist.)

CLEMENCE: Armand! Armand, no!

PRUDENCE: She'll miss the last act!

(*But ARMAND takes CLEMENCE off.*)

BELA: (*To SOPHIE.*) Where did you go?

SOPHIE: If you must know, Dieppe.

BELA: (*Laughs, highly amused.*) Dieppe?! A long way for a crochet hook.

PRUDENCE: Please, Prince!

(*He unpins a large diamond brooch from his lapel, pins it on SOPHIE's shoulder.*)

BELA: For service. But I think I shall kill you.

SOPHIE: For Armand Duval? No need. He's left me. As he will leave you, *Monsieur le Prince.*

BELA: You think so?

SOPHIE: It's what he enjoys.

BELA: Then we make him jealous.

(*She moves away.*

He pursues her.)

Why not?

SOPHIE: Because I choose for myself – *Monsieur le Prince.*

(*BELA's attention is diverted by the return of ARMAND, followed at a discreet distance by CLEMENCE.*)

BELA: Ah…back again, so soon?

(*But ARMAND walks over to PRUDENCE, standing over her with an odd, glowering awkwardness. She squints up at him warily. He sits abruptly on the arm of her chair and begins to stroke her arm.*)

PRUDENCE: (*Purrs.*) Armand…why can't you treat us decently?

ARMAND: (*To BELA.*) Have you noticed women's arms? There's something honest about them.

(*He bends and bites PRUDENCE on the arm, making her scream.*)

PRUDENCE: Stop it! You're a brute!

ARMAND: Ah, flesh…so white – so mature –

PRUDENCE: I mean it, Armand, you're too rough.

ARMAND: But worth your while.

PRUDENCE: The pawnbroker doesn't think so.

ARMAND: What do you want then?

PRUDENCE: From you? It won't be emeralds.

(*He looks at her, blank-faced.*
She returns his gaze.)

What's the matter? (*Gently.*) What is it? Home comforts…is that what you want? (*She strokes his hair briefly.*) All right, my dear… *Au 'voir, mes enfants.* A little business to arrange for this young man – what I don't do for my friends…!

SOPHIE: The last act is in ten minutes, Prudence!

(*But PRUDENCE waves airily. She and ARMAND walk apart.*)

PRUDENCE: Armand, why must you be so cruel?

ARMAND: Cruel?

PRUDENCE: With women. Why?

ARMAND: They disappoint.

(*MARGUERITE appears.*
She is followed by an older man, HONORÉ DE SANCERRE.
ARMAND sees MARGUERITE.
MARGUERITE sees ARMAND.

There is a long, still pause as they regard each other.
Then MARGUERITE inclines her head the merest fraction and moves on.
ARMAND gazes after her, turns to PRUDENCE.
As he does so, MARGUERITE turns her head for another swift glance.)

ARMAND: Who is that?

PRUDENCE: Marguerite. Come away, she's not for you.

ARMAND: Why not?

PRUDENCE: You couldn't afford her.

ARMAND: Why not?

PRUDENCE: No-one can.

MARGUERITE: (*To DE SANCERRE, looking past him to ARMAND.*) Who is that?

DE SANCERRE: Armand Duval, why?

MARGUERITE: Will you forgive me...I must talk to some friends. Shall I see you later?

DE SANCERRE: Perhaps. (*He walks off.*)

SOPHIE: (*Calls.*) Marguerite!

(*They embrace warmly.*)

MARGUERITE: You're back! How are you?!

BELA: (*Kissing MARGUERITE'S hand passionately.*) Bellissima...

MARGUERITE: Ah...Prince... (*But her attention is distracted. She notices ARMAND, at a distance.*) Who is that?

SOPHIE: No-one.

BELA: A friend of mine. (*Sulky.*) You wish to meet him?

MARGUERITE: (*Laughs at him, teasing.*) I wouldn't deprive you.

(*She takes SOPHIE's arm and they move apart together.*)

(*Serious urgency.*) Are you all right?

SOPHIE: Yes, I've stopped bleeding.

(*They wave seductively at their friends.*)

MARGUERITE: Here. (*She gives SOPHIE her purse.*) No, take it, you'd do the same for me.

SOPHIE: (*Pocketing the purse grimly.*) I doubt it.

(*MARGUERITE smiles, and moves away, to go.*)

ARMAND: *Mademoiselle...*

(*MARGUERITE turns.*)
Your flowers…
MARGUERITE: Yes?
ARMAND: (*Gazing at her.*) They're beautiful.
MARGUERITE: Thank you.
(*She moves away, he follows. She turns. PRUDENCE approaches.*)
PRUDENCE: Camellias. Marguerite always wears them. My dear, may I present Armand Duval?
ARMAND: (*Bows.*) Why camellias?
MARGUERITE: Why not?
ARMAND: They have no scent.
MARGUERITE: (*Raising her eyebrows at his knowledge of flowers, then smiling.*) Ah, but you see, I'm an optimist. Please don't do that. (*As he blocks her path.*)
ARMAND: I must. When can I see you?
MARGUERITE: Please…
ARMAND: What do you want? Just tell me what you want.
MARGUERITE: From you, nothing. (*She attempts to pass.*)
ARMAND: What's the matter, don't you like me? Tell me what you want!
MARGUERITE: (*To BELA.*) Your friend is impatient. (*She puts a gloved hand on ARMAND's cheek, speaks gently.*) Like a child.
ARMAND: No, wait! (*To PRUDENCE.*) You, get her back for me!
PRUDENCE: She won't come.
ARMAND: Why not?
PRUDENCE: For one thing, I think she likes you.
ARMAND: What do you mean?
PRUDENCE: Armand, don't be obtuse. A woman in her position can't afford to like a man.
(*He goes, abruptly.*)
I shall begin to suspect that young man of a romantic disposition.
(*They laugh.*)
SOPHIE: Duval?
BELA: Duval??
SOPHIE: Supper! I'm hungry!

PRUDENCE: Another time, my dears.

(*She exits with DE SANCERRE. SOPHIE joins CLEMENCE, who is gazing after ARMAND.*)

SOPHIE: Don't tell me you've lost your heart to Armand Duval. (*She turns to PRINCE BELA.*) Only fools do that.

(*Angry, he turns on his heels and goes.*

The TWO WOMEN are left unescorted.

The OLD DUKE enters assisted by ERNESTINE who swerves away from them, guarding her prize. The OLD DUKE waves vaguely, but is borne away.

Music up and CLEMENCE and SOPHIE promenade, displaying their gowns and their charms in formal splendour.)

Scene 3

Screams, off. JANINE, Marguerite's maid, rushes on, pursued by MARGUERITE.

JANINE: I never touched them!

MARGUERITE: Then why were they under your bed, you bitch?

JANINE: It wasn't me, it wasn't me – leave off…Marie!

MARGUERITE: Nothing but trouble from the day you –

JANINE: It ain't fair! (*Sobs noisily.*) I was the one found *Señor da Costa*, if it was up to me he'd still be –

MARGUERITE: Well it ain't, so shut your gob –

JANINE: My nose is all swolled up –

MARGUERITE: The only trouble with your nose is the sodding great hole underneath it. Come on, where's the rest?

JANINE: Ow – what?

MARGUERITE: The moonstone collar and the pearls – if you've sold them –

(*She grabs JANINE by the hair and they fight, rolling on the floor.*

PRUDENCE enters, shown in by JEAN, carrying hatboxes. He puts them down, stands and grins at the fight, spits and goes.)

PRUDENCE: (*Voice of brass.*) That's enough…that's enough!

(*She lays about her with her parasol, parts them expertly.*)

MARGUERITE: Robbing me from cellar to attic – you're going home to your pig-faced mother!

JANINE: (*Throwing stuff on the ground from her pockets.*) Go on, take it! I hope it sticks in your great mush and chokes you!

MARGUERITE: Hang on, where do you think you're going?

JANINE: I'm not staying where I'm not appreciated! Who was it found *Señor da Costa*...me! (*She goes.*)

MARGUERITE: I'll bang her bloody head through that door.

PRUDENCE: They're all the same.

MARGUERITE: The linen slips through her hands like tiddlers...well, I've never met a laundress yet who wasn't light-fingered.

PRUDENCE: (*Sotto-voce.*) You should know, dear. (*Aloud.*) She's right about da Costa, though. My dear, the uglier the better...they pay up.

MARGUERITE: I hate her.

PRUDENCE: Well that's because she's a little turd. But a good maid.

MARGUERITE: Biggest scroungers in the village. I only took her to show off.

PRUDENCE: Playing the lady – well, why not? With those bones there isn't a door you couldn't kick open. I always had too much flesh. Flesh will take you so far, but after that it's bones – ooh, I like this. (*Swooping on a brooch on the floor.*)

MARGUERITE: (*Without bothering to look.*) Have it. (*She tries on a bonnet as PRUDENCE pins the brooch on her collar swiftly.*)

PRUDENCE: (*Prompt.*) Now that's nice!

MARGUERITE: You don't think it makes me look pale?

PRUDENCE: All the better – class!

(*They look in the mirror together.*)

MARGUERITE: As long as you don't want ready money.

PRUDENCE: I'll put it on your account.

(*SOPHIE enters from the bedroom, bangs another of the bonnets on her head.*)

SOPHIE: Selling you for a bonnet is she? (*Looks at herself in the glass.*) Ugh!

PRUDENCE: (*Snatching the bonnet from SOPHIE's head.*) It makes your face look crooked.

SOPHIE: (*To MARGUERITE.*) She'll get you in so deep –

PRUDENCE: What are you talking about, I'm the best friend Marguerite's ever –

SOPHIE: Fishtrap, you mean! –

PRUDENCE: She doesn't throw herself away –

SOPHIE: – till the fish begins to stink. Where will you be the day you can't raise money on her name?

PRUDENCE: You're glad enough to act the cadger –

SOPHIE: And you're asking for a mouthful of loose teeth!

PRUDENCE: Shut up! (*She fends SOPHIE off with her parasol.*)

MARGUERITE: (*Mildly.*) Come on, it sounds like a snipe bog in here. (*Lifts a hand as SOPHIE makes to go.*) Where are you going…shall I see you?

(*They exchange a small, yearning embrace then SOPHIE goes, goosing PRUDENCE, making her shriek with fury.*)

PRUDENCE: (*Calls.*) She's in for more than a bonnet, unlike some!

MARGUERITE: She's teasing.

PRUDENCE: (*Darkly.*) You want to watch that girl. You shouldn't let her sleep with you for a start –

MARGUERITE: Oh? Why not?

PRUDENCE: She coughs.

(*JEAN appears at the door.*)

JEAN: The woodman's here. (*He advances.*)

MARGUERITE: Damn. (*She goes to the desk drawer, takes a note, gives it to him.*)

JEAN: There's last month's and all.

(*She pulls a face, gives him another note.*)

JEAN-PAUL: (*Runs on, fast.*) Tan' Marie…Tan' Marie! (*He jumps into MARGUERITE's arms, followed by YVETTE.*)

MARGUERITE: Jean-Paul! Ohh! (*Swinging him round.*) Yvette...I wasn't expecting you! Everything all right?

(*YVETTE bobs and nods, smiling.*)

Your mother...?

YVETTE: Yes, Madame, thank you, *Madame.*

(*She bobs. MARGUERITE waits patiently.*)

Boots.

MARGUERITE: Ah! He's growing! (*Yearning.*) You're growing! (*She fetches some money for YVETTE.*) Put it somewhere safe. (*To JEAN-PAUL.*) What would you like? I know – cake!

JEAN-PAUL: Yes, please!

YVETTE: Oh good, you said please.

MARGUERITE: Jean, fetch some milk – and bring up the chocolate cake.

JEAN: The one for tonight? Cook'll put a knife in me –

MARGUERITE: Oh go on – here...

(*She gives him a cigar. He goes.*)

PRUDENCE: No need to give him good cigars, you spoil them!

MARGUERITE: (*To YVETTE.*) He's been well?

YVETTE: Ooh yes. Been climbing trees, 'aven't you?

JEAN-PAUL: Yes!

MARGUERITE: Here...littlun...

(*JEAN-PAUL gives the hat he has been playing with to YVETTE, who smooths it.*)

PRUDENCE: Ooh, be careful! (*Making YVETTE jump.*) You'll pull the threads... (*To MARGUERITE, who gives her a venomous look.*) ...her hands are rough, she'll pull the threads!

MARGUERITE: (*To JEAN-PAUL.*) I've been keeping it for you.

(*She gives him a miniature carousel, then turns a handle and makes it play.*

The BOY's face is full of wonder.

She watches his face.

He takes the toy, turns the handle.)

JEAN-PAUL: Will it go backwards?

MARGUERITE: No, you'll break it.

YVETTE: What do you say?
JEAN-PAUL: Thank you, Tan' Marie.
YVETTE: That's it.
MARGUERITE: (*Lifts him up.*) Are you still my little man?
JEAN-PAUL: (*Throwing his arms about her neck.*) I'm your man.
JEAN: (*Runs on.*) It's the Duke – he's here!
MARGUERITE: Where?
JEAN: On the stairs.
MARGUERITE: God in heaven… (*She hugs the BOY and runs, returns in anguish to kiss him again and flies out, gesturing to PRUDENCE to see to things.*)
PRUDENCE: (*To JEAN.*) Quick, down to the kitchen…not that way…here…shoo!…
(*As the BOY takes his carousel firmly under his arm…she pushes YVETTE out firmly.*)
YVETTE: What? (*Confused, she is pushed out with the BOY.*)
PRUDENCE: Ah, *Monsieur le Duc…*!
DUKE: (*Enters.*) M' lead horse went lame, so I walked!
JEAN: Glass of wine, Your Grace?
(*JANINE, in full regalia, ribbons flying, swoops on with a silver tray.*)
DUKE: Ah, Janine! And how is Janine today…sweet little thing!
PRUDENCE: Oh adorable.
JANINE: Wicked Jean, not making you comfortable – (*She fills a glass for him.*)
JEAN: Hop it, you – clear off. (*To a MAN who sticks his head through the door.*)
UPHOLSTERER: Three hundred francs or that sofa goes.
JEAN: Out!
UPHOLSTERER: Oh no, sonny…this foot remains.
JANINE: (*Stamping on it.*) No it don't.
(*They push him out as PRUDENCE refills the DUKE's glass.*)
PRUDENCE: Glorious weather, Duke!
DUKE: Is it, by God? Steady on, gal. Don't want to be hors de combat.
PRUDENCE: These early evening visits, so much more satisfactory.

UPHOLSTERER: (*Pushing through the door again.*) Can I have my three hundred francs!

(*JANINE looks to MARGUERITE who enters and pulls a face, she has no more money.*)

JANINE: No, you can't. Here…

(*She gives the UPHOLSTERER a big, juicy kiss.*)

UPHOLSTERER: (*Stumbling.*) Yes…well…

(*The DUKE, seemingly unaware, puts his hand in his pocket, hands MARGUERITE a roll.*

She gives some to JANINE, who palms half and puts it down her front, gives the rest to the UPHOLSTERER and pushes him out, followed by JEAN.

MARGUERITE slips a note to PRUDENCE.)

MARGUERITE: (*To the DUKE.*) *Mon cher*…no, don't get up – that's an order.

DUKE: Yours to command…she's so strict! I walked!

MARGUERITE: Good…did you? Then you must be rewarded. However, if you haven't been behaving yourself I shall find out…let me say goodbye to Prudence –

DUKE: Ah, Prudence…settling up, eh? Busy as ever?

PRUDENCE: *Plus ça change*, Duke… (*Sotto voce.*) you old fool. (*To MARGUERITE, at exit.*) Shall I say yes to Armand?

MARGUERITE: Armand?

PRUDENCE: Duval. You said he might call.

MARGUERITE: No I didn't!

(*The DUKE becomes restless, they giggle mechanically.*)

Prudence, I shall tell! Prudence is being very wicked about you, Monsieur le Duc! (*Sotto voce.*) Why should I?

(*The DUKE hems.*)

Oh all right, bring him with the others. (*She turns to the DUKE.*) *Mon cher Hercule*, what are we going to do with you, hmm?

(*PRUDENCE slips away.*)

DUKE: Something special?

MARGUERITE: Only if you're good.

DUKE: I am, I am!

MARGUERITE: Are you? No, I don't think so. I think you're telling me a lie. And you know what happens to little boys who tell lies, don't you?

DUKE: I *am* a good boy, I *am* a good boy...

(*She helps him out.*)

Oh, my lovely Camille...oh...

Scene 4

Light change. The same evening. JANINE and JEAN come and go, preparing the room for a party. They move furniture and bring on flowers and glasses. JEAN opens the piano. They bump into each other and she curses irritably. He pulls a face at her. They finish and stand, surveying their work. She tweaks a flower arrangement and is satisfied.

JEAN: Fancy a duck's wing?

JANINE: Asso to you.

JEAN: Yeah, that'll do.

(*He gooses her, she yelps.*

They go, separately. Pause.

MARGUERITE enters, a glass of water in her hand. She strolls, sips, inspecting the room lazily. She touches a piece of furniture. And another.)

MARGUERITE: My things. My lovely things.

(*She takes another turn, throws herself down in a chair. She leans back, enjoying the rare moment of quiet.*)

(*Puzzled.*) I'm happy. Why am I happy?

(*DE SANCERRE, in the shadows, draws on his cigar so that we see the glow. He walks up behind her.*)

I'm expecting guests.

(*But he stands, immovable.*)

(*In a resigned voice.*) You bastard.

(*She rises and crosses, he follows.*

They exit.

Lights down.

JEAN enters with a candelabrum, sets it down and goes.

JANINE enters separately and idles, 'tidying'. She steps forward as DE SANCERRE enters, tying his stock.)

JANINE: Let me do it, sir.

(*She ties his stock. He nods in thanks.*)

Not at all, *Monsieur.* Anything you wish, *Monsieur.*

DE SANCERRE: (*Inspecting her coldly.*) Bones of a pigeon.

JANINE: Oh yes. I'd crack ever so easily…*Monsieur.*

(*She waits in his path, looking up at him with cool expectancy.*)

DE SANCERRE: You want to be careful.

JANINE: Oh I'm ever so careful, *Monsieur de Sancerre.*

(*He glares at her dangerously. But he puts his hand in his pocket and gives her money. And goes.*

JANINE goes.)

MARGUERITE: (*Off, furious.*) Janine! You devil!

JANINE: (*Off.*) I didn't know he was here!

MARGUERITE: (*Off.*) How much did he give you, I'll murder you –

(*JANINE runs on with an armful of crumpled sheets.*)

JANINE: How was I supposed to know!

(*She stops short at the sight of the YOUNG MAN who has entered with a large bunch of flowers and a package.*

JANINE changes key effortlessly.)

Oh… Count. What a surprise. (*Flat.*) *Mam'selle* will be pleased.

(*The YOUNG MAN, stiff and awkward is the same YOUNG MAN who has been frightened off by CLEMENCE in Scene Two. He is Swedish, with an accent.*)

COUNT: You think so? That is good.

JANINE: Take a seat. Wine?

(*He shakes his head, clutching his package and the flowers.*)

How are you?

COUNT: I am very well. Apart, of course, from my heels.

JANINE: What? Oh…yes. Didn't you try the hog's lard? Oh well, I expect they'll get better soon. (*She gestures, offering to take the flowers but he resists.*) You're in for a jolly time.

COUNT: (*Alarmed.*) Oh?

JANINE: We're having a party.

COUNT: (*Blanching.*) But I thought –

JANINE: No, you'll enjoy it – never mind, perhaps they won't stay long. Tell you what, I'll try and get rid of them for you. (*She stands over him till he understands and gives her money. It is not enough.*) Well, I'll try. Trouble is, they'll all be giving me something to let the party run on. If you see what I mean.

COUNT: (*Gives her more money.*) This is enough?

JANINE: Oh, aren't you nice! I'm always telling *Mam'selle* what a sensitive man you are, *Monsieur le Comte.*

COUNT: Yes, that is true.

JANINE: I know, I just said so. (*Hiatus.*) Oh…ah – the weather…

COUNT: (*Brightening.*) Ah! The weather! This morning was cold, I think one, maybe two degrees of frost, this is not unusual for time of year but damaging with these plants which are began their grow. I am thinking to wear Ulster for the possibility of rain because when I am looking outside window…hoop! (*He makes her jump.*) Black cloud! But when I have eaten my good breakfast and I am performed my exercises, hullo…black cloud is no more, so now perhaps it is possible no rain, but maybe later, so must I wear my good Swedish jacket for sure and – ow! (*As JANINE clouts him over the ear.*)

JANINE: Oh! No, it's all right, thought I saw a spider in your ear…there it is! (*Clips him another one.*) Oh, it's only a bit of fluff…

COUNT: Oof!

JANINE: …still – don't want spiders in your ears, do we? (*She dusts him down.*)

COUNT: (*His hand to his reeling head.*) Ooh…!

JANINE: All right?

(*He nods, dodging warily.*)

Uh…let's think – I know, how are the coins?

COUNT: (*Smiles happily.*) Ah, my good coins! (*But he lapses into silence.*)

(*An agonizing pause for both of them. She slides a look of inspection.*)

JANINE: Perhaps if you was to part your hair at the side –

(*JANINE is saved by MARGUERITE who enters, sees the COUNT, tries to withdraw but it is too late.*)

MARGUERITE: Dear Canute! (*She pulls a face at JANINE.*)

COUNT: (*Loses his composure.*) Ah…ah…er…ah…

MARGUERITE: Still afflicted? And I thought we were making progress.

COUNT: Ah…oeer…er…ah… (*He thrusts the flowers at her.*)

MARGUERITE: How lovely! For me? Oh – chrysanthemums.

COUNT: They are not fresh?…but I was assured –

JANINE: They're funeral flowers! For your grave.

COUNT: This is true? In Sweden not so.

JANINE: Well it is here. (*She sweeps them away and goes.*)

COUNT: Forgive me, please. (*He proffers a wrapped box.*)

MARGUERITE: It's nothing. (*She opens the box.*) Oh, what beautiful shoes!

COUNT: They are fitting? Please to try.

MARGUERITE: I'm sure they'll fit.

COUNT: Please to try. (*With an effort.*) My dear.

MARGUERITE: There, that wasn't so difficult, was it?

(*He kneels, puts a shoe on her foot. In the second shoe is a diamond necklace.*)

Canute? Canute! – oh, they're lovely!… (*Genuine. She jumps to her feet.*) Like raindrops!

(*He does up the clasp.*)

Like tears.

COUNT: Yes, as in Sweden when is melting the snow –

MARGUERITE: Yes…

COUNT: – first comes little drops, plink, plink, so…

(*The piano plinks.*)

…yes!…and then plink, plink, plink…and quickly now…plink, plink, plink, plink…and now running, plinkety plonk, plinkety plonk, plinkety plonk…

(*The piano drowns him.*)

…yes, that is so…exactly this!

(*He hops about, still plinking, and pulls her into the dance. BELA lurches in, drunk, followed by PRUDENCE and CLEMENCE.*

Their laughter brings the COUNT up short and he bows, stiff with embarrassment.)

MARGUERITE: The Count was showing me an old Swedish dance.

BELA: Throw him out of the window.

MARGUERITE: (*Makes a face at him.*) Clemence, I believe you've met Count Druftheim, from Sweden. *Ma'moiselle Clemence de Villeneuve*...from Boulogne.

CLEMENCE: What's it called, your dance? (*She tries a hop.*)

COUNT: It is called the hopping dance.

(*She hops, he hops, and she shrieks happily as he hurls her round in a galumph, ending with her giving him a hearty push which sends him flying. She pulls him up, laughing.*)

CLEMENCE: I enjoyed that!

COUNT: Yah!

(*They join hands to start again.*)

PRUDENCE: Enough! Dear Count! How lovely to see you again – (*Pulling a face at MARGUERITE behind his back.*) – so soon. We thought that Marguerite was going to keep you all to herself. (*She wheels MARGUERITE out of the PRINCE's way as he looms.*) My dear, you look enchanting. Duval couldn't keep his eyes off you last night.

MARGUERITE: Well I hope he means to be more amiable this evening.

BELA: Who?

PRUDENCE: Armand. He's joining us.

BELA: No, no, no.

PRUDENCE: Why not?

BELA: I don't think so.

MARGUERITE: Ah, but can you assure me, my dear?

BELA: Absolutely. He's at the tables, enjoying the greatest pleasure in the world...he's winning.

CLEMENCE: (*Arch.*) And what's the second greatest pleasure in the world, Prince?

BELA: (*Inspecting her coldly.*) The second greatest pleasure in the world, *Mam'selle* – is losing.

(*He moves away.*

CLEMENCE, out of face, crosses to the COUNT.)

CLEMENCE: Not bored, Count?

COUNT: (*Ill at ease.*) Oh no…

CLEMENCE: Only I know you foreigners…all that travel, you're bound to be debonair.

COUNT: Yah.

CLEMENCE: It must be nice coming from a long thin country like Sweden. Cold though.

COUNT: Oh yah! For example now in Sweden we are still in the muff and the gaiter and many degrees of frost, also fug –

BELA: (*Dangerously polite amid stifled laughter.*) Fug?

COUNT: Oh yah, very wide fug –

PRUDENCE: Marguerite for God's sake play something!

MARGUERITE: For my friends? I wouldn't be so cruel –

(*SOPHIE enters.*)

– Sophie, where were you? I left a note, I couldn't find you, where were you? (*Apart.*)

SOPHIE: Montmartre.

MARGUERITE: Why? It's dangerous.

PRUDENCE: She'll end up in the river.

MARGUERITE: My dear – why be at risk?

(*SOPHIE pulls away.*

MARGUERITE pursues her, speaking low.)

Prudence can make an arrangement for you –

SOPHIE: No.

MARGUERITE: Is it money? Have these. (*Lifts the diamonds at her neck.*)

(*But SOPHIE laughs, backs away, and breaks into a savage dance.*

The OTHERS applaud as she finishes.)

(*To SOPHIE, sotto voce.*) All right – suit yourself. (*She crosses to BELA.*) My wicked Prince – tell me something pleasant… (*Frowning at SOPHIE.*) …something agreeable.

BELA: Tra la la la la! (*Sings, indicating CLEMENCE and the COUNT.*) Keep an eye on your investments!

(*But MARGUERITE merely laughs, throwing back her head in genuine amusement at CLEMENCE's single-minded pursuit.*

BELA leaves her side and stalks and prowls about CLEMENCE and the COUNT…
CLEMENCE fends him off with her fan.
BELA pulls ferocious faces behind the COUNT, making MARGUERITE laugh.)

CLEMENCE: How many castles?

COUNT: Seven. My favourite is Druftenen –

CLEMENCE: Ooh, is that the biggest?

COUNT: Yes, and here is the bestest collections of me and my father and my grandfather –

CLEMENCE: Collections? Of jewels?

COUNT: Please? No, no, harness of horses of my family since many hundred years, also wheels and implements –
(*BELA picks up a decanter and refills the COUNT's glass, and spills wine on his trousers.*
The COUNT jumps up.)

SOPHIE: (*Claps.*) Bravo! (*To BELA.*) Done with the subtlety of a servant.

BELA: Indeed, Mam'selle?
(*He crosses to her.*)
And how is the lady from Dieppe?

SOPHIE: Unencumbered, *Monsieur.*

BELA: Perhaps I shall see you, in the Park.

SOPHIE: Very likely. I'm there every morning. For my dogs to relieve themselves.

BELA: Why don't you smile at me?

SOPHIE: Why should I?
(*She looks up at him steadily. He looks down at her.*)

BELA: Everyone smiles at me. I am a Prince.
(*She rises and walks away.*
MARGUERITE moves to the piano, sings.)

MARGUERITE: Let me forever in tenderness lie,
Though doubt and darkness invade and enfold.
Here in your arms let me know no despair –
(*As the song begins ARMAND enters quietly and stands by the door, watching MARGUERITE. Unaware of him she moves about, singing. On the third line of the song she turns, and sees him. She breaks off at once and comes to greet him with friendly formality.*)

MARGUERITE: *Monsieur Duval –*

ARMAND: Good-evening, *Ma'moiselle Gautier.*

(*MARGUERITE contemplates him for an instant. Then she breaks into a cheerful, vulgar song, dancing and swaying round the room.*)

MARGUERITE: (*Sings.*) The Major's on the doorstep,
The Colonel's on the stair,
The Brigadier's in the chamber,
His corsets in the air…
But here's the cavalry captain,
A galloping at full stride,
With a bump de bump de bump de bump,
To take me for a ride.
(*The OTHERS join in.*)
Bump de bump de bump de bump!
The Admiral's in the arbour,
The subaltern's in the hall,
And two or three more outside the door,
And one perched on the wall…
But here's the cavalry captain,
A galloping at full stride,
With a bump de bump de bump de bump,
To take me for a ride!

(*She circles ARMAND, ending before him with a curtsey and a mocking smile. The COUNT claps fervently, rising to his feet. His applause dies away before ARMAND's cold stare. ARMAND walks away. Silence.*)

PRUDENCE: Bravo! (*She claps, the OTHERS join her.*) Hungry, Count?

COUNT: Yah, most hungry!

CLEMENCE: Come on, then! (*Taking his arm.*) What's your favourite…mine's game pie…well, I like everything …there's nothing I don't like!

(*She takes him off.*)

BELA: Good. He can tell her all about the sewage systems of Stockholm. (*Raises his voice.*) What's the matter?

MARGUERITE: (*By the piano, suppressing a cough.*) Nothing, I caught my breath.

BELA: Is she ill?

PRUDENCE: Marguerite? Heavens no…strong as a racehorse.

(She waits for his arm but he stares across to ARMAND. PRUDENCE exits alone.)

BELA: *(To ARMAND.)* Are you coming?

(A slight pause. Then BELA exits.)

MARGUERITE: *Monsieur Duval?*

(But she is taken with a prolonged fit of coughing. He fetches water. She drinks. The spasm subsides.)

I must have swallowed a feather. Thank you.

ARMAND: *(Takes the glass, sets it down.)* Why do you sing that song?

MARGUERITE: You prefer something more sentimental? You surprise me, *Monsieur Duval.*

ARMAND: Why, have you been studying me?

MARGUERITE: No more than the door handle.

ARMAND: It's not your style.

MARGUERITE: What would you like me to sing? Something more elevated? Don't delude yourself, *Monsieur* –

(But she coughs again. He gives her his handkerchief as she waves away the water. She recovers, attempts a smile.)

ARMAND: Shall I send them away?

MARGUERITE: Of course not! *(She crosses, looks at herself in the glass.)* Heavens, how pale I look!

ARMAND: May I stay?

(She shakes her head.)

Why not?

MARGUERITE: It's impossible.

ARMAND: Why? *(She lifts her hand with a smile of apology.)* Is he coming back? De Sancerre?

MARGUERITE: Have you been spying on me?

ARMAND: Why can't I stay?

MARGUERITE: I'm not obliged to give you reasons.

ARMAND: Don't you like me?

MARGUERITE: No.

ARMAND: I think you do.

(MARGUERITE walks about, inspecting him from time to time.)

MARGUERITE: (*Pause.*) You lack grace, *Monsieur Duval.* it might do for some. Not for me.

ARMAND: (*Coarse.*) Allow me to put myself in your hands.

MARGUERITE: (*Slight pause.*) Why do you seek to be less than you are?

ARMAND: You think I should aspire?

MARGUERITE: It might be more interesting.

ARMAND: Don't tell me you require virtue?

MARGUERITE: That would be provincial, would it not?

(*She walks away from him again. He watches her.*)

ARMAND: Are you going to name your terms? And allow me to fill them?

MARGUERITE: What I should require from you is not, I think, yours to bestow.

ARMAND: And what is that?

MARGUERITE: Respect.

(*He laughs aloud.*)

I mean, towards yourself.

ARMAND: (*Slight pause.*) Myself.

MARGUERITE: And a little honour.

ARMAND: (*Cold.*) You accuse me of lack of honour?

MARGUERITE: Oh I daresay you keep faith with those of your sort. I'm talking of another kind of honour.

ARMAND: And what kind is that?

MARGUERITE: Between a man and a woman.

ARMAND: Ah, you want gallantry?

MARGUERITE: Just mutual courtesy. You find that bizarre?

ARMAND: I don't know what you're talking about.

MARGUERITE: No. Because you have a black heart. You're a monster.

ARMAND: (*Blocking her path urgently.*) Permit me to prove that I'm not.

MARGUERITE: Then begin by allowing me to pass. Which you are preventing.

(*He bows, offers her his arm.*)

Thank you, *Monsieur Armand.* (*She pauses.*) Why are you smiling?

ARMAND: You called me Armand.

(A game of hide and seek. SOPHIE and CLEMENCE hide. BELA hides under CLEMENCE's skirt.

The COUNT enters, they tease him, then lift their skirts, BELA emerges.)

CLEMENCE: Oh, Count, you're blushing!

BELA: *(Kisses CLEMENCE's hand.)* Congratulations, *mademoiselle,* on your most original legs!

CLEMENCE: He didn't see a thing, it was dark! *(She bears the COUNT away.)*

(A waltz. The COUNT dances with MARGUERITE, ARMAND with SOPHIE, BELA with CLEMENCE.

The mood is languid.

Light change.

ARMAND dances with BELA.

The OTHERS pass the opium pipe.

MARGUERITE dances alone.

ARMAND, sitting with BELA, watches. He rises, takes her in his arms, they dance.

Light change.

ARMAND and MARGUERITE, dancing together.

The OTHERS are sleepy…only BELA looks on watchfully.)

MARGUERITE: Why?

ARMAND: Because I must.

MARGUERITE: Is it so important?

ARMAND: Yes.

MARGUERITE: Oh, if it's so important…

ARMAND: Not if it isn't to you.

MARGUERITE: To me? You *are* sentimental! Such games come expensive in this house.

ARMAND: I don't want to play games.

MARGUERITE: *Monsieur Armand,* what do you want from me?

ARMAND: I want the truth.

MARGUERITE: The truth? Oh I don't think you can afford that.

ARMAND: Nevertheless it's what I want.

MARGUERITE: Please go away. Your friend is waiting. Go away with him, please.

ARMAND: No.
MARGUERITE: You see? You are a monster.
ARMAND: If I am, you make me so. (*He stands before her, refusing to move.*)
BELA: Armand, are you coming?
MARGUERITE: Please go away.
ARMAND: No.
(*Pause.*)
MARGUERITE: Very well. One night. If you insist. Then you can say that you knew Marguerite Gautier. And that she disappointed.
ARMAND: Why should I say that?
MARGUERITE: I don't mind what you say so long as you go!
ARMAND: Very well.
MARGUERITE: I have your word?
ARMAND: I promise to do whatever you want.
BELA: Armand –
ARMAND: I'm staying!
(*He lifts his head briefly in triumph, then follows MARGUERITE off.*
BELA crosses. He pauses, and PRUDENCE puts a consoling hand on his arm. He thrusts her away angrily and goes.
CLEMENCE and the COUNT leave together.
PRUDENCE wakes SOPHIE, and they go.)

Scene 5

The bedroom. ARMAND and MARGUERITE in bed. They are making love. ARMAND gasps. MARGUERITE groans.

ARMAND: (*Soft.*) What is it?
MARGUERITE: Nothing, nothing.
(*Pause.*
He whispers.
She laughs very softly.
They murmur. then silence.
Lights to black.)

Scene 6

The bedroom. ARMAND and MARGUERITE.

MARGUERITE: How many?
ARMAND: None. Till now.
MARGUERITE: Liar. You must have been in love. Tell me. (*Pause.*)
ARMAND: I did love someone once.
MARGUERITE: Who? Who?
ARMAND: My father's riding master.
MARGUERITE: (*Tips back her head, laughing.*) Was he handsome?
ARMAND: No. He was short and bandy, had a foul tongue, and a head as flat as a badger. (*He lies back, remembering.*) He lived with his mother and farted a lot.
MARGUERITE: Why did you love him?
ARMAND: (*Shrugs.*) I don't know. He turned my bowels.
MARGUERITE: No-one else?
(*He thinks, shakes his head.*)
I see. So that's why you're unhappy.
ARMAND: (*Rearing up on his elbow in surprise.*) I'm not unhappy!
MARGUERITE: My dear, you're full of grief.
(*She strokes his hair. He looks at her and then leaps off the bed and prowls round the room, touching everything in turn with ritualistic affection.*)
ARMAND: I love it here. Everything in this room. I love everything you see, everything you touch. (*He looks in the mirror, touches the surround.*) I love this mirror because it sees your face. (*He picks up one of the silver-lidded bottles.*) I love these –
MARGUERITE: Look at the crests. The initials. All different. Remember that when you start to feel sentimental.
(*He returns, leaps on the bed and stands over her.*)
ARMAND: Why did you let me stay?
MARGUERITE: Because you were a nuisance.
ARMAND: You could have had me thrown out.

MARGUERITE: Yes.

(*He embraces her passionately.*

Light change.

MARGUERITE and ARMAND in bed together.

A pause.

Then she lifts her head and regards him levelly.)

Very well. If you must. (*Slight pause.*) My mother was a laundress. On a big estate.

ARMAND: Where?

MARGUERITE: (*Vague.*) Oh…in the country. My father died when I was nine. I have four younger brothers. (*Slight pause.*) And I have a son.

ARMAND: (*Slight pause.*) You have a child?

MARGUERITE: Yes.

ARMAND: Where is he?

MARGUERITE: With a farmer's wife.

ARMAND: Is that why you…how you came to…to be…do you live this life because you love it…is that why you – ?

(*MARGUERITE throws back her head and laughs at him.*)

Go on…tell me – I want to know!

(*MARGUERITE leaps off the bed and walks about like a tiger.*)

MARGUERITE: You want to know? You want to know? What do you know! I know the way you live! Hothouses, stables, libraries…a fire in your room. (*She lopes, fiery and restless.*) I used to clean the grates with my mother at five o'clock in the morning, on tiptoe while you all snored. I saw them! The rugs, the pictures, the furniture…hot baths and nine course dinners, all a hundred metres from where we lived on potatoes and slept, the seven of us, in a coach-house loft.

ARMAND: (*Slight pause.*) Are you accusing me?

MARGUERITE: Yes. (*Pause.*) When I was thirteen I became a housemaid. I shared an attic…my own bed, you can't believe the bliss!

(*Pause.*

He shakes her gently to make her continue.

She looks at him oddly and away.)

After two years *Monsieur le Marquis* took me into his bed. It was his habit with the younger maids. A year later I had our son.

(*She plays with the quilt for a moment and then speaks with musing objectivity.*)

You have no idea what difference a child makes. Your life is changed…forever.

(*She smoothes the quilt gently.*)

You're connected…with someone who is, and isn't you. Your own flesh. I love my brothers of course…but…you grow up…you go away, you're on your own. Until, if you're a woman, you have a child. Then you're never alone again. Whether you wish it or not…whether you're with the child or not. It's there. Part of you. Of your body.

(*Pause.*)

I hardly ever see him. He thinks I'm his aunt.

(*She pauses…then, as ARMAND starts to speak.*)

I was dismissed, of course. I went to my mother's sister and sat by the river wondering what to do. The most sensible thing seemed to be to drown myself.

(*Pause.*)

And then, one morning, my cousin came into my room. I was putting on my stockings, and he started to shake. I didn't have the strength of push him away. Afterwards, he put his finger to his lips, and he gave me a gold coin. And there it was. I knew. All of a sudden. How to do it. How to go through the magic door. How to be warm, how to be comfortable…eat fine food, wear fine clothes, read fine books. I had the key, a golden key. (*She laughs.*) After all…what had I got to lose? Innocence? That had gone before I was five.

(*He leans on his elbow abruptly.*)

Look at me. I was a pretty child – do you know what that means? It means that when your neighbour sits you on his lap and gives you sweets he puts his thumb in you. But who can you tell? Who will believe you?

(*She pauses, dreamy.*)

My mother sent me for some vegetables one day. A gift. It was Sunday, the church bells were ringing. The gardener was in one of the hothouses, pruning the peaches. He said I looked flushed – I was hot, I'd been running. And then he said 'Come over here'...and sat on some sacks. So I sat down. And he said 'Well, my little maid, are you ready for me yet?' God, you should have seen the mess. I put up a terrible fight...I had the whole tree down on him, but he took me anyway. He made me get a bucket of water after to clean up the blood, in case the dogs came sniffing.

ARMAND: I'm surprised you don't hate us.

MARGUERITE: Hate...love... (*She shrugs.*)

ARMAND: Yes. What about love?

MARGUERITE: Love? (*She laughs aloud.*) Love? Seven pregnancies in nine years? Arms swollen with soda from washing stains from other people's linen? Ask my mother. No. No love. Anyway, I had a child to support.

ARMAND: What happened? What did you do?

MARGUERITE: I took a chance. I went back to the house...the family were away...let myself in...and helped myself. I filled a valise and two basket trunks with what I needed – clothes, wraps, jewellery...even books. I took from that profusion what wasn't wanted, needed...or regarded. I equipped myself. Then I called up the butler. I said that *Monsieur le Marquis* had been kind enough to make provision for my change of address, and gave him the name of a hotel I'd found on the morning room table. I fetched my son, took him where I knew he'd be well cared for...and I came to Paris!

ARMAND: And?

MARGUERITE: I sat in a hotel room for five days crying for my baby, and waiting for the police to arrive. I laid it all out...the ribbons, the shoes, the garnets that had never been worn, the turquoises that made Milady's skin look yellow. I sat, with my tortoiseshell brushes, the box with the violets from Parma on the lid, the bonnets... You have no idea of the magic of things when you've never had any. (*She pauses.*)

ARMAND: What happened?

MARGUERITE: Nothing! Nobody came! I got tired of waiting, put on one of Milady's dresses, and took a walk. And met him...in the park...*Monsieur le Marquis*!

ARMAND: What did he do?

MARGUERITE: Got out of his carriage, and hit me in the face. I still have the scar from his ring.

(*He inspects her face.*)

Now you know.

ARMAND: You're a lion. A tiger. A leopard. I honour your courage...and I respect your choice.

MARGUERITE: Choice.

ARMAND: To be a huntress, a marauder. (*But he looks away.*)

MARGUERITE: Nonetheless...

ARMAND: Nonetheless?

MARGUERITE: There is always a nonetheless. Nonetheless how can I bear it...it's what you all want to know. (*She laughs.*) I bear it very well. At first you shut your eyes, dream of the handsome valet. But then, if you're successful, who has time to think? And who is to say what goes on in our heads?

ARMAND: What do you think of when we make love?

MARGUERITE: Of you.

ARMAND: How can I be sure?

MARGUERITE: You can't.

ARMAND: 'Nonetheless'! (*They laugh.*) What is it between us? From the moment I saw you no gap...no distance. We inhabit the same world – how is that? (*Plays with her hand.*) You accept my ugliness –

MARGUERITE: (*In surprise.*) You're not ugly! –

ARMAND: Oh, believe me, I am. (*Studies her face.*) You understand my disgust...my resentment...you don't judge, you don't condemn...more than that you imply...what? A possibility. Of something...other. (*Accusingly.*) I'm happy.

MARGUERITE: Is that so alarming?

ARMAND: I'm at home with you. I've never had a home before.

MARGUERITE: (*Sardonic.*) You? No home?

ARMAND: I was sent away to school at seven.

MARGUERITE: Seven? But – your mother – ?

ARMAND: Came into the nursery occasionally.

(*MARGUERITE rears up in horror.*)

My dear, you speak of the daughter of a duke. (*He lies back again.*) Beyond excluding the rest of the world, my mother thought, my mother said, my mother did nothing. Why should she? My mother was a Lady.

(*Slight pause.*)

MARGUERITE: (*Unobserved, she watches him with a snake-like gaze.*) And your father?

ARMAND: Like me. A cold devil.

(*She shudders.*)

What is it?

MARGUERITE: You remind me of something.

(*She bends, kisses him.*)

ARMAND: When you kiss me I come to life.

MARGUERITE: (*Kisses him.*) Wake up, Armand.

(*Crossfade.*

MARGUERITE sits on the side of the bed, putting on her stockings.)

ARMAND: (*On his stomach, sleepy.*) Where are you going?

MARGUERITE: I'm not, but you must.

ARMAND: Why?

MARGUERITE: Because I ask you.

ARMAND: Why? I'm never going, you know that – I tell you every minute of every day. Do you want to go out? Shall I drive you? Tell me what you want, I'll get it for you.

MARGUERITE: You know you must go.

ARMAND: No-one is to touch you.

MARGUERITE: Please.

ARMAND: I won't have it.

MARGUERITE: My dear, how am I to live? How can I afford you if –

ARMAND: I can afford you!

MARGUERITE: No. Never. The day you pay for me I'm a dead woman. (*As he makes to protest.*) Please…don't. Take what there is, what we have.

ARMAND: You mean…go on as before?
MARGUERITE: (*Light.*) Why not?
(*He shakes her.*)
ARMAND: I shall give orders that no-one is to enter.
MARGUERITE: If you do you'll never see me again –
ARMAND: (*Loud.*) No!!
MARGUERITE: Armand, how can you be jealous? I've known so many men, what difference does it make? Armand!
ARMAND: That's over, for both of us.
MARGUERITE: For how long? A month? Three? Six? You'll betray me…yes you will, you'll betray me like the rest of them when desire fails. D'you think I'd lend you my heart for an instant? I'd be a fool.
ARMAND: You think I'd –
MARGUERITE: Give up my life? For what? Don't you know what I'm risking as it is? Prudence tells me I'm wasting my time, Bela refuses to speak to me…even Clemence has stolen my most reliable attachment, I don't know what to do! (*She starts to cry.*)
ARMAND: (*Irritable.*) Oh stop that!
MARGUERITE: The bank never leaves me alone, I have creditors at the door – (*Sniffing.*)
ARMAND: How much do they want, I'll pay it!
MARGUERITE: No. Nothing. Can't you understand? If you pay it's finished between us. I can afford you, for a little while at least.
ARMAND: Have I not made myself clear? I mean to stay. Forever.
MARGUERITE: Forever? Oh my dear, however short my life, it will last longer than your love.
ARMAND: Trust me. Come away with me.
MARGUERITE: No.
ARMAND: Why?
MARGUERITE: I can't leave Paris.
ARMAND: Why not? You're free.
MARGUERITE: You think it's so simple? For Armand Duval, perhaps. Armand Duval trips and there's a

goosedown pillow to break his fall. The winds blow colder for me.

ARMAND: You have my word –

MARGUERITE: Oh? And what guarantee can you give me? Your heart? Can I burn that to keep out the cold? Armand, this is a house of business. It runs on credit. When my creditors hear I'm no longer seeing de Sancerre there'll –

ARMAND: But you can't bear him!

MARGUERITE: His mother was a Rothschild, I can bear him very well. Oh Armand. Don't ask me to be poor again.

ARMAND: (*Slight pause.*) Marguerite. Marguerite, I am prepared to change my life for you.

MARGUERITE: And my life?

ARMAND: I am asking you to marry me.

(*Silence.*)

MARGUERITE: You're mad. You don't know what you're saying! (*She bursts into wild laughter and cannot stop.*)

ARMAND: (*Startled.*) Very well. Since you find the idea so ludicrous, we won't marry. It's all the same to me. Being *Madame la Marquise* would undoubtedly bore you within a month...so...my beloved lion...don't you understand – don't you understand – we're free! To do as we please! (*He grasps and embraces her, rolling her on the bed, teasing her.*) Too much love, that's what it is...too much love... (*He kisses her.*) I'll arrange everything.

MARGUERITE: No.

ARMAND: Why not?

MARGUERITE: They won't let us.

ARMAND: They can't prevent it.

MARGUERITE: Can't they?

ARMAND: Trust me.

MARGUERITE: (*Sad.*) I do.

ARMAND: Then live with me!

MARGUERITE: Oh, if I could, if I could! If everything were different – no! There is no world, no way that you and I can connect...except in the moment. There's nothing for us. I could look over the wall at you all my life and never get to touch your coat-tails. Don't be a fool, Armand. Only a fool believes a lie.

(*She turns away from him and has a spasm. She tries to stifle it, but coughs, loud, rasping sounds.*)

ARMAND: Stop that. Stop it!

(*She gasps, astonished at the harshness of his tone.*)

Breathe! Breathe...you can if you choose!

(*She gazes at him, mesmerised. But then she smiles, a helpless, sickly smile, gesturing with her hands. And haemorrhages. He leaps, finds a napkin and is at her side. She tries to turn away, then puts out an urgent hand for the napkin. There is another dreadful spasm, and the napkin is red with blood. Silence, but for MARGUERITE's rasping breath. She gazes transfixed at the napkin drenched with blood.*

They both gaze at it. Then he steps forward, takes the napkin from her, and, looking into her eyes, raises it to his lips and kisses it.)

MARGUERITE: (*Intake of breath.*) No!...

ARMAND: (*Throws down the napkin, snarls.*) Now will you listen to me!

MARGUERITE: It's from the throat...it's from the throat!

ARMAND: You mean there's been blood before?

MARGUERITE: It's not the relentless form of the disease, the doctor assures me!

ARMAND: We'll go away, to the country, I know just the place, it's high, the air is good...we'll find a house, walk, ride, and sit in the sun and you'll be well –

MARGUERITE: No...

ARMAND: My love, what is to prevent us?

MARGUERITE: Everything.

ARMAND: No! We decide. Our lives. Our decision. You can live...if you wish...if you choose.

MARGUERITE: (*Tired.*) Choose...

ARMAND: Yes, choose! Choose it – your life! Demand it. Then I can make you well. Find a coat, this minute, come away, I know the very house, there are fields, poplar trees, a stream – and the air! – you'll breathe!

MARGUERITE: Is that a promise?

ARMAND: Yes!
MARGUERITE: Well, why not?
ARMAND: No! Not like that –
MARGUERITE: Perhaps a month…six weeks –
ARMAND: No! Decide…for yourself! (*He forces her to look at him.*)
MARGUERITE: Very well. If it's what you want… (*As he makes to speak.*) …no – I understand. I choose.

(*He buries his head in her shoulder and she smiles sadly, unconvinced.*)

ARMAND: You see? Was it so difficult?

(*She shakes her head.*)

So simple. All you had to do was –

(*But his face is suddenly shocked and he steps back from her.*)

MARGUERITE: What is it?
ARMAND: (*Stammers.*) Your eyes!
MARGUERITE: What is it, what's wrong?
ARMAND: Your eyes, I can't see your eyes!
MARGUERITE: My dear. A trick of the light! It's nothing.

(*They embrace quietly.*)

Oh, is it possible? Could it be? A life together? A dream.

ARMAND: No. Real. (*He kisses her.*) What else is it all for?
MARGUERITE: (*Murmurs.*) Oh my beloved…
ARMAND: What else…?

ACT TWO

Scene 1

A graveyard, night. ARMAND and GASTON enter, followed by an old GRAVEDIGGER.

GRAVEDIGGER: Here we are, *monsieur*, it's over here in the new plots. You'll see how nice and neat it is, not all higgledy-piggledy…now, where are we? There – you can see your party as easy as anything in the moonlight…it do look lovely. I wish they all took as much trouble with their dead as you do, *monsieur* – begging your pardon, it was you left the orders for the camellias?
(*GASTON gestures towards ARMAND.*)
Ah – you, *m'sieu*? As you see, fresh as the milk from the cow. Whenever a bloom fades, I picks him off. (*He whispers to GASTON as ARMAND moves away.*) Little friend of his, *monsieur*…? I hear she was one of that sort of lady…

GASTON: I'm sorry?

GRAVEDIGGER: Very civil of you to come, she do appreciate it…well, nobody else comes near her, you can't expect it. If I was to tell some of them who their late ones was lying by, ooh dear, they'd carry on…we should have to be moved about again, and 'tis all work. (*He calls to ARMAND.*) As you see, sir, it's a fine plot. Nothing wrong with this plot. Not like down there where the water lies. (*To GASTON.*) Not that I minds the moving sir…to tell the truth…this one's the dead body I do love the best – we're obliged to love the dead, you see sir, we're kept so busy we don't hardly have time for the living. My brother now, he had the job before me, but he took to melancholy and had to be moved to a baker…the dough, you see, sir…reviving. (*Calls to ARMAND.*) Why disturb the young lady, sir? Let her lie. She'm decently buried – not like some poor young things, throwd in without so much as a bit of pine, let alone oak around them. Still, if you've made your mind to shift,

(*GASTON gives him money.*)

shift we shall. I better go and wait for the Inspector, make sure he don't lose his way. Course, with a bit of luck he might fall in one of the diggings.

GASTON: The man's right. I beg of you…abandon the endeavour…what object, where's the point?

ARMAND: (*Neutral.*) Why was it done?

GASTON: You were ill.

ARMAND: So they put her here.

GASTON: My dear Duval, what difference where she lies? There's a fine plane tree…the view is good –

ARMAND: Unacceptable.

GASTON: Is it not more appropriate that she lies here, in this simple spot? Will she not be happier with those of her own kind…people she knew and understood and had affection for? You think she would prefer a grand vault…is that what you truly believe?

(*Voices off.*)

They're coming.

(*An INSPECTOR arrives, followed by the GRAVEDIGGER and a COLLEAGUE.*)

INSPECTOR: (*To GASTON.*) *Monsieur Duval?*

ARMAND: I am Armand Duval.

INSPECTOR: Good morning, sir. Cold morning. You have written permission?

(*ARMAND gives him a paper. He scrutinises it by the lantern.*)

And the certificate?

(*He reads this too, hands it back.*)

This you retain. The other we keep. Very well. Open the grave.

(*The DIGGERS move the flowers from the lid of the coffin.*)

GASTON: (*Draws ARMAND aside.*) It's still not too late. Stop them, I beg you. At least come away!

ARMAND: No.

(*The MEN bring up the coffin.*)

INSPECTOR: (*To ARMAND.*) You understand, sir, that it is my duty to have the coffin opened in cases of request for reburial of remains. The law demands that we identify the corpse.

(*ARMAND nods.*

The GRAVEDIGGERS open the coffin.

The MEN step back, put handkerchieves to their faces, at the stench.

ARMAND groans.)

Get on with it, man!

(*The OLD DIGGER unloops the shroud…revealing the body.*

ARMAND backs away. He pushes his scarf into his mouth.

He staggers and almost slips.

GASTON supports him.)

ARMAND: (*Whispers.*) Her eyes? Where are her eyes?

INSPECTOR: Sir? You identify the remains?

ARMAND: I can't see her eyes. (*He howls, breaks away from GASTON.*) No! No! (*He throws himself down beside the coffin.*) No – no…no…no…no!

(*GASTON and the MEN drag him away.*

Lights to black.

Music.)

Scene 2

ARMAND's rooms. A large open trunk. BELA, in a dressing gown, and with his wrists bandaged in stained, untidy bandages torn from sheets, is drinking brandy. PIERRE, Armand's valet, pads quietly to and fro, filling the trunk with clothes. He pauses, looks at BELA and approaches.

PIERRE: Breakfast, Your Highness?

(*BELA ignores him.*

ARMAND enters with clothes, which he gives to PIERRE, who packs them.)

ARMAND: (*To BELA.*) Where is the doctor?

BELA: Gone. With my boot in his back.

ARMAND: You'll die of septicaemia.

BELA: Oh, poor Bela! And will you grow a rose on my grave?

ARMAND: Go to hell for all I care.

BELA: (*Murderous.*) Where were you?

ARMAND: You know where I was –

BELA: I waited –

ARMAND: No-one asked you to make a nuisance of yourself –

BELA: My apologies, for the mess. I'll make a better job of it next time.

ARMAND: There won't be a next time.

BELA: Oh?

ARMAND: I'm leaving Paris. For good.

BELA: Ah. I see. (*Laughs.*) The line of lunacy in my family seems not to be exclusive. Armand! For love? For love?

(*ARMAND goes.*)

And the whole of Paris reels with boredom. (*Calls.*) It does nothing for your looks.

(*PIERRE enters, followed by the MARQUIS, Armand's father.*)

PIERRE: The *Marquis de Saint-Brieuc.* (*To MARQUIS.*) The usual, Milord?

MARQUIS: Yes, yes. (*To BELA, cold.*) Good-day.

BELA: Ah, the Marquis. An early call.

MARQUIS: Late more like, from the looks of you. What have you done to your wrists – riding accident?

BELA: You could say so.

MARQUIS: (*To PIERRE.*) Is my son in bed?

PIERRE: I'll get him Milord. At once, Milord.

MARQUIS: I hear you distinguished yourselves at the tables last night?

BELA: I?

MARQUIS: What happens to you is of the least importance to me or to France but I will not have you assist my son to ruin.

BELA: I entirely agree.

MARQUIS: What?

BELA: Our dear Armand is gambling to win. Fatal.

MARQUIS: Then what do you propose?

BELA: (*Shrugs.*) Nothing to be done. For the present.

MARQUIS: Run its course, you mean?

BELA: It won't last.

MARQUIS: (*Approaches.*) Could you get him away – abroad?

BELA: For you?

ARMAND: What do you want? (*At the door. He approaches the MARQUIS.*)

MARQUIS: (*Genial.*) Good morning. I've been trying a new horse...a black devil. Bit of a rig, I believe I shan't take him.

ARMAND: Why are you here?

MARQUIS: Matter of business.

ARMAND: Profitable?

MARQUIS: That remains to be seen.

ARMAND: Is there something you wish to discuss with me?

(*Hiatus.*

BELA rises.)

BELA: Ah...a *tête-à-tête.* (*He bows insolently to the MARQUIS.*) You have my permission.

ARMAND: (*To BELA.*) I'll see you before I go? You'll be at the course?

BELA: Or in hell.

MARQUIS: Sorry about your wrists.

BELA: An *affaire du cœur.*

(*He kisses ARMAND full on the lips, slides a smiling glance at the MARQUIS and goes.*)

MARQUIS: I note that you take the trouble to find the most vicious company in Paris.

ARMAND: Oh come. Surely his pedigree's good enough, even for you...finest quarterings in Europe.

MARQUIS: Degenerates, the lot of them. (*To PIERRE who is filling his coffee cup.*) Be careful, dammit, you nearly scalded my hands! (*He waves a letter at ARMAND.*) What is this?

ARMAND: (*Crosses looks.*) You find it unclear?

MARQUIS: Unfortunately I cannot stop you from realising your capital –

ARMAND: It is mine, to dispose as I wish –
MARQUIS: Your mother was ill-advised.
ARMAND: I am in need of funds. Marguerite has debts.
MARQUIS: The best kept woman in Paris?
ARMAND: Be careful.
MARQUIS: The money's flowing out like the Rhine! What are you both doing out there in your love nest – burning it to keep warm? Eh?! You cannot continue to run through funds which rightfully belong to the estate – no – (*As ARMAND turns to leave.*) – please…you will do me the courtesy to hear me out.

(*ARMAND pauses, turns back.*

The MARQUIS walks about, taking his time, used to people waiting on his pleasure.)

My boy… (*He pauses for a moment, begins again.*) My boy, don't think for a moment that I don't understand. (*Slight pause.*) We are somewhat alike, you and I. Women are necessary to us. However, placed as we are, to buy affection is the sanest solution. (*Slight pause.*) The right woman, with understanding, sympathy…beauty… (*He sighs reminiscently.*)

ARMAND: Have you finished?
MARQUIS: I'd care for you to hear me out. There is no objection to a permanent mistress. However, in our position one must beware the wire, the low branch. Can't afford to take a fall. Responsibilities.
ARMAND: Any responsibilities I care to assume will be of my own choosing.
MARQUIS: Ah, the Bohemian life! Well, why not? time enough for the halter.
ARMAND: What do you want?
MARQUIS: I have come to settle your debts, and to offer you a draft for twenty thousand francs.
ARMAND: That's remarkably generous.
MARQUIS: In return we ask that you maintain the lady discreetly and in a manner that will not embarrass your family. Surely that's generous.
ARMAND: A fair bargain, you mean?

MARQUIS: If you want to put it that way.

ARMAND: (*Pause.*) There is something you need to know. (*Pause.*) I intend to marry Marguerite.

(*Silence.*)

MARQUIS: That, as you know, is utterly out of the question.

ARMAND: She says the same. Nonetheless…that is what I intend to do.

(*Silence.*)

MARQUIS: I forbid it.

ARMAND: You can't prevent it.

MARQUIS: (*Pause.*) Armand…none of us is here by choice. If we're wise we play the hand dealt. I'd like to have been a gamekeeper. However. You're my heir. You are to have the guardianship of twenty thousand acres and the souls who live on them – some of whom have been on the land as long as we have. They've spilt blood for us. Do you intend to dispossess, to abandon them? Is their well-being of no consequence to you? My boy, you are the heir to a kingdom!

ARMAND: The land is not entailed. Let my brother have it.

MARQUIS: He's not the heir! You're young. Tradition means nothing to you. At your age it's necessary to smash everything to pieces, start again. Listen to me. Trust me. Permanence, continuity, the preservation of the line – they're of the utmost value. What else is there? What else stands against chaos and dissolution. Land and blood. It's all that matters.

(*Pause.*)

ARMAND: To you. Not to me. I do not intend to live as you.

MARQUIS: Have you no thought for your family?

(*ARMAND grimaces.*)

Do we mean so little to you? Do you want to break your sister's heart? Her engagement has just been announced. De Luneville will break it off at once…what's to happen to that poor girl? It's a love match. She's in love with him.

ARMAND: If it's a love match he'll marry her.

MARQUIS: And destroy himself? You know better than that.

(*Pause.*)

ARMAND: You don't begin to understand. I have to marry her.

MARQUIS: Why?

ARMAND: It's my only chance.

MARQUIS: For what?

ARMAND: Life.

MARQUIS: I see...you intend to create a new universe – above the aspirations of the rest of us. (*Savage.*) What do you think marriage is? Some sort of beatified love affair, impervious to the winds that blow...you think society runs on love? Hah! Talk to me of love in six months' time, when the money's run out.

ARMAND: Once our debts are settled we shall not be concerned with –

MARQUIS: She'll leave you.

ARMAND: (*Slight pause.*) Six months ago I should have agreed with you. With every word. Now, I'm the most fortunate man in the world because Marguerite Gautier loves me. Because Marguerite Gautier is prepared to spend her life with me. It is not a question of love even – though that goes without saying. It is a question of friendship. Of respect.

(*The MARQUIS turns on him in a towering and frightening rage.*)

MARQUIS: Respect? Respect?! For a whore?!! You dare to talk of love...you dare to talk of friendship – with a whore? You dare to come to me, talk of marriage? Introduce a harlot into my family! Are you seriously suggesting...that you want...as your life's companion... before God and the Church...as the mother of your children...my heirs...a woman who has felt the private parts of every man in Paris?

(*ARMAND lunges at the MARQUIS, who stumbles.*)

You become as depraved as the company you keep. (*Rises, dusts himself down.*) Good God, boy, what does it matter? One woman's slot or another?

ARMAND: Get out.

MARQUIS: Very well. (*He puts on his gloves.*) I shall stop your allowance and disclaim all responsibility for your debts. If I post that publicly you may whistle for credit, there won't be a door open to you. Give the matter some thought. I shall expect you tomorrow. Three o'clock.

(*He puts on his hat, PIERRE ushers him out.*

ARMAND crosses at once to the trunk.)

ARMAND: Pierre...Pierre!

(*PIERRE hurries back on, ARMAND manhandles the trunk eagerly, with PIERRE's help. They go.*)

Scene 3

The garden of the cottage. MARGUERITE and JEAN-PAUL, playing with a pair of doves in a cage.

MARGUERITE: What are you going to call them?

JEAN-PAUL: Plume...and Hat.

MARGUERITE: Which one is which – be careful, they'll peck you!

JEAN-PAUL: That one's Hat...after *Madame Prudence.*

MARGUERITE: You rogue!

(*YVETTE enters with JEAN-PAUL's jacket. She and MARGUERITE swing him round and collapse, laughing.*

MARGUERITE tickles JEAN-PAUL, who shrieks with laughter.

YVETTE, smiling, holds out the boy's jacket.

ARMAND strolls on in his shirtsleeves.)

ARMAND: (*Catching JEAN-PAUL.*) Got you!

MARGUERITE: Will he need his coat?

YVETTE: Be on the safe side. (*She picks up her basket.*)

MARGUERITE: Now be careful with the eggs!

YVETTE: Oh he's good! He finds them quicker than me, don't you?

(*JEAN-PAUL dodges behind MARGUERITE and ARMAND chases him.*)

MARGUERITE: Don't go in the water!

ARMAND: He's all right.

(*He swings JEAN-PAUL around.*
JEAN-PAUL runs off, followed by YVETTE.
MARGUERITE crosses to ARMAND and they embrace.)

Now I have you all to myself.

MARGUERITE: You're jealous.

ARMAND: Of course.

MARGUERITE: Don't be jealous.

ARMAND: Not if you ask it.

(*They kiss.*)

MARGUERITE: And you're happy?

ARMAND: Yes.

(*He nods. But he looks away.*)

MARGUERITE: You're not sure? What is it. What's the matter?

ARMAND: Nothing.

MARGUERITE: Tell me!

(*He looks at her soberly, shakes his head.*)

What?

ARMAND: I've been misled.

MARGUERITE: Misled? Who by – me?

ARMAND: No. By love. I have been misinformed.

MARGUERITE: You are disappointed?

ARMAND: No.

MARGUERITE: What then?

ARMAND: Surprised.

MARGUERITE: Surprised? What did you expect?

ARMAND: Agony…sighs…letters in mauve ink – an urgent involvement with poetry to the extremities of picking up a pen. Instead…

(*He sighs.*)

MARGUERITE: Instead?

ARMAND: None of the old rank paths. A garden, with tall trees, oak and ash and cedar –

MARGUERITE: Not cedar, they're for graveyards.

ARMAND: An olive grove then, and water – very fierce – spray all over the rocks!
MARGUERITE: And flowers?
ARMAND: You won't be able to walk for them.
MARGUERITE: It's a dream.
ARMAND: No. Real. (*He kisses her fingers.*)
MARGUERITE: For how long?
ARMAND: (*Looks up.*) I know what you mean. To be the custodian of something so precious – how to keep it safe?
MARGUERITE: We can't.
ARMAND: We can. We will. Why not, if we choose. We choose!
PRUDENCE: So this is where you're hiding!
(*She sweeps on, followed by CLEMENCE and SOPHIE.*)
MARGUERITE: Oh!! (*Embraces them.*) Clemence, you look splendid! I never saw such pearls, they're as big as pigeons' eggs!
CLEMENCE: I know! They keep you ever so warm – worth the neck-ache.
PRUDENCE: (*To MARGUERITE.*) Bought by the Count – for you.
CLEMENCE: (*Fondly.*) Ye-es, we had a laugh about it…you don't mind, do you, Marguerite?
(*MARGUERITE laughs, tipping back her head, then shakes it, smiling.*)
I knew you wouldn't. I knew we'd still be friends… anyway, all the best friendships are where you never see each other.
SOPHIE: (*Embracing MARGUERITE.*) Are you well?
MARGUERITE: As you see…blooming.
SOPHIE: (*To ARMAND.*) Suits you, does it, country life?
ARMAND: I shall be indistinguishable from the hayricks in six months.
SOPHIE: Six months is a long time.
PRUDENCE: Wait until the winter!
SOPHIE: Mud –
CLEMENCE: Chilblains –

SOPHIE: Ice on the washing water –
(Laughter.)
PRUDENCE: They'll be back.
ARMAND: *(To CLEMENCE.)* And how is the Count?
CLEMENCE: Ooh, we've been travelling!
MARGUERITE: Where?
CLEMENCE: Heaven knows! We kept having to be somewhere to get to somewhere else. I think it was the Mediterranean, but you're so busy drinking it all in.
PRUDENCE: They were at the Duchess's ball last night.
MARGUERITE: Really!
PRUDENCE: She went as a powder puff, and he went as a brush. Still.
MARGUERITE: And you like him?
CLEMENCE: Oh yes! He says such interesting things! – not like any other Swede who likes time-tables – if you see what I mean.
(The OTHERS laugh.)
MARGUERITE: You must look at the garden – there's a pond!
CLEMENCE: A pond – ooh! Can we punt?
ARMAND: Afraid not.
CLEMENCE: Never mind. People in boats are such hooligans.
(ARMAND goes, with CLEMENCE and SOPHIE.)
MARGUERITE: *(After a pause.)* How much?
PRUDENCE: Ten thousand.
MARGUERITE: What?!
PRUDENCE: Marguerite, selling is not buying.
MARGUERITE: You saw the Duke?
PRUDENCE: Nothing.
(YVETTE enters with a tray of drinks.
PRUDENCE assesses her shrewdly as she bobs and goes.
MARGUERITE smiles.)
MARGUERITE: Janine left me – she didn't take to country life again. I told her you might find her something.
PRUDENCE: I already have. *(Slight pause.)* My dear, how long can this go on?

MARGUERITE: As long as the money lasts.
PRUDENCE: What then? The landlord's repossessed.
MARGUERITE: There was cash in hand!
PRUDENCE: Not any more. I can't get a penny on your name, even the little woman in the glove shop gave me her account. There are new stars rising. If you continue this nonsense I shall be forced to abandon you.
MARGUERITE: I thought we were friends.
PRUDENCE: Friendship is based on good sense. You can't expect the rest of us to follow you to ruin. For God's sakes, Marguerite, do you want to end up like me…everybody's catspaw? There's nothing so vacated as being a woman of my age. Take my word, it won't last forever!
MARGUERITE: I know. (*Pause.*) He's asked me to marry him.
PRUDENCE: Has he, by God? So that's why his father is in Paris.
MARGUERITE: What?
PRUDENCE: He didn't tell you? There's a devil of a row. You'd be a Marquise, of course, but there's no profit in it, the way things stand. You'd have to leave France, and he'd go into drink, I've seen it all before.
MARGUERITE: I don't think so.
PRUDENCE: You love him, is that it?
MARGUERITE: Yes. Yes, that's it.
PRUDENCE: Good, then you won't want to ruin his life. He'll be ostracised, cut off from everything he knows. What about the boy, you want him schooled, don't you? Your brothers, just lifting their heads above water, thanks to you…your mother, she's not getting any younger. You're a beauty. Men desire you. You keep us all afloat… servants, seamstresses, shoemakers…not a bad achievement for a girl who couldn't write her name. My dear, don't throw it all away.
MARGUERITE: Prudence…
PRUDENCE: How are *we* to survive? (*Slight pause.*) Listen. I've met this charming wine merchant. He saw you at the

Opera and he's dying to meet you. Not young, but very soundly based. You could still see Armand – why not? He must learn to share! You'll afford him a lot longer if you give up these foolish notions of love in the attic. My dear, you can't trust it. I know these aristocrats. They're finished off in the cradle. He's like his father. Cold.

MARGUERITE: He's changed.

PRUDENCE: I doubt that. I doubt that very much. No man's constant, Marguerite, it isn't in their nature. I kept a rogue for twenty years, he couldn't wait to deceive me, not a week without it. Come back. Once it's known that Marguerite Gautier is returning to Paris – new address…new wardrobe…my dear, you should see the silks this year…colours like light, you won't be able to resist them.

MARGUERITE: Prudence…I truly appreciate your coming to see me…

PRUDENCE: But you're not coming back?

MARGUERITE: No.

PRUDENCE: We'll give it another month.

MARGUERITE: No.

PRUDENCE: Very well, my dear. If you change your mind, let me know. *Au revoir*, I don't want to drive back in the middle of the day, the horses will get hot.

(*She goes.*

SOPHIE enters.)

SOPHIE: What's the matter?

MARGUERITE: Can't you guess?

SOPHIE: You're a fool.

MARGUERITE: How's Paris?

SOPHIE: Amusing. (*Pause.*) Marguerite…

(*MARGUERITE turns her head away, with a smile.*)

It's not going to last. Why ruin yourself, for a man? You're free!

MARGUERITE: Am I?

SOPHIE: You mean you like him? You like Duval?

MARGUERITE: There seems to be *some* sort of necessity. I am, almost, persuaded. Some of the time.

SOPHIE: (*Slight pause.*) I'm thinking of going abroad.
MARGUERITE: (*Dismayed.*) Oh! Where?
SOPHIE: To the sun. Africa. Will you miss me?
MARGUERITE: Very much. Who with?
SOPHIE: A man.
MARGUERITE: Will he treat you well?
SOPHIE: As badly as I shall treat him.

(*They laugh and embrace.*)

MARGUERITE: But you'll be safe?
SOPHIE: Safe enough.

(*ARMAND returns with JEAN-PAUL on his shoulders followed by CLEMENCE, and by YVETTE who goes in.*)

CLEMENCE: Look what we've found!
JEAN-PAUL: Eggs! (*He shows MARGUERITE the basket of eggs.*)
CLEMENCE: (*Touching the eggs.*) Ugh, they're still warm... ugh! Do they lay anything else?
ARMAND: Diamond bracelets, but only on Sundays.

(*She chases him with her sunshade.*
JEAN-PAUL laughs.)

CLEMENCE: (*Stops short.*) Mmm, what's that gorgeous smell?
MARGUERITE: Roast lamb.
ARMAND: Slaughtered in your honour.
CLEMENCE: Ahh, poor little thing!...how could you?
ARMAND: With rosemary sauce –
JEAN-PAUL: And new potatoes!
CLEMENCE: Oooh!

(*She and ARMAND take JEAN-PAUL between them and whisk him off to luncheon.*)

MARGUERITE: You're looking well.
SOPHIE: Yes, I'm not coughing. And you?

(*MARGUERITE shakes her head with a smile.*)

(*Rising.*) Then life here suits you?

MARGUERITE: It seems so.

(*They go, arm in arm.*
Pause.
The PARTY return, replete after a meal, and sit under the parasol on cushions.

Music.
Pause.)
JEAN-PAUL: A.
MARGUERITE: (*Lazily.*) Azure.
JEAN-PAUL: B.
SOPHIE: (*Slight pause.*) Black.
JEAN-PAUL: C.
ARMAND: Chrome yellow.
CLEMENCE: That's two words. Oh, all right. D. Damson.
JEAN-PAUL: Damson? That's not a colour.
CLEMENCE: Yes it is.
JEAN-PAUL: What colour's damson?
CLEMENCE: Everyone knows what damson looks like, silly – how old are you?
JEAN-PAUL: Seven.
CLEMENCE: (*Scornful.*) Is that all?
SOPHIE: He's right. Do you mean the skin, or the flesh –
MARGUERITE: Or stewed damsons –
CLEMENCE: I mean damson and cream, like when people say something's raspberry coloured they mean raspberry fool –
SOPHIE: Oh come on, whose turn is it? Jean-Paul –
JEAN-PAUL: But are we having fruit?
MARGUERITE: We ought to have a policy –
CLEMENCE: Oh let's not have policies, we don't want policies –
SOPHIE: All right, we accept damson. (*She whispers to JEAN-PAUL, who cannot think of a colour beginning with E.*) Evergreen...
JEAN-PAUL: E. Evergreen!
ARMAND: Rejected.
(*JEAN-PAUL wails.*
MARGUERITE throws a cushion at ARMAND.)
What about eiderdown...
(*As JEAN-PAUL attacks him with a cushion.*) Eggy? Ellow?
(*They shout him down.*)
Very well.
(*He whispers to JEAN-PAUL.*)

JEAN-PAUL: Emerald.

(*They clap.*)

MARGUERITE: Flame.

SOPHIE: Garnet.

CLEMENCE: Garnets come in lots of colours.

ARMAND: Reject.

SOPHIE: Grey then.

CLEMENCE: H. Oh I thought of one just now…now I've forgotten it.

SOPHIE: Double marks to me if I give you one.

CLEMENCE: Oh we're not having marks are we?

ARMAND: H. House…home…happy…

(*Light change.*

JEAN-PAUL runs off.

ARMAND, hat in hand, waits as MARGUERITE kisses CLEMENCE goodbye.

She turns to SOPHIE.)

MARGUERITE: Write to me!

(*They kiss. CLEMENCE and SOPHIE go. MARGUERITE turns to ARMAND.*)

Must you go?

ARMAND: I've a few things to settle.

MARGUERITE: But I've spoken to Prudence. There is money.

ARMAND: I'll be back tonight.

MARGUERITE: Will you?

ARMAND: Marguerite! They can't hurt us – they can't touch us…there's no way they can pull us apart. Trust me.

(*They stroll, arm in arm.*)

It's simple. We're strong…engines of possibility! Here we stand, openly, for all to see…to live, to have our children… (*He grasps her hand eagerly.*) I shall do as we planned, become a printer – write, perhaps, if I've the talent for it…if not, print the works of those who have. We'll work and live together, side by side…without ambition, except to excel, without greed, except to offer the best of ourselves. Our aim – to find our true work...to live, support our children...to read...think – and to be as clear as we can.

(*They embrace. She draws back.*)

MARGUERITE: Must you see him again?

ARMAND: My father? I said I would.

MARGUERITE: Be careful.

ARMAND: (*Kisses her.*) Don't wait up.

MARGUERITE: You know I shall.

(*They embrace and he goes.*

MARGUERITE walks back and forth, troubled.

JEAN-PAUL runs on, followed by YVETTE.)

JEAN-PAUL: Tan' Marie, Tan' Marie, we're going to catch frogs!

MARGUERITE: (*As he runs past.*) You...didn't finish your lunch!

JEAN-PAUL: It was only the cabbage!

YVETTE: Only the cabbage!

(*MARGUERITE laughs, watching them go. But she resumes her walk, anxious and reflective.*

The MARQUIS enters behind her.)

MARQUIS: There was no-one to announce me so I took the liberty of walking round.

(*He bows.*

MARGUERITE turns.)

MARGUERITE: *Monsieur le Marquis?*

MARQUIS: Good-day, Marie.

(*He stands, easy, and surveys her with an unhurried stare.*

MARGUERITE moves, rings a bell.

PIERRE appears.)

PIERRE: *Monsieur le Marquis?*

MARQUIS: Armagnac and water.

(*PIERRE goes.*)

Pretty spot. (*He gazes out at the view.*) Fine view of the river. Damned hot dusty drive though.

(*PIERRE returns.*

The MARQUIS waves him away, and mixes his own drink.

PIERRE goes.

MARGUERITE watches in silence as he measures the drink without haste.)

Fine old Armagnac...can you afford it?
MARGUERITE: We keep it for creditors.
MARQUIS: (*Inspecting the bottle.*) Not a lot left.
MARGUERITE: As you see.
MARQUIS: I hear you're being sold up.
MARGUERITE: And what are you going to do about it?
MARQUIS: I? Not my affair. If my son chooses to ruin himself, that's his concern.
MARGUERITE: How is he to live?
MARQUIS: How indeed, since he's cashing up, it seems, on your behalf.
MARGUERITE: I've not asked him to do so. I've tried to prevent it.
MARQUIS: So much so that he's gone through his mother's inheritance in a month. A pity, since I'm withdrawing financial support, including my name to all his bills.
MARGUERITE: You can't!
MARQUIS: The disclaimers are in my pocket.
MARGUERITE: He has as much right to the money as you have. You didn't earn it!
MARQUIS: Come, no need to lose your temper. Wearing thin already, is it?
MARGUERITE: You'd like to believe so.
MARQUIS: No pleasure for me, watching my heir make a fool of himself before the whole of Paris...let alone upsetting his family.
MARGUERITE: So you've come to offer me money.
MARQUIS: Of course.
MARGUERITE: How much?
MARQUIS: Fifty thousand.
MARGUERITE: You have a sense of humour.
MARQUIS: I'll go to seventy-five.
MARGUERITE: You're wasting your time.
MARQUIS: A hundred then. That's the top.
MARGUERITE: Have you got it with you?
MARQUIS: Don't play the fool with me, girl. There's a closed carriage outside, waiting to take you back to Paris. Come with me now and I'll pay the rest of your

debts and set you up again. Come, be honest, Marie, aren't you bored? After Paris? (*Pause.*) Armand will understand – if not now, later. He'll respect your sacrifice for the rest of his life. (*Slight pause.*) You surely can't stand by and see him ruined if you truly and genuinely love him. Come, take my arm –

(*And he touches her.*

She springs away as if burnt.)

MARGUERITE: No! Get away from me! I don't want to see you, ever...don't you ever come here again! I don't want to see your face, I don't want to hear your voice, I don't want you near me! You've no right to come here threatening me under my own roof, do you think I can't take care of myself –

MARQUIS: Don't get hysterical –

MARGUERITE: You have no authority here –

MARQUIS: No authority? I could have you arrested within the hour.

MARGUERITE: On what charge?

MARQUIS: Does it matter? Do you think you matter? You will leave with me now. That is what I wish, and that is what –

MARGUERITE: No! Go away! You think I'm nothing? Something to be pulled out of the way like a piece of wood in the road? We don't need you. You poison the air you breathe, the ground you walk on. You have no control, no influence over us. So take your foul breath and your rotting teeth and your stinking ass out of my house! Go on...get out!

MARQUIS: I can place your name on the list of undesirables, you won't see Paris then –

MARGUERITE: Get out! Get out...get out! (*She picks up a knife.*)

MARQUIS: (*Going.*) You'll be put away as a madwoman –

(*YVETTE returns with JEAN-PAUL.*

He carries a jar.)

JEAN-PAUL: (*Running on.*) Tan' Marie, look...

(*He stops at the stranger.*

MARGUERITE freezes.

She waves YVETTE to take the BOY away but the MARQUIS approaches.)

MARGUERITE: Don't touch him!

MARQUIS: That's a fine frog, my boy. A fine frog like that deserves a louis. (*He takes it from his pocket, gives it to the BOY, who, nudged by YVETTE, bows.*)

JEAN-PAUL: Thank you, sir. Oh, a gold one! (*He shows YVETTE.*)

MARQUIS: (*To YVETTE.*) Boy's a credit to you.

YVETTE: Thank you sir. (*She curtsies and smiles.*)

MARGUERITE: (*Harsh.*) Take him in, Yvette.

(*They go.*

Silence.)

MARQUIS: A fine child. Good-looking boy.

MARGUERITE: Leave him out of it.

MARQUIS: I had no idea. A little rough in his speech, perhaps, but that's soon amended.

MARGUERITE: He is not your concern.

MARQUIS: Is he not? What plans do you have for him?

MARGUERITE: My plans are none of your affair.

MARQUIS: He'll need decent schooling...that's not cheap.

MARGUERITE: Will you go?

MARQUIS: A fine boy, I'm taken with him. He has an air of Armand at the same age. (*Slight pause.*) I see you still have the scar from my ring.

MARGUERITE: (*She seems exhausted.*) Go...just go.

MARQUIS: I'll strike a bargain with you Marie. Come back to Paris in the coach with me, here and now, and I'll give the boy an education.

MARGUERITE: No.

MARQUIS: What's his future to be? Hawked about with you and my son, not a sou between you? A couple of years schooling if he's lucky...to become a labourer in the fields...an ostler...with an aging mother to support?

MARGUERITE: I tell you no.

MARQUIS: I might even be prepared to take him...accept him, publicly, as my natural son. Give him my name – after all, in a way it's his birthright. We'll hire a tutor, start him on his declensions.

MARGUERITE: You devil. You're the devil.

MARQUIS: He'll be reared as a gentleman.

MARGUERITE: You think I want him to be like you?

MARQUIS: Do you want him able to read, think for himself, carry on a profession? Able to keep a decent household...live a civilized life? It's in your hands, Marie. It's for you to choose. You're his mother. What shall it be? Will you choose for yourself? Or for the child?

MARGUERITE: No...no...

MARQUIS: I am, after all, his father.

MARGUERITE: No! No!!

MARQUIS: Very well, then I shall get a magistrate's order stating that you are an unfit mother. Good God, woman, what do you think you're playing at? Have you forgotten your place?

MARGUERITE: Don't – oh don't! Don't...no...don't...no... please, sir, don't!

(*She becomes hysterical.*

JEAN-PAUL runs on, followed by YVETTE.

MARGUERITE clasps JEAN-PAUL to her feverishly.)

No! No!

(*The MARQUIS takes the BOY from her, gives him to YVETTE.*)

MARQUIS: Take the boy away and pack his clothes.

(*YVETTE, frightened of him, obeys.*

They go in.)

JEAN-PAUL: (*Offstage, wails.*) Maman!

MARGUERITE: No...no... (*She weeps.*)

MARQUIS: Be reasonable, Marie. You've no choice in the matter. (*Pause. He approaches her.*) Take what you can get.

(*She weeps.*)

You were always realistic – courageous, I admired your spirit!

(*He laughs in reminiscence.*

A long pause.)

MARGUERITE: (*Low.*) I want him educated.

MARQUIS: As I've said.

MARGUERITE: You'll adopt him? Give him your name?

(*He nods.*)

I don't want him left to servants!

MARQUIS: I am about to marry again. An Italian. I believe they are fond of children.

MARGUERITE: Oh please…

MARQUIS: He will be well-treated.

MARGUERITE: Shall I…shall I see him again?

MARQUIS: Perhaps…when he is a man. Let time create him for us. Then we'll see. A fine child. I do congratulate you. (*He gives her his arm.*) Come…we'll go into the house and you can write the note.

MARGUERITE: The note?

MARQUIS: To Armand. Saying that you have returned to Paris. That you are bored with the country, with your present life. That you prefer your former existence. There must be no confusion. No doubt as to your intentions. Afterwards we'll drive into Paris together…and the boy can come home, with me.

(*He helps her inside.*

The light goes. Pause.

PIERRE comes out to light the garden lantern. He looks off, for ARMAND, sees nothing, goes inside again.

Lights to black.

The slow light of the moon.

ARMAND enters, wearing a cloak.)

ARMAND: Marguerite?

(*PIERRE enters, hands him a letter and goes in again. ARMAND opens the letter and reads it. He falls to his knees, crushing the letter and uttering a loud, eerie, prolonged howl of anguish.*)

Scene 4

The foyer of the Opera. The TWO WAITERS prepare for the entr'acte. The sound of a woman singing as the doors open and CLEMENCE enters, fuming, followed by COUNT DRUFTHEIM.

CLEMENCE: I'm just not standing for it!

COUNT: My Snowdrop, you are not enjoying the opera?

CLEMENCE: Letting him pester her like that, it really riles me!

COUNT: But it is the makings up, not the true…and the singing, oh, so full and round –

CLEMENCE: Well it makes me go outraged –

COUNT: Beloved –

CLEMENCE: She should punch him in the head.

COUNT: You have the soft, warm heart. (*He kisses her hand.*)

CLEMENCE: We'll go again tomorrow, see the rest.

COUNT: No. We will not. You shall choose.

(*He bows as the old DUKE enters, squiring ERNESTINE, but the DUKE, busy, does not see him.*

ERNESTINE and CLEMENCE exchange a laconic nod.)

CLEMENCE: (*Sitting.*) I would have enjoyed it more only one of my stays went and I lost the drift a bit.

COUNT: Ping, ping!

(*Heads together, they giggle and whisper as the DUKE and ERNESTINE promenade.*

PRUDENCE enters with JANINE, her new protegée, now dressed to kill.)

JANINE: We'll miss the ending!

PRUDENCE: Nonsense, what do you care, anyway I've seen it, she kills herself. (*She looks round.*) Where's Armand, what's happened to Armand?

(*She turns, retracing her steps.*)

JANINE: (*Surly.*) He's at the bar.

PRUDENCE: Now why did you allow that – (*Sees CLEMENCE and the COUNT, screeches.*) – Count! Clemence! What a wonderful surprise! (*She embraces CLEMENCE.*) Wicked! When did you arrive?

CLEMENCE: Yesterday.

PRUDENCE: You should have left a note! How well they look (*Introducing her.*) – Olympe, my new protegée – don't they look well!

CLEMENCE: Janine?

JANINE: Yes. Like a couple of Parma hams. What? (*As PRUDENCE digs her in the ribs to mind her manners.*)

CLEMENCE: We saw every country in Europe except Japan –

COUNT: (*Embarrassed by her error.*) My darling –
CLEMENCE: – we even saw an octopus, (*Scornful.*) but I didn't believe it!
COUNT: *Madame Prudence*, you are from the opera? (*Kissing her hand.*) So fine, is it not?
PRUDENCE: Oh yes.
JANINE: Miserable though.
COUNT: *Jah, jah.* First we see the young girl, so happy and innocent. Then is coming the father, and –
PRUDENCE: (*Quick.*) How was your voyage?
CLEMENCE: Lovely. Every minute.
(*She and the COUNT exchange a doting smile.*)
PRUDENCE: You enjoyed yourselves then?
COUNT: Oh yah. The first day was warm, but not so warm that we are without the jackets, then on the second day is coming little shower –
(*PRUDENCE flees, pursued by the COUNT.*)
JANINE: How are you getting on with him?
CLEMENCE: Like a couple of roosting hens, you should see us!
JANINE: There you are, I told you, didn't I? Who put you up to it, remember?
CLEMENCE: He's ever so clever, he can saw a woman in half!
JANINE: Get away!
CLEMENCE: Of course he doesn't really, it's a trick. Mind you, he eats a lot. I expect that's to feed his mind.
JANINE: Yes. Build it up.
CLEMENCE: Tonight he ate half a side of venison! (*She belches, eases her stays. Queasily.*) I ate the other half.
(*The COUNT, having lost PRUDENCE, wanders on again.*)
JANINE: Count – over here!
COUNT: (*Bows.*) How do you –
JANINE: It's Janine! Don't you remember? Only I'm called Olympe now. (*Aside, to CLEMENCE.*) You'll never guess who's paying my bills. (*To the COUNT.*) How did you find Italy?
CLEMENCE: It took quite a while.

COUNT: Florence is a most beautiful city with many statues and paintings which, of course, we have seen all.

JANINE: I hear you've been eating well.

COUNT: The food is good, yes. But it is not so agreeable to look up and see swimming before you in the river, rats...also cats...sometimes swimming and sometimes dead.

(*PRUDENCE enters and is caught.*)

Ah, *Madame Prudence*! I have been sending to the Mayor documents and diagrams for the disposal of –

(*PRUDENCE is saved by the appearance of SOPHIE and BELA.*)

SOPHIE: Prudence!

PRUDENCE: Sophie! Prince!

(*PRUDENCE and SOPHIE embrace and kiss each other.*)

Well, Now the season can begin!

(*BELA lifts PRUDENCE off her feet, swings her round, making her screech.*)

Prince! Ouf! How was Africa? You look like a pair of Zouaves. Very unfashionable – pale is the thing. Pale is the last word. Duke!

DUKE: (*Passing.*) It will suit *La Gautier* then, eh?

PRUDENCE: Ah Duke, always the wit!

BELA: Pale?

(*SOPHIE draws PRUDENCE aside.*)

SOPHIE: What have you heard?

(*PRUDENCE moves away. SOPHIE follows.*)

Is Marguerite ill?

PRUDENCE: Never more sparkling.

(*SOPHIE pursues her.*)

SOPHIE: She's ill.

PRUDENCE: I haven't said so. You should see the Russian bear she has in tow!

SOPHIE: How ill?

PRUDENCE: (*Shrugs.*) Skin like watered milk.

SOPHIE: What is it, opium? The lungs? Tell me!

(*ARMAND enters.*)

ARMAND: Well! Well!

(*BELA bows ironically.*)

Two blackened faces from the past. (*To BELA.*) I thought you were dead.

SOPHIE: Sorry to disappoint.

JANINE: Armand! (*She runs across to ARMAND, takes his arm with a familiar gesture.*) Armand, we missed you!

BELA: (*To ARMAND.*) What's this?

JANINE: Where did you go?

(*She whispers in ARMAND'S ear.*
He laughs, and looks challengingly at BELA.)

BELA: I see.

ARMAND: (*Throws JANINE off abruptly.*) Get out.

PRUDENCE: He adores her.

(*Furious, she walks off and joins PRUDENCE.*)

BELA: Do you – adore her?

ARMAND: Of course. She is disgusting.

(*BELA throws back his head in a shout of laughter.*)

BELA: Bravo! Bravo!

(*He leaps on ARMAND and embraces him.*
ARMAND smiles, and kisses him full on the lips and then crosses and sits, apart.
JANINE joins him, taking his arm.)

JANINE: (*To SOPHIE.*) Surprised?

SOPHIE: Not in the least. (*She laughs.*) God help us all.

JANINE: Do you like my dress?

SOPHIE: You look like a firework.

(*JANINE waltzes in circles, throws herself on ARMAND's lap. SOPHIE crosses to PRUDENCE.*)

What have you been up to? That bitch? Are you desperate? (*She laughs grimly.*) You're wasting your time. Those two mean devils have no more for you than for each other.

PRUDENCE: I know that. Why do you think he does it? (*She gets up, crosses.*) He does it to spite her!

(*SOPHIE follows.*)

SOPHIE: Marguerite? You mean Marguerite?

(*There is a sudden hush.*
SOPHIE turns, and there is MARGUERITE.

She is in black and gold, and is accompanied by a heavily-built OLDER MAN in highly-ornamented Russian clothes.)
(*Shocked, whispers.*) God in heaven!

PRUDENCE: Quick, he mustn't see her –

(*She moves to cut MARGUERITE off, but is too late.*)

SOPHIE: Too late.

(*ARMAND and MARGUERITE meet. ARMAND comes forward, bows low.*)

ARMAND: Good evening…good evening. Up for a breath of air, *Mademoiselle Gautier*?

MARGUERITE: *Monsieur Duval.*

(*She tries to pass him, but he blocks her path, calling out to the MAN behind her.*)

ARMAND: How are you, tonight, Prince? Ah, out of action, I see.

(*The PRINCE is paralytic.*)

MARGUERITE: Please.

ARMAND: Your servant. I compliment you on your choice of transaction. The perverse…the elderly…the *hors de combat* – a convenient clientele, *Ma'moiselle.*

JANINE: Well, if it isn't Marie – *you* look old. Armand, come and dance! I could dance all night…you won't tire me out!

(*ARMAND and JANINE dance.*
MARGUERITE, trapped on the PRINCE's lap, is forced to watch.)

ARMAND: (*Calls, to the PRINCE en passant.*) You'll find the lady wanting, *Monsieur le Prince*…failing in contractual commitment –

PRINCE: (*In Russian.*) Fuck off before I kill you.

(*SOPHIE dances with BELA, CLEMENCE with the COUNT.*
The old DUKE hobbles on, waves his stick happily at PRUDENCE, and hops round the floor with her.
The PRINCE rises majestically, takes MARGUERITE in his arms, spins her to the centre of the room, and crashes to the ground with her.
Laughter and applause.)

ARMAND: Throw them some buns! Come on, *Mademoiselle*, up on your haunches, let's see the next trick.

JANINE: Don't waste your time, Armand...who wants yesterday's mackerel?

(*The music stops as she speaks and her voice rings out.*

SOPHIE steps forward. She approaches JANINE like a tiger stalking its prey.

JANINE withdraws.

But SOPHIE strikes, and boxes JANINE's ears.

The two girls fight, rolling over and over, screaming and clawing and going for each other's hair.

JANINE begins to get the worst of it.

SOPHIE is cheered on as JANINE begins to dodge about, evading.

MARGUERITE manages to extricate herself from the PRINCE. She makes unobtrusively for the exit.

But ARMAND, who seems absorbed and delighted in the fight, moves swiftly to cut her off, as PRUDENCE and CLEMENCE pick up the snivelling JANINE.)

ARMAND: You're leaving us, *Mademoiselle Gautier*?

MARGUERITE: Don't.

ARMAND: *Honoré de Sancerre* waiting with his whips and his costume trunk?

MARGUERITE: Armand, there's no point. Let go.

ARMAND: The monster obliges.

(*He bows, and, somewhat drunk, slips and almost falls over. She is obliged to help him up. In each other's arms, they cannot move.*)

MARGUERITE: No. Armand, please...

(*She looks up at him. It looks as though they will embrace. Then he cracks her across the face. BELA and the COUNT run to her assistance.*)

COUNT: No!

BELA: For God's sake, Armand!

COUNT: Please, this is not possible!

JANINE: (*Bursting into tears.*) Armand...Armand!

PRUDENCE: Shut up, you.

(*She gives JANINE a clout and runs after SOPHIE, who goes to MARGUERITE's assistance.*)

BELA: For God's sake… (*Pulling ARMAND away.*)

SOPHIE: (*Bending over MARGUERITE.*) Are you all right?

(*MARGUERITE, in pain, holding the side of her face with both hands, nods. PRUDENCE and SOPHIE help her to her feet.*)

CLEMENCE: Armand!

(*MARGUERITE takes SOPHIE's arm and they leave as the old DUKE hobbles across.*

He pauses and peruses MARGUERITE, shakes his head.)

DUKE: Too thin, too thin! (*Assisted by a WAITER, he walks away as MARGUERITE goes.*)

BELA: (*To ARMAND.*) A public scene, for that?

PRUDENCE: (*Crosses and confronts ARMAND.*) That was ill-done.

ARMAND: (*Bows.*) I beg your pardon. Deepest apologies.

PRUDENCE: She is ill.

ARMAND: So am I. So am I. (*He goes, pushing JANINE aside.*)

PRUDENCE: Why did he do that? There was no need…he shouldn't have done that.

(*They leave.*

Music.)

Scene 5

MARGUERITE's bedroom. MARGUERITE being helped into a dressing gown by YVETTE, who then gives her water to sip. SOPHIE walks about, angry. YVETTE goes quietly.

MARGUERITE: I'm perfectly well.

SOPHIE: You don't look it. Have you thought of going south?

MARGUERITE: (*Quick.*) I can't leave Paris!

SOPHIE: Why not? You should think of your health. If not for you, for the boy.

MARGUERITE: (*Slight pause.*) I… I've had him adopted.

SOPHIE: What?!

MARGUERITE: So…as you see…I don't see him any more.

SOPHIE: Why did you do that?!

MARGUERITE: He'll be educated – (*As SOPHIE makes to reply.*) – it's more than we are!

SOPHIE: Is it? Well I wouldn't let him go. I'd rather he was a pimp than let him go if he was mine.

MARGUERITE: Well he isn't so there's an end of it.

SOPHIE: (*A whine.*) I liked playing with him!

MARGUERITE: Have one of your own then.

SOPHIE: Hardly likely, after all the knitting needles.

(*SOPHIE bends over MARGUERITE to kiss her goodbye.*)

MARGUERITE: (*Quick.*) No, don't kiss me. (*She covers.*) Is it serious, you and Bela?

SOPHIE: The fact that he owns half Moldavia's serious.

MARGUERITE: That doesn't sound like you.

SOPHIE: (*Laughs.*) No.

MARGUERITE: Does he treat you well?

SOPHIE: We understand each other. (*She stands over MARGUERITE.*) Get over it.

MARGUERITE: How?

SOPHIE: I knew!!

MARGUERITE: Well don't glare at me like a cross Pekinese.

SOPHIE: More like a cowpat the watercart's run over. Mind you, I left my mark on the bitch. Forget him, Marguerite.

MARGUERITE: I already have.

(*SOPHIE goes.*

Voices.

MARGUERITE, exhausted, checks her hair in the glass, coughs.

YVETTE enters.)

PRUDENCE: (*Offstage.*) I'm not intending to stop, girl! (*Enters.*) My dear, what a fracas! Unforgivable! The whole of Paris is talking about it, are you recovered, you're looking very pale.

MARGUERITE: Nonsense. Yvette, a glass of cognac for *Madame Prudence*!

PRUDENCE: Clemence sends her love, I've left them below.

MARGUERITE: She's a duck.

PRUDENCE: A goose, you mean. But more sense than I gave her credit for...she's going off to Sweden as his Countess...yes! I daresay he's been turned down by all the Swedes, well, half a minute and you're gasping but she thinks he's a wit, they're studying wasps now. (*Shouts of laughter, off, she lifts her eyes in resignation.*) You're all right?

MARGUERITE: Of course!

PRUDENCE: Good, because the Prince is on his way up. I've told him it was his fault, he thinks he's the one who slapped you – well, does no harm. He's bringing them round.

MARGUERITE: Who?

PRUDENCE: The emeralds, you fool!

MARGUERITE: (*Awed.*) No!

PRUDENCE: Necklace, ear-rings, bracelets...the whole parure! I told you it could be done. *Niet, niet,* was all I got from the drunken wretch – so – what did I do? I told him they were out of fashion! I said you'd never wear them! Well, you know the Russians...can't bear to be thought provincial – he's had them all reset!

(*Noise and laughter, off.*)

I'd better go before they turn your place upside down. I'll be in tomorrow to settle up. Get out the brandy bottle. Tomorrow you can tell him what a stallion he was and get another night off and the next quarter's rent paid into the bargain.

MARGUERITE: Yes, why not? Thank you!

(*PRUDENCE embraces her, makes to kiss her, but draws back.*)

PRUDENCE: Good. Well, I mustn't keep the horses. We're all off to the *Varietés. Au 'voir* my dear – heavens, what a noise they're making!

(*She goes, to the sound of laughter and banging.*
The crash of an outer door.
Silence.
YVETTE enters.
MARGUERITE looks up with a smile.)

MARGUERITE: They've gone?

YVETTE: Yes Madame.

(*MARGUERITE leans back, exhausted.*)

Is there anything I can get you, *Madame*?

MARGUERITE: Oh a shawl, Yvette, I'm so cold!

YVETTE: (*Surprised.*) But – (*She finds a shawl, puts it about MARGUERITE's shoulders.*)

MARGUERITE: Thank you. (*She touches YVETTE on the cheek.*) You're so good to me.

YVETTE: Shall I go for the doctor?

MARGUERITE: Whatever for?

YVETTE: We wouldn't have to pay him. He'd come for you.

MARGUERITE: I don't need him! (*She laughs at YVETTE happily.*) You see? I'm perfectly well!

YVETTE: Good, I'll bring supper!

MARGUERITE: No!

YVETTE: A little soup...just a little?

MARGUERITE: No, no.

(*But YVETTE stands over her.*)

Well, if you must.

(*YVETTE, triumphant, rushes out.*

A door clangs.

The sound of voices.

ARMAND bursts into the room.)

ARMAND: What's the matter, she ran down the stairs like a weasel!

MARGUERITE: Nothing's the matter. The silly girl's got a soft heart.

ARMAND: Did I hurt you? You look pale.

MARGUERITE: No, I'm just cold.

ARMAND: Cold? The room's stifling. Have you a fever? (*He puts a hand on her cheek.*) You're icy!

MARGUERITE: It's nothing.

ARMAND: I hit you.

(*He looks at her, then takes off round the room, prowling restlessly, looking at everything, touching things.*)

The room! (*He spins round, taking it in.*) It's exactly the same as before! – I thought everything had been sold!

MARGUERITE: I bought back some of the furniture. The rest I had copied.

ARMAND: Why? (*He inspects the room, checking.*)

MARGUERITE: I wanted everything to be the same.

(*Pause.*)

ARMAND: (*Low.*) I should like to burn this room. And you with it.

MARGUERITE: Do it, then.

(*Pause.*)

ARMAND: Why?

MARGUERITE: (*Slight pause.*) You know why.

ARMAND: I don't believe it.

MARGUERITE: It's the truth.

ARMAND: All a lie? All those days, all those nights? Coming up for air, not just from love but from the ecstasy of talk? All nothing? Do you know what I've been through? I'm a dead man. Look at me. I'm uglier than before. At least then there was no possibility.

MARGUERITE: Forget me. I'm useless to you! If I loved you the best thing I ever did was to let you go.

ARMAND: Is that why? You thought you'd ruin me – ?

MARGUERITE: (*Harsh.*) No. It's as I said in my letter. I'd had enough.

ARMAND: I don't believe you. Look at me. Look at me. Do you know what it's cost me to come to this house? What am I doing in this room…?

MARGUERITE: Don't… (*She weeps.*) …don't…

(*He sweeps her into his arms.*
They hold each other in a desperate embrace.)

ARMAND: Oh my love…my own love! I've been dead… everything dry, everything smelling of metal in my head…I see, I hear people's voices but I'm cut off, I'm not part of it any more… Please…oh please…please, please, please, please…

MARGUERITE: No. You mustn't. You don't understand, Armand – oh, your dear, beautiful face –

ARMAND: Nothing…all I…just to…never, never let me go…

MARGUERITE: No, never! No! I don't care! Armand…!

ARMAND: You won't go away again? You won't go…?

MARGUERITE: No, of course not. Never. It was…I won't leave you…I'll never leave you, how could I –

(*They kiss.*)

We'll be together, what does it matter all the rest – unimportant. I'll fetch Jean-Paul –

ARMAND: Where is he?

MARGUERITE: I'll get him back. We'll go away, the three of us. Just us. Our life. On our own.

ARMAND: Yes! We'll go to Italy! (*He kisses her hands.*) To Venice…Venice! Together! My love, you're so cold!

MARGUERITE: No, I'm warm!

ARMAND: We'll sail the Bosphorus. And Greece…the Parthenon…Egypt – what is it?

(*To YVETTE, who stands at the door.*

YVETTE looks from ARMAND to MARGUERITE.)

YVETTE: (*Soft.*) It's the Prince, Madame.

MARGUERITE: Send him away.

(*She turns, smiles at YVETTE. Then she pauses, looks from one to the other.*)

Wait.

YVETTE: Madame…?

MARGUERITE: Wait…why not? Why not? Oh!

(*She laughs, full of life and energy and waves to YVETTE to bring up the PRINCE. YVETTE nods and goes.*)

ARMAND: What are you doing?

MARGUERITE: My love! A gift! I shan't come to you empty-handed! (*She kisses him feverishly.*) We'll buy a fleet of gondolas…a palazzo! In Venice!

ARMAND: (*To YVETTE.*) Tell him to go.

MARGUERITE: No! Armand – emeralds! Rivers of emeralds! To buy a lifetime of freedom! You see? My love, I bring you a dowry! Go – just for now.

ARMAND: What?

(*He breaks away from her.*)

MARGUERITE: Oh Armand! He'll fall asleep on the carpet! It has nothing to do with us! It's not important! Don't! No, don't…you can't…not now…

(*He throws money in her face and goes.*

MARGUERITE, on the floor, becomes hysterical.
YVETTE enters.
MARGUERITE looks up.)
Is he still there? The Prince?

YVETTE: Yes.

MARGUERITE: (*Feverish and imperious.*) Then show him up!
(*YVETTE goes.*
MARGUERITE crosses to her dressing table. With an effort, she makes herself beautiful. She turns from the dressing table, smiling, alight and alive as YVETTE opens the door and the PRINCE lurches into the room.)

PRINCE: (*In Russian.*) My beautiful shining, bright-eyed herring…

MARGUERITE: Sergei… (*She takes his arm.*) My dear… (*She manhandles him across to the elbow chair.*) You look tired…Yvette, what are you thinking of…brandy, for His Highness…

PRINCE: (*In Russian.*) Don't talk shit, where's the brandy.

MARGUERITE: (*Helping him off with his coat, coos over him.*) You've been in a skirmish again…
(*The lights begin to go.*)

PRINCE: (*In Russian.*) What have you got your clothes on for?

MARGUERITE: My bear…
(*She begins to fondle him.*)
You'll feel better… So much better…
(*The PRINCE grunts. He falls asleep, half trapping MARGUERITE.*
A pause, he breathes heavily.
The MARGUERITE begins to struggle, trying to free herself. She half rises from the bed. And has a massive haemorrhage.)

Scene 6

MARGUERITE is in bed. YVETTE moves about the room quietly. A MAN comes to the door. She goes to him, speaks to him quietly, indicating MARGUERITE. But he insists, and she stands back, to allow him in. He begins to take an inventory of the room. Eventually he approaches the bed.

MAN: Begging your pardon, miss. (*He makes an inventory of the bed and its hangings.*)
MARGUERITE: (*A whisper.*) How much for me?
MAN: Beg pardon?
MARGUERITE: (*Sighs.*) Not a lot.

(*The MAN goes.*
A PRIEST arrives and begins to murmur.
The REST OF THE COMPANY arrive severally and sit about at a distance.
The PRIEST finishes his prayers and rises quietly.
A long silence.
Only MARGUERITE's breathing can be heard.)

MARGUERITE: (*Half rises.*) Jean-Paul?

(*The OTHERS half-rise, but MARGUERITE subsides.*
YVETTE tidies the bedsheet swiftly.
MARGUERITE's breathing rasps. It strengthens and falters, becomes irregular.
MARGUERITE dies.)

Scene 7

The Tuileries Gardens, very early morning. The birds sing. The sun becomes stronger, slanting through the trees. A clock strikes six. Pause. Then GASTON and ARMAND appear. They stroll, side by side, without speaking. ARMAND pauses, looks up.

ARMAND: What time is it?
GASTON: (*Consults his watch.*) Just after six.
ARMAND: We've walked all night. You're not exhausted?
GASTON: Not in the least.
ARMAND: Nevertheless I have exploited your good will.
GASTON: My dear Armand, if I have been of the least assistance I am more than delighted to have missed a few nights sleep.
ARMAND: Thank you for your friendship.
GASTON: The feeling is mutual. I only wish, now that the lady lies in peace, that you were…that you were able to –
ARMAND: To what?

GASTON: To forgive yourself. There is no doubt that *Mademoiselle Gautier* was a sick woman. And…forgive me…her way of life. I imply no criticism but alas, we are the sum of our circumstances and our past. Your pardon if I seem harsh.

ARMAND: I wish you had known her.

GASTON: Yes. (*Pause.*) It's a fine day. Spring.

(*He turns at the sound of voices.*

PRUDENCE enters, followed by BELA, SOPHIE, CLEMENCE and the COUNT. They are all in evening clothes.)

PRUDENCE: My dear Armand! What a surprise! We all thought you were abroad! (*Politely.*) *Monsieur…* (*She inclines her head to GASTON.*) Bela – Armand, he's here! We've been celebrating an engagement! Clemence has captured Canute, what a coup!

(*A WAITER serves brioches to CLEMENCE and the COUNT and they eat stolidly.*)

BELA: (*To ARMAND.*) Where have you been hiding?

PRUDENCE: (*Enjoying the sunshine.*) How splendid! Glorious weather!

CLEMENCE: Yes, makes you glad to be alive!

SOPHIE: Why don't you shut up?

(*CLEMENCE remembers ARMAND, claps her hand over her mouth.*)

PRUDENCE: We've been making plans for the summer. We're all off to Sweden for the wedding. Come with us, Armand.

CLEMENCE: I can't wait to hear them call me Milady!

BELA: Come to England, for the racing.

GASTON: I think *Monsieur Duval* wishes to remain in Paris.

PRUDENCE: Nonsense.

CLEMENCE: He can't stay in Paris, he'll die of the heat.

SOPHIE: Let him stay if he wants. Go to hell if he wants. (*She walks away.*) Well he finished her, didn't he?

PRUDENCE: Sophie!

GASTON: Your friends are right. Why not Sweden – a fine country, fine people, and a fairy tale in the summer –

ARMAND: No.

GASTON: Then where you will – I should be delighted to accompany you – Spain, Switzerland – or Italy – Venice – ah Venice!

(*ARMAND breaks down.*)

PRUDENCE: Dear God…

COUNT: My friend!…

(*ARMAND sobs.*)

CLEMENCE: Armand don't!

SOPHIE: Let him enjoy himself.

(*PRUDENCE pushes CLEMENCE aside.*)

PRUDENCE: Leave him to me – (*To GASTON.*) – A moment, Monsieur, if you will.

(*The OTHERS draw away.*
PRUDENCE allows ARMAND to cry.)

Ah, my friend, no more rapture? No more grand passion? Well, can it last? At least you lived it. For a while. What more do you want? What more is there? Armand, don't betray what you had by destroying yourself. Do you know what she would have done if you had died? She would have gone away for a season – wasted a year of her looks. And then she would have remade her life. From necessity.

ARMAND: I have no life.

PRUDENCE: Poor boy. You thought to rescue Marguerite Gautier and you lost her. (*He does not reply.*) Perhaps, after all, she preferred her freedom.

(*He looks up.*)

Has it never occurred to you that some of us might prefer the life – given the alternatives?

ARMAND: No. No. (*He rises.*) You killed her.

PRUDENCE: I?

ARMAND: It was the wrong transaction. No profit to be made, so we must be done out of it. Were we so threatening? One man? One woman? There was a chance. Something real. Something honest – ordinary – there for the taking like an apple on a tree.

PRUDENCE: A dream.

CLEMENCE: (*Calls.*) Prudence – are you coming?

ARMAND: What do you want from us?

(*Pause.*

PRUDENCE looks at him, and then across to GASTON.)

PRUDENCE: Don't be tiresome.

ARMAND: We're your creatures. You make us. What do you want?

PRUDENCE: Since you ask – who is your friend? Is he well placed?

ARMAND: You make us ugly. Monsters. Very well. If that is what you want…

(*He looks at her savagely, then turns on his heels and goes. PRUDENCE looks after him, frowning in the sunlight. Then, dismissing the thought of him, she puts up her sunshade.*)

PRUDENCE: *Eh bien, mes braves…*a little beauty sleep! *Monsieur Gaston*, my card. Call on me – no, I insist! I am at home every afternoon at five. You need enjoyment – you see, I can tell. Trust Prudence.

(*She turns away.*)

Bela? Sophie? Where's the Countess? *Au'voir, M'sieu – au'voir.*

(*CLEMENCE and the COUNT, eating steadily, look up. PRUDENCE descends on them and bears them away. SOPHIE laughs and walks off, BELA turns, bows ironically to GASTON and follows SOPHIE.*

GASTON, alone, looks after them. He looks at the card, puts it in his pocket, puts on his hat and goes, separately.)

QUEEN CHRISTINA

Foreword

WOMEN'S THEATRE GROUPS ARE ADEPT AT SELF-HELP. They have to be. It is harder and harder for any group of artists to find patronage, public or private, when they most need it, that is, at the beginning. People like to back favourites – more chance of first past the post and who needs losers? As is said in America, 'To know a loser is to begin to be one.' A strange system, a system where only winning matters. Being a winner means beating...to win connotes losers. You can't have one without the other. So, like the traditional class system, which exists to support the few at the expense of the many, so the new 'success' ethic similarly promotes success at the expense of the defeat of others. A new imperialism. Can we ever get off it?

The Women's Company, in the seventies, came by a 'dark' week at the Roundhouse...one of our members, Shirley Stone, was working there as a publicist, and, amazingly, gained permission for us to play a week there. (We didn't realise at the time that the builders would be in, banging loudly, all day as they removed and dropped huge sleepers from a height.) I was asked to write a piece and went to France for a week on an out-of-season French railways holiday, very good value except that it rained every day. Which meant that I was able to research and write the piece *Go West, Young Woman*, about the pioneer women who crossed America, without interruption. Not so the first night of our week, when the play was interrupted twice by two separate groups of feminists who objected to the fact that we had men in our cast. The performances, not surprisingly, lacked focus. But by Thursday we were running in and Ann Jellicoe, writer of *The Knack* and *The Sport of My Mad Mother* and creator of community plays in Dorset, came in to review the piece for *Kaleidoscope*. As a result she offered me a commission, my first, at the Royal Court...she was at the time, all too briefly, literary manager there. I asked if the commission was for Upstairs or the main space. The Court said either. So I thought I'd do a 'big' piece...if it was to be rejected, let it be rejected for the main space. I wrote *Queen Christina.* By the time the script was submitted, a year later, Ann had left the Court, and there was a new management. The play was rejected as 'sprawling, unattractive...it appealed more to women than men,' said the letter of rejection to the agent's office.

Why a play about Queen Christina? I'd seen the Garbo movie... I had the idea, like, I suspect, many people, that Christina had been a shining, pale intellectual beauty, who had, romantically, chosen freedom. The reality is harsher. The real Christina was a dark, plain woman with a crippled shoulder, daughter of a beautiful mother whose health and nervous system had been ruined by yearly pregnancies in the effort to provide a male heir. Since Christina was the only survivor, she was, at her father's instruction, reared as a man, that is to say, educated, and taught all the male necessities, how to ride, fence, shoot, how to lead an army. And then, on her accession, told to marry and breed, that is, to be a woman. By which time, of course, like males of her era, she despised women as weak, hysterical, silly creatures. The confusion seems to have been too stressful. She abdicated and went to Rome, at the time a place of seeming warmth and freedom of thought after the cold, Lutheran north. It is a confusion which seems as apposite as ever. In the past, relatively few women were able to develop the cognitive or artistic sides of their nature. The role of women was confined, necessarily, to the production and rearing to maturity of children. Pregnancies were inadvertent, frequent, often fatal for both mother and child. It is only in this century that the undertaking has become reasonably safe, that it has become possible not to breed. Women are now living longer...single-parent families are not a new phenomenon...disease took parents of both sexes until very recently. Now a woman has many years after birthing and rearing her children. She has the choice to avoid childbirth, or to rear children on her own. Wonderful freedoms? Or trappy dilemmas? To read contemporary literature, magazines, novels, is to be aware of dichotomy. A whole movement which emphasizes women's rights, the right to join, to have equal opportunity, to represent. At the same time torrents of romantic novels, proliferating magazines on the traditional 'female' roles and skills...cooking, sewing, interior decorating, the art of cosmetics, fashion. Given the needs of manufacturers to sell their goods, it is still a colliding mixture of signals. Having our cake and eating it? Freedom, with security? Whichever way we look at it, the old norms won't do any more. More and more people are having children, for example, without the formality of marriage. Why not? We are no longer a Christian society, why bother with a piece of paper from a registry office? We love each other, we love our children. Nonetheless, when love goes, if the relationship fails, where is the structure to protect the children? The structure to represent the father's right of access? Should one oppression be replaced by another? We have a lot of thinking to do. Is it possible to create a multi-society which accepts, equally in society, gay relationships, the motherly man, the fatherly woman, the chaste, the sexually needful. Perhaps, if we can hang on to the best of permissiveness, and not backlash into our old, beloved Puritanism, this anarchic, chaotic time in England's history, when the consent to be governed has given way, new norms, new models might emerge. The alternative, the new brutalism, the new pagan, cornered greed, just isn't good enough. Some of us, thirty years ago, when the high-rises were going up, predicted a future of mindless vandalism. We have to learn from it. We can change things. Who else? We can decide what the bottom line should be, what our demands should be. And women are the new breed. We need to put our oar in. We have to think, hard, about what's essential, not for our own personal happiness, 'success', but what's good for all of us...maybe, for example, what we can do without. There are encouraging signs. The young, the energetic, thanks to mass communication, have circled the world clawing in money for Ethiopia...the despised yobs, the rock and rollers...those known earlier for their drugged exploits, their conspicuous spending, their iconoclastic nihilism. It's a breathtaking turn-around, no wonder the politicians are bemused. I think, as women, just as citizens, that we have to stop thinking of 'them' and 'us'...as a working-class woman it bedevilled the first part of my life, being afraid of 'them'.

If we believe there is only Us, then something is released, something egalitarian, sisterly. With so much to be done, can we waste energy on friction? We know, in the particular, that in many spheres we have to be better than our confrères, even to be reckoned. To be reckoned, to feature, is fair, necessary. But is not the real work towards the creation of a society more suited to both sexes, and to the happiness of children? And if that is sentimental, long live senti-mentality...it is on our side.

Pam Gems

Characters

QUEEN CHRISTINA

CHRISTINA as a child

CHANCELLOR AXEL OXENSTIERNA

KING GUSTAVUS ADOLPHUS

GERMAN PRINCE

GERMAN AMBASSADOR

LADY EBBA SPARRE

QUEEN MOTHER

DESCARTES

MAGNUS DE LA GUARDIE

PRINCE KARL

GIRL

CHANUT

SECRETARY

COPLEMAN

DUKE

BISHOP

MARQUISE

MARIANNE

FOOTMAN

CATHERINE DE ROHANT

COUNT OF BREVAYE

POPE

MONALDESCHO

CARDINAL AZZOLINO

CAPTAIN

SOLDIER

LUCIA

ANGELICA as a child

ANGELICA

RUFFINO

ROMANO

SALVATOR

MUSICIAN

Queen Christina was first produced by The Royal Shakespeare Company at The Other Place, Stratford-upon-Avon, in October 1977. The cast was as follows:

QUEEN CHRISTINA, Sheila Allen
CHRISTINA as a child, Erin Tyler
CHANCELLOR AXEL OXENSTIERNA, Bernard Brown
KING GUSTAVUS ADOLPHUS, Barrie Rutter
GERMAN PRINCE, Iain Mitchell
GERMAN AMBASSADOR, John Burgess
LADY EBBA SPARRE, Charlotte Cornwell
QUEEN MOTHER, Valerie Lush
DESCARTES, John Burgess
MAGNUS DE LA GUARDIE, Nigel Terry
PRINCE KARL, Ian McNeice
GIRL, Fleur Chandler
CHANUT, Barrie Rutter
SECRETARY, Iain Mitchell
COPLEMAN, Nigel Terry
DUKE, Iain Mitchell
BISHOP, John Burgess
MARQUISE, Valerie Lush
MARIANNE, Fleur Chandler
CATHERINE DE ROHANT, Charlotte Cornwell
COUNT OF BREVAYE, Iain Mitchell
POPE, Bernard Brown
MONALDESCHO, Nigel Terry
CARDINAL AZZOLINO, Ian McNeice
CAPTAIN, John Burgess
SOLDIER, Barrie Rutter
LUCIA, Valerie Lush

ANGELICA as a child, Erin Tyler
ANGELICA, Fleur Chandler
RUFFINO, Iain Mitchell
ROMANO, Barrie Rutter
SALVATORE, Nigel Terry
MUSICIAN, Robin Weatherall

Directed by Penny Cherns
Designed by Di Seymour
Music by Guy Woolfenden
Lighting by Leo Leibovici
Choreography by Gillian Lynne
Fight directed by Nick Stringer
Company voice work by Cicely Berry

Queen Christina was written in 1975. The play is not a documentary, thus characters have been concertinaed, and some events changed. All plays are metaphors, and the dilemma of the real Christina, reared and educated as a man for the Swedish throne, and then asked to marry and breed for the succession, is perhaps not irrelevant today.

The play may be performed with a cast of three women, five men and a child.

Chronology of the Life of the Real Queen Christina

1626 Birth of Christina

1632 Death of her father, King Gustavus Adolphus

1644 Christina comes of age

1648 Peace of Westphalia, the end of the Thirty Years War

1649 The succession of Prince Karl Gustav confirmed

1650 Descartes visits Sweden (and dies there)

1650 Coronation of Queen Christina

1654 Abdication of Queen Christina

1655 Christina confirmed as a Roman Catholic in St Peter's

1656 Christina attempts to secure the throne of Naples

1657 Death of Monaldescho

1658 Christina returns to Rome

1666 Christina bids for the Polish crown

1689 Christina dies

ACT ONE

Scene 1
Succession

A SMALL CHILD crouches in a huge fireplace, lit by the glow from the fire. TWO MEN, one dressed as a soldier, pace. Off, there is screaming, ending in a howl of pain. AXEL OXENSTIERNA, Chancellor, exits. He returns after a brief pause. The KING looks across at him bleakly. As bleakly, he shakes his head.

KING: Dead?
AXEL: As before.
KING: Was it a boy?
AXEL: I believe so.
KING: How is she?
AXEL: Losing blood.
KING: What is it with women? Weak!
(*The QUEEN begins to sob, and the low sobbing continues throughout the scene.*)
AXEL: There's always next year.
KING: If she breeds again it'll finish her, I'm surprised she's alive this time.
AXEL: I'm sorry. If it weren't for the succession...
KING: I'm well aware.
AXEL: What about the Palatinate alliance...good strong girl...
KING: We have a queen – goddammit man, she's not dead yet. (*He moves away, notices the CHILD.*) We do *have* an heir. (*Gestures the CHILD.*)
AXEL: A girl.
KING: She's fit enough. Intelligent.
AXEL: But the wrong sex! With a weak succession it'll be anybody's game, we can't have a woman.
KING: Make a man of her then.
AXEL: How?

KING: Training.

(*Pause.*)

AXEL: I'd need legislation for that.

KING: Draft it. (*Looks at the CHILD.*) I want her fit, educated, able to lead an army if necessary.

AXEL: We'll talk about it later.

KING: No. I shall be with the army tomorrow – God knows when we'll meet again.

AXEL: Just the thing for you.

KING: Yes. All this howling, I'd rather face a brigade of guards. Make a man of her, for my sake.

(*AXEL bows and leaves.*

The KING turns to the CHILD.)

What did you think of that...were you listening?

CHILD: Why is Mama crying?

KING: We're going to make a queen of you.

CHILD: (*Flinches.*) No, I don't want to.

KING: Don't worry, not like your mother...like me, like a king. You'll be living with the Chancellor from now on. Do as he says, and be good, for my sake. Oh, and try not to fidget in church...we mustn't upset the Lutherans.

(*He lifts and kisses her. She throws her arms about his neck and won't let go.*)

CHILD: Don't leave me here.

(*He prises her off, sets her down.*)

KING: A king must fight. Now remember, look after your mother. Take care of her, she's a woman.

(*He makes to go in one direction, then turns and exits towards the sound of sobbing.*

The CHILD moves after him, then stops. She hugs her doll.

AXEL enters and stands apart, frowning at her.

She looks back, and they appraise each other with level stares.)

Scene 2
Betrothal

The Swedish Palace. A bare, bleak interior. Enter a GERMAN PRINCE, a small man, waiting to be received as a suitor. He wears Swedish ribbons on each shoulder. He is followed by AXEL, now grizzled, who is talking to the Prince's AMBASSADOR.

AMBASSADOR: As I say, we are fully empowered to negotiate.

AXEL: Good. Good. We might even touch on trade talks…if it's within the brief.

AMBASSADOR: The visit of your ambassadors to the Flemish court has been noted.

AXEL: Oh, purely formal. Fishing rights, that sort of thing.

AMBASSADOR: Glad to have your assurance. Of course… everything depends… (*He looks toward the PRINCE.*) … His Royal Highness was most impressed with the miniature. We hear nothing but the most glowing reports of Her Majesty's beauty.

AXEL: (*Neutral.*) What?

AMBASSADOR: It will greatly facilitate negotiations if… if ah… (*He smiles, waggish, at AXEL, who returns a gloomy stare.*) if the royal consorts…ah…

PRINCE: He means if we fancy each other. Absolutely, you bet…I'm a man of feeling, Chancellor.

AXEL: I trust Your Royal Highness has the interests of your country at heart.

PRINCE: Of course. Oh don't worry, we know the score… the hard work you chaps have put in on behalf of…of…

AMBASSADOR: Of a fruitful and enduring relationship between our two great nations.

PRINCE: Right. Speaking of which, where is the wench?

AXEL: Her Majesty always hunts before breakfast, Sire. Perhaps Your Highness would care to inspect the Flemish tapestries.

PRINCE: Bugger the Flemish tapestries, I've been here an hour, we're getting into protocol!

AMBASSADOR: Patience, Sire. Never known a woman to be on time, eh Chancellor?

AXEL: What? Oh, here they are.

(*He sounds surprised.*

A beautiful YOUNG WOMAN enters. She is wearing a simple but beautifully cut riding habit. Her pale ringlets fall about a beautiful but thoughtful face. She smiles as she approaches, and the PRINCE, enchanted, moves forward, smiling in delight.)

MAN: (*At the door.*) What's all this?

(*He enters, a battered figure in hunting clothes. He slouches up to the young woman, moving louchely...he appears to be slightly crippled, or perhaps it is that one of his shoulders is out of true, giving him a swivelled, crooked appearance. He puts a familiar hand on the young woman's shoulder.*)

Who the hell's this?

(*The PRINCE, deeply insulted, nonetheless steps forward to present himself.*

The MAN bursts out laughing.

The PRINCE puts his hand to his sword, glaring at AXEL, who stands grim and unmoving. Nonplussed, the PRINCE kisses the young woman's hand with a flourish.)

Steady on...steady on!

(*The PRINCE is now totally affronted.*)

PRINCE: (*Through his teeth to his AMBASSADOR.*) Do something!

(*The AMBASSADOR whispers to him, agitated and placating.*)

MAN: (*To AXEL.*) Who is it?

AXEL: (*Through his teeth.*) It's the royal suitor! Put up your sword, man – (*As the PRINCE, outraged at the MAN's snigger, draws his sword.*)

PRINCE: I see...I see! So this is our future consort... trailing a fellow about her like a common...a common...

AMBASSADOR: Sire...

PRINCE: It's outrageous...bloody outrageous...

MAN: At least there's some spunk in him. (*He thumps the PRINCE genially on the shoulder, sending him reeling, then turns to AXEL with a murderous face.*) Some sort of joke?

AXEL: You've been fully aware of the negotiations.

MAN: And you're developing a sense of humour.

AXEL: May I remind you that we are talking of royal connection – this is not a personal area.

MAN: And may I remind you that there is a limit. For God's sake, man. I mean – look!

(He…she…that is to say, CHRISTINA, takes the PRINCE's nerveless arm and stands beside him in wifely stance. Even AXEL masks a momentary smile.)

CHRISTINA: You'll have to do better than this. I'm sorry, little fellow.

AMBASSADOR: *(Faintly.)* Are we…are we to understand…?

AXEL: You are in the presence of Her Majesty.

CHRISTINA: Nothing like a formal introduction. I suppose they've been showing you some fancy-assed painting – think yourself lucky we weren't married off by proxy – oh, get rid of them, Axel, I've taken one fall already this morning. There is one matter.

(They pause.)

No more Swedish troops. You can have a few forests instead…believe me, timber lasts longer.

(To AXEL, hard.) See to it.

(She bows the visitors out with courtesy. AXEL glares and goes.)

EBBA: You've upset him.

CHRISTINA: He'll get his own back.

EBBA: You're well-matched.

CHRISTINA: Not surprising – I'm his boy. Sending me notes to dress up like a monkey's arse.

EBBA: You knew perfectly well they were coming.

CHRISTINA: And what they were after. I'll end this bloody war if it's the – ahh! *(She groans, pressing her abdomen.)* My bloody period. Of all the ludicrous patterns in nature, hens are better off.

MOTHER: *(Off.)*…let me pass, I know she's in there…

CHRISTINA: Quick, get rid of her.

(EBBA shakes her head helplessly as CHRISTINA's MOTHER enters. She is fine-boned, dressed in messy finery. She presents the picture of an intensely unhappy woman,

near anguish. She is often coarse, trivial, out of place, even comic. But the intensity of unhappiness, and her bewilderment, prevent us from finding her just a figure of fun. A beautiful woman who has now lost her looks.)

MOTHER: There you are...there you are! Why do you keep avoiding us? (*Curtsies...waits.*) If we don't sit down we shall scream.

CHRISTINA: (*Motions her to sit.*) Not too upset to forget the royal we, you notice.

MOTHER: Turned you down, has he?

CHRISTINA: Other way round!

MOTHER: Took one look, couldn't run fast enough, well don't blame me. (*To EBBA.*) What did he say, is he off? (*EBBA turns away, with a look at CHRISTINA.*) ...oh, I should know better than to ask her. I saw you in the stables this morning, the pair of you. At least I could get a man.

CHRISTINA: What do you want?

MOTHER: Nothing you can give me. Oh, what does she look like? All those babies, and she had to be the one to live!

CHRISTINA: (*Scuffles across, jerking her crippled shoulder at her MOTHER.*) Did your best to do me in, crippled me for life.

MOTHER: Stop it!...the nurse dropped you! Anyway, what difference does it make, you're so ugly –

CHRISTINA: As you never tire of telling me.

MOTHER: It's true! (*Weeps.*) I'm not staying in this hellhole another winter, I shall go to Italy.

CHRISTINA: Clear off, the sooner the better.

MOTHER: What? But we shan't see you then!

CHRISTINA: Good.

MOTHER: But we're your mother!

CHRISTINA: (*Doubles in pain.*) Ohh!

MOTHER: I've a right to grandchildren, the same as any other woman – what's the matter, can't you bear to look at us?

EBBA: Her Majesty is not well this morning.

MOTHER: What?

EBBA: (*Leading the QUEEN MOTHER off.*) She's very tense.

MOTHER: Tense? What's she got to be tense about? Wait till you're my age, ignored, no pension, treated without respect – wait till you've got wrinkles on your face, see how much notice they take of you then! Tense! When have I had a night's rest with the neuralgia…

(*EBBA steers her out, returns.*)

CHRISTINA: Ugh.

EBBA: You know what she wants.

CHRISTINA: Money.

EBBA: She wants your love.

CHRISTINA: What! You've had your hair done.

EBBA: I was wondering when you'd notice. It's still damp, do you like it?

CHRISTINA: You look like a young birch tree. Oh!

(*She dives at EBBA roughly, going for her breasts like an importunate baby.*

EBBA lets her nurse briefly.

CHRISTINA becomes calmer.)

EBBA: You were cruel – no I mean it, Pixie.

CHRISTINA: Hah, seen the new casualty lists?

EBBA: Yes.

CHRISTINA: Thirty years at war. Now they want me to breed for it.

EBBA: Why NOT Prince Karl? At least as your cousin he's in the family.

CHRISTINA: (*Absently.*) Be like fucking your own sword handle. What sort of litter do you think we'd produce, by God, when I'm with you I forget, *you* become my mirror, I see *your* face, *your* eyes.

EBBA: Beauty isn't everything.

CHRISTINA: Isn't it? I hear you've got a new beau.

(*EBBA is startled, as CHRISTINA has intended.*)

Is he handsome?

EBBA: Yes. May I present him?

CHRISTINA: All right, but don't love him too much.

(*Walks.*) Christian war!…connote me that phrase. Yesterday we hanged five boys – ah, says Axel, when order's restored we can relax the severity. Who shall we *BE* when we've killed and mutilated half Sweden?

EBBA: No-one blames you.

CHRISTINA: They should.

EBBA: It's your duty.

CHRISTINA: Another word of unfathomable meaning.

EBBA: Pixie why go against the grain? Play by the rules, you are still free to think.

CHRISTINA: Live like a toad under a stone? And since when have you had a reflective nature…I saw your eyes on the boys last night.

EBBA: If you did you shouldn't have – *I* don't care to show.

CHRISTINA: Except to me.

EBBA: Except to you, of course.

CHRISTINA: I love you.

EBBA: I know.

CHRISTINA: I often wonder what you think about that.

EBBA: I'm honoured.

CHRISTINA: Is that all? Don't punish me. Why should I endure her? I tell you, I begin to find endurance insufficient.

EBBA: Is it hard.

CHRISTINA: No, it's too easy, that's the trouble! Oh Belle. Why are we given life? In order to suffer…to be stoic? If so, why the larch tree? Why you? I think! To what purpose? For to believe we're here *because*…or *in order to* – why that's to accept the most horrifying malignancy or the unbelievably inept! Pestilence…the murder of children – by design? Better no meaning at all, I begin not to believe in anything…oh, don't worry, I keep it to myself. Still, no doubt about it – the idea of a First Cause begins to look like a Swiss cheese.

EBBA: What?

CHRISTINA: The notion of the Creation, my dear, has acquired a distinct wobble. D'you know what they're saying?

EBBA: No.

CHRISTINA: They are saying…that the earth is round …and hangs, like a ball, in space.

EBBA: Nonsense! Oh, you read too much! Christina life is for living! Life! We must live!

CHRISTINA: Well, we'll see what our Monsieur Descartes has to make of it.

EBBA: I insist that you dress up for him. We can't have a Frenchman putting us out of face.

CHRISTINA: That little man's going to unlock doors for me or I'll kick him for a fraud.

EBBA: What about the Italian dress? (*She runs off.*)

CHRISTINA: No. (*She walks, restless. Catches her reflection in the glass.*) Even my bitch is in love. You fool, take your pick. He'll come unwilling either way so choose the best pair of legs in Europe.
There must be someone willing to prance with me.
No man who wants a person?
No such luck.
(*She turns abruptly and leaves.*
EBBA enters, the dress over her arm.
MAGNUS DE LA GUARDIE, young and handsome, enters separately.
They glance to make sure that they are not observed and embrace briefly.)

MAGNUS: When? When?

EBBA: Not yet...we must be careful. I'll catch her in the right mood.
(*They go.*
Blackout.)

Scene 3
Welcome, Monsieur Descartes

A chair for the QUEEN, another for the QUEEN MOTHER, seats for AXEL and DESCARTES. Enter the QUEEN MOTHER. She is eating from a large, ornate box of chocolates. DESCARTES attends her, followed by AXEL.

MOTHER: Chocolate, Mossoo Desscart?

DESCARTES: Thank you, gracious *Madame*, but no.

MOTHER: They're soft centres, from Prague!

DESCARTES: (*Disguising a belch.*) I have been fed most... royally at your table.

MOTHER: Yes, nice piece of cow, we enjoyed it. Of course, meat isn't at its best this time of year, but with a few turnips, and a boiled potato –

AXEL: (*Sourly.*) Her Majesty enjoys her food.

MOTHER: What else is there for me to enjoy? I still miss him, you know, Mossoo...my lovely husband. I have his clothes put out every night. (*She dives into her bosom and fetches out a miniature.*) His likeness! Pretty man, doncha think?

DESCARTES: A noble countenance.

MOTHER: Split clean down the middle on the field.

DESCARTES: *Chère Madame*!

MOTHER: He'd eat a side of beef for starters – well, you have to keep out the cold in this icehole.

DESCARTES: A most beautiful man.

(*The QUEEN MOTHER kicks her DWARF who presents the box she carries to DESCARTES, who assumes it to be a gift.*)

My most gracious thanks, *madame.*

MOTHER: (*Peals of laughter.*) Oh, it's not for you! He thinks it's for him, what a gaffe Mossoo, never mind, we forgive you. You can have a look.

(*She watches fondly as he opens the lid.*)

We never go anywhere without it.

(*DESCARTES looks inside, claps the lid shut.*)

There! What do you think of that! The heart and member of a king! I bet you've never seen that before.

(*DESCARTES shakes his head weakly.*)

I've precious little else, Mossoo, a woman in my position has no-one to protect her. Tell me, are you a married man yourself?

AXEL: (*Heavy.*) I think the dance is about to begin.

(*CHRISTINA hisses and gestures. They sit. Loud gigglings and whisperings, off, then CHRISTINA erupts onto the scene. She is wearing a costume and looks like nothing on earth.*)

CHRISTINA: My Lords and Ladies...in honour of *Monsieur Descartes*, our distinguished guest...we present ...our Masque! I shall play –

MOTHER: What's it about?

CHRISTINA: War and peace, I keep telling you! I shall play Peace. I am Peace. Magnus is War – Magnus...

(*MAGNUS enters.*)

The part of War is played by our friend Duke Magnus de la Guardie. (*She gives him a kiss.*)

MOTHER: He's only a Duke.

CHRISTINA: Belle!

(*EBBA enters.*)

The Lady Ebba Sparre plays Venus...ooh! (*She gives EBBA a hug and a kiss.*) Oh and there's Karl. What's Karl playing, Magnus?

MAGNUS: Sweden, Ma'am.

CHRISTINA: Yes, he's Sweden, the Swedish people, that sort of thing. I play Peace. Right, we'll start. Mars, the God of War, descends on the people. Venus tries to help but that's no good. Then I come on and peace conquers all.

(*Music.*

The Masque begins.

The QUEEN MOTHER provides a running commentary, to CHRISTINA's wrath.)

MOTHER: (*As KARL, with clumsy good will, does his dance.*) Oh Karl! Oh, isn't he good! (*On MARS' galvanic entrance.*) Ooh, oh, ooh! (*Clutching DESCARTES for protection.*) Oh Mossoo...oh poor Sweden! Ahhh! (*As EBBA descends, trailing draperies.*) Oh, isn't she sweet...so pretty...how enchanting! Oh dear. (*As CHRISTINA makes her entrance.*) Oh. Oh well, never mind.

(*The Masque ends in a gigue.*

It becomes a romp as CHRISTINA, breaking the steps, twirls with MAGNUS. She shrieks with pleasure as the music ends, throwing her arms about MAGNUS' neck.)

CHRISTINA: (*Reeling.*) Anyone would think we were drunk!

(*MAGNUS crosses swiftly, whispers to EBBA.*)

EBBA: No please...not yet!

(*MAGNUS whispers briefly to AXEL.*)

CHRISTINA: Come on, no whispering – by God, what a handsome fellow!

MAGNUS: A mere shank to the pearl of Your Majesty's radiance.

CHRISTINA: Get off, you sound like a Frenchman...oops, sorry! My two dear friends! (*She embraces them.*) Where's the brandy, we'll put some fire in your feet, little philosopher...did you like the painting? (*Throws herself on the throne.*)

DESCARTES: My thanks again, Majesty. Your Majesty has a marvellous eye!

CHRISTINA: Surprised eh? Not much culture in this cold country. We've another for you.

MOTHER: She's been spending again.

CHRISTINA: Why not? No point if we can't share our love, eh Magnus?

AXEL: Your Majesty is in a mood for good news.

CHRISTINA: Look at him, sober as a judge...yes, come on, let's have it man. And give us a smile, melt the Pole!

AXEL: I ask your formal permission for a projected marriage.

CHRISTINA: (*Intense suspicion.*) Marriage? What have you been up to, Karl?

KARL: Nothing, cousin, I assure you.

AXEL: I make formal request, for the betrothal of two of your most devoted subjects.

CHRISTINA: Splendid, who is it?

AXEL: We ask your formal consent to the marriage of the Lady Ebba Sparre with the Duke Magnus de la Guardie.

(*Silence.*

Then CHRISTINA lurches to her feet. She glares, then begins to screech, becoming hysterical.)

CHRISTINA: Bitch...bitch! Liars...cheats!

MOTHER: You see? You see? It's always the same!

CHRISTINA: Vicious, hateful cow!

(*KARL tries to restrain her.*)

Get off, you fat fool…get off!

(*She grapples with him, clouting him savagely and pulling his hair. Everyone seeks to go, but she hauls DESCARTES back, clinging to him for a second.*

He waits, while she howls and sobs.

She throws herself down on her throne at last, sniffing, and blowing her nose loudly in her skirt. She becomes aware of his presence and flinches. Pause.)

(*Mutters.*) Good of you to sit with us.

DESCARTES: The honour is mine.

CHRISTINA: I've made a fool of myself. We were hoping to impress you with our qualities of mind.

DESCARTES: Your Majesty is young. You bear a special burden.

CHRISTINA: Yet who more privileged? Most people struggle for mere existence. Don't you find that inept – that the most suffer the most?

DESCARTES: It is a puzzle.

CHRISTINA: Then you imply solution. I wish I had access to it…by God, I can't even secure my own happiness. Am I, in my privilege, to derive contentment solely from the nourishment of others? Do you not consider that to be unjust? And, if unjust, does it not call for action?

DESCARTES: If the action be just.

CHRISTINA: Good, I'll have his head for it.

DESCARTES: Can the road to happiness lie thus?

CHRISTINA: Be careful, I'm not in the mood for the cold shale of endurance.

DESCARTES: Madame, there is choice.

CHRISTINA: Choice? Hah. Between circumstance and the flesh we are all slaves.

DESCARTES: In part. We know that we must die. Which does not absolve us from the challenge of choosing.

CHRISTINA: The making of decision, little Frenchman, is my daily burden.

DESCARTES: But with choice there is possibility. For change. And the concept of change implies the very world within our grasp. It is we who decide.

CHRISTINA: (*Pause.*) You may be right. (*She chews her nails.*) I loved him. I let him see that I loved him, they all saw that I loved him. Now tell me how he can live.

DESCARTES: Through the mercy of princes.

CHRISTINA: (*Groans.*) And how do I survive? (*She stands, and begins to shake uncontrollably.*) How...how?

DESCARTES: Perhaps, in the end, we must learn to love those things we CAN have.

(*CHRISTINA groans again.*)

CHRISTINA: Tell me how to live! I cannot go forward to the next moment in my life!

DESCARTES: Pain passes.

CHRISTINA: All very well for you, little philosopher. You tip the world on its head and leave the rest to us to reset the pieces. It's we who decide, is it? Can't see the priests approving of that. Well, we'll talk again.

(*He bows, dismissed, makes to go.*)

And wrap up warmly. We don't want the world saying Sweden finished you off.

(*He bows again, goes.*)

Yes, well...a man...a philosopher. Runs down a pink road while the world gets the wheat in. What about me, the worms in my belly? Coming to me with the salt of a man on her, swearing her love – what do you want?

(*As KARL enters and coughs politely.*
She crosses to him, flicks the ribbons on his shoulders.)

What's this, the ribbons of a suitor, Karl?

KARL: Forgive me, I must speak.

CHRISTINA: Don't presume too far on old acquaintance.

KARL: I want you to know that I'm here.

CHRISTINA: Clever timing. The popular solution. Our feelings, of course, are irrelevant.

KARL: I think you know mine.

CHRISTINA: What?

KARL: I said, I think you know mine, Christina. I can understand that I don't please you. I'm not well-favoured.

CHRISTINA: What am I supposed to say…that we're not a pair of uglies? The flies will fall off the wall on our wedding night, there isn't a tavern joke I haven't thought of already.

KARL: I do so love your vicious intelligence.

CHRISTINA: Yes, well, that almost reached me. Possibilities. Perverse, of course, but then you always did like me beating you up. (*She grabs his hair, as before.*)

KARL: I'm sorry, I don't know what you mean.

CHRISTINA: No, you wouldn't – oh, clear off. For Christ's sake, what is there in my fat face that gives you a tremble?

KARL: I wish you wouldn't. Christina, you have such a wonderful countenance. I never tire of the wit and life in your eyes. And did you know…you have very pretty ears.

CHRISTINA: Ears? What sort of fool d'you take me for? Ears? You – are fat. Your lips pout like a girls, your legs are bandy and you walk with your ass cocked up like a turkey. What makes you think I could fancy a squat little asshole like you? I've got the pick of Europe! (*Her voice breaks, she turns away.*)

KARL: (*Pause.*) You CAN trust me.

CHRISTINA: That's true.

KARL: Then you consent?

CHRISTINA: It's all the same to me. I suppose so.

KARL: Oh, Christina, if you knew how I loved you!

CHRISTINA: What? We'll have none of that.

KARL: But I mean it. I love you!

CHRISTINA: Love? You? Do you think I want to be desired by the likes of you? A man who fancies a long-nosed cripple? Since there's no sap of ambition in you, and I doubt you've the wit for contrivance, it must be aberration!

KARL: Christina…

CHRISTINA: Get away!

KARL: Christina, please…

CHRISTINA: No! There's one freak on the throne…no need to perpetuate the joke. The answer's no.

(*Pause.*
Then he bows and goes.
CHRISTINA paces, then sits.)
(*Pause.*) What do they mean…a ball hanging in space? It's almost imaginative. (*A pause.*) Why not? Make a widower of him tonight – tell him to shut his eyes and call me Belle? Two sons and a thousand gifts later he won't even remember the difference. Why not? (*She breaks briefly, then recovers herself.*)
One. Create Karl Commander in Chief of the Army. Two. Make Magnus ambassador to Paris. Give, Christina, give, give! And watch your position. Guard the throne. It's all you have. (*She goes.*)

Scene 4
A Warm Wind From the South

CHRISTINA's bedchamber. The bedcurtains drawn. The QUEEN MOTHER sits by the bed huddled in fur and sheepskins. Still cold, she pulls the rug from the floor over her knees. AXEL enters with a scroll.

MOTHER: She's ill.
AXEL: I am assured that Her Majesty is well enough to receive me. Pray inform her.
MOTHER: Certainly not. If you approach the Queen's bed we shall call the guard and have you arrested for an attack on the Queen's person.
AXEL: Madam, will you return to your embroideries and not try my patience.
MOTHER: Oh yes, wouldn't you love to get your hands on me.
AXEL: Hardly, madam.
MOTHER: Oh? Times have changed! Where's the notorious straying hand? The last time was in Church, and it was Lent.
AXEL: I must have been drunk.
MOTHER: (*Gloomily.*) You were too incapable to do anything. I suppose it's young flesh you want to prick

you up like pepper. They're only after your money – d'you think they'd roll with you if you were a button-maker?

AXEL: I'm prepared to pay for my pleasures – alas, we men are not romantics, ma'am. Perhaps a closer contact with the world makes us less susceptible than ladies to the lures of the imagination.

MOTHER: He'd have my fantasies off me now. I'd trade them, for a life.

AXEL: Your Majesty's life is the envy of most women.

MOTHER: Where does that put them? What have you ever done for the women of this country?

AXEL: I have the satisfaction of seeing this nation immeasurably stronger than when I took up the reins of office thirty years ago.

MOTHER: We've been at WAR thirty years!

AXEL: The voice of Sweden speaks to the world –

MOTHER: Never mind the voice, what about the eggs, where are the eggs?

AXEL: You have never understood the nature of war economy.

MOTHER: And when should I have learned that – I was pregnant for fifteen years.

AXEL: Precisely.

MOTHER: The women of this country don't need to understand theory. They're too busy keeping their families alive against the day you expose them to the sword.

AXEL: You spit on the shield that defends you.

MOTHER: You? Defend US?

AXEL: Who else?

MOTHER: The Queen! My daughter! Who's taking us out of this war? Not you!

(*CHRISTINA thrusts back the curtains.*)

CHRISTINA: Shut up, or I'll throw you both in the bloody clink. (*To AXEL.*) What do you want?

AXEL: I've delayed council as long as possible. They insist on decision.

CHRISTINA: I will sign no edict that bans the mass – Goddammit, man, the Catholic countries are our major allies.

AXEL: That is foreign affairs. Matters of dogma touch on internal security. To allow mass to be celebrated is to increase nests of spies from one end of the country to the other.

CHRISTINA: But we can't break the law…as ambassador, the man's on his own territory.

AXEL: It sets a precedent.

CHRISTINA: By God, is a man not to be allowed the thoughts in his head? Do you want a nation of dissemblers? What does it matter if we listen to dog latin or mournful sermons? No religion can be put to the proof.

AXEL: (*Barks.*) What?

CHRISTINA: I merely point out that the picture is relevant to the point of view. A matter of perspective.

AXEL: I am aware of Your Majesty's recent attachment to modern painting. May I ask that these extreme views be confined to the Royal quarters?

CHRISTINA: Oh, don't be a fool.

MOTHER: It's time they got a slap in the face. When are they going to vote my pension?

(*Pause.*)

AXEL: I must ask you to reconsider. There is a good deal of…restlessness since we ended the war.

CHRISTINA gives him a sharp look. Pause.

AXEL: The nobles are speaking for a fresh campaign.

CHRISTINA: And I wonder who gardened that notion.

(*Pause.*)

I will not have our Catholic allies disaffected. There will be no more adventures…campaigns.

(*Silence.*

A prolonged battle of wills.)

On the matter of my marriage…

MOTHER: My love?

AXEL: On the matter of Your Majesty's marriage, the demand for decision becomes insistent. As Your Majesty well knows.

CHRISTINA: (*Pause.*) Why all the fuss? They know I'll marry Karl.

MOTHER: Oh my love, at last! A wedding at last! We must begin preparations for the ceremony at once.

AXEL: If it could be announced on a formal basis.

CHRISTINA: Very well. If you insist.

(*He kisses her hand, to her surprise.*

The QUEEN MOTHER promptly offers her hand, which is kissed.)

And tell them to tear up their edict. You'd better send him in. The French ambassador.

MOTHER: He's a doctor, my love. Consult him.

AXEL: He is also a Catholic. I must ask Your Majesties to maintain reserve.

(*He bows and goes, triumphant.*

CHRISTINA and her MOTHER make vile faces at his back, united for once.)

MOTHER: A wedding!

(*She embraces CHRISTINA and kisses her.*

CHRISTINA flinches at the unexpected embrace, and extricates herself clumsily. To evade her MOTHER she climbs back into bed, disturbing the bedclothes, and revealing a lightly clad, pretty girl.)

I should have known better than to expect a moment's happiness from you. I suppose I must be grateful you haven't got a donkey in there.

(*She goes.*

CHRISTINA cuddles the girl.

CHANUT, the French ambassador, enters, clears his throat politely.)

CHRISTINA: By God, you were quick! Ain't there no-one to present you?

CHANUT: Your Majesty's betrothal is being announced. My felicitations.

CHRISTINA: Oh that. They haven't wasted much time. Meet my bedfellow.

CHANUT: *Enchanté.* Your Majesty's taste is poetic. I trust that you are feeling better.

CHRISTINA: And I trust you've the wit to see I'm not.

CHANUT: May I? (*CHANUT examines her discreetly and deftly.*) You feel sick...bilious?

(*CHRISTINA nods.*)

It feels tender here?

(*She nods. He completes his examination.*)

A crisis of the liver. What have your doctors ordered?

CHRISTINA: Hot cream, spiced meat and brandy.

GIRL: Which Her Majesty, being unable to stomach, forces me to eat.

CHANUT: Then you, too, lady, will be in a heated state before long.

(*CHRISTINA smiles, dismisses the GIRL.*)

CHRISTINA: This business of the mass.

CHANUT: I deeply regret to have caused you embarrassment.

CHRISTINA: Discretion, *Monsieur*! What news of Paris, I hear I'm known as a rake.

CHANUT: And as an intellectual.

CHRISTINA: They flatter me. Mere restlessness. I've been tricked into this marriage, you know.

CHANUT: The thought is not pleasing to you?

CHRISTINA: My dear Chanut, the prospect of royal marriage is about as attractive as a forced march through mud.

CHANUT: Very graphic, ma'am.

(*They laugh.*)

CHRISTINA: How others adapt to it is beyond me.

CHANUT: Your Majesty is too perceptive.

CHRISTINA: Then you predicate the need for royal fools. Not that I haven't sought achievement. In the accident of my estate. Peace...prosperity...a shining light from the north. And as I reach for the pinnacle, they will push me off into the byre.

CHANUT: Surely there are...options? The world is full of possibilities.

CHRISTINA: So poor *Monsieur Descartes* had it, before our cruel Swedish winter finished him off. You Catholics disturb me. You bring a sweet, warm air from the south. Possibilities, eh? Perhaps I should change my condition. After all, it is the meek who will inherit the earth, are we not told?

CHANUT: A queen may practise humility, Your Majesty is a witness to that fact.

CHRISTINA: Our practise, *Monsieur Chanut*, is power… humility mere hobby. Which we have no wish to extend to humiliation. You're a handsome man. No, if I must marry I must…but I'm damned if I'll breed for them and be destroyed, like my mother. He'd make a fine king, you said? The Prince Karl.

CHANUT: A thousand pardons, Majesty. I meant, of course, King-Consort.

CHRISTINA: I'll proclaim him my heir, that should placate – oh, don't be alarmed, Karl won't threaten my position. Amazing as it may seem he has an affection for us.

CHANUT: Why amazing?

CHRISTINA: Come, don't tell me that a man of your wit and style isn't amused at the thought of little Karl and me.

CHANUT: I see that Your Majesty horribly under-rates herself.

CHRISTINA: And I see that you seek to flatter like the rest of them. Look at me, man.

CHANUT: You find your appearance wanting? Is there a woman who does not?

CHRISTINA: Then it is a general condition.

CHANUT: *Madame?*

CHRISTINA: We live on sufferance. To your desires. I find you a cruel sex.

CHANUT: Madam, a man is powerless. Where his body stands, there must he follow.

CHRISTINA: No man follows me. They follow symmetry, and all the thought in the world won't give me that. No,

I'm damned if I'll breed for them. I pollute enough space as it is.

CHANUT: For which I prescribe two days of fasting, followed by a diet of fruit and vegetables.

CHRISTINA: What?

CHANUT: Not an immediate cure. Chronic Puritan conscience tends to persist but we can make a start.

CHRISTINA: Fast, for two days?

CHANUT: Three would be better but Your Majesty is a beginner.

CHRISTINA: Three it shall be then.

CHANUT: With respect, ma'am, I prescribe two. We must try to secede from the stoic.

CHRISTINA: By God! We agree so well we shall be enemies in no time! Vegetables? Hardly a diet for a Queen.

CHANUT: Ah, but this is for the woman – forgive me, I spoke without thinking.

CHRISTINA: Oh I don't think you'd do that, *Monsieur Chanut*. You'd better be as good as the promise in those dark eyes. Good. I can't wait to start.

(*She strokes his cheek, then goes quickly without ceremony. CHANUT's SECRETARY appears, to take dictation.*)

CHANUT: You will be pleased to hear that we maintain a most cordial climate with Snowdrop. Our personal relations are…no…erase that. Spiritually there is growth, but soil conditions remain poor and the outlook is bleak. However, I have to report a unique climatic possibility. Our flower now refers, albeit indirectly, to transplantation. In which case there is the possible replacement of Snowdrop by Cabbage. Is this in our interest? Underline that please. I request instruction with urgency…we remain, etc, etc. PS, we now hold mass openly. Attendance this morning, twenty-four, including two German converts and an elderly Swede. No question about it – she's coming our way.

SECRETARY: Very puzzling, sir.

CHANUT: Puzzling? It's downright dangerous. You'd better keep a valise packed. We may need to make a sudden journey.

SECRETARY: Sir?

CHANUT: If there's one thing Protestants enjoy as much as good Catholics, dear boy, it's a scapegoat. I wonder if this is the right job for you. (*An arm about the YOUNG MAN's shoulder as they leave.*)

SECRETARY: I beg your pardon, Uncle?

Scene 5
Impasse

A table, formal. AXEL enters, followed by KARL, the DUKE, an OLDER MAN, and COPLEMAN, a merchant. CHRISTINA follows on their heels.

CHRISTINA: Good morning!

(*They sit.*)

Let me see the agenda. Good. We'll reverse the order. Propose the last motion.

(*Silence.*)

AXEL: Very well. Proposed.

CHRISTINA: Copleman?

COPLEMAN: Seconded, ma'am.

(*The DUKE glares at him.*)

CHRISTINA: On the matter of the succession, are we ready to ratify? The matter lies on the table.

(*Silence.*)

DUKE: The succession of His Highness, the Prince Karl, in advance of the royal nuptials, could hardly be agreeable to the Swedish people.

CHRISTINA: Oh? And since when have they been asked? (*Slight pause.*) The object is to secure succession in case of accident. Suppose I break me neck on the hunting field? Copleman, you speak for the merchants.

COPLEMAN: It is our humble opinion that His Royal Highness, Prince Karl, would be more than worthy to…ah…reign over Sweden, should that unhappy eventuality arise.

CHRISTINA: Good. Good, then that settles it. I have the casting vote.

AXEL: No.

(*Silence.*)

CHRISTINA: Why?

AXEL: The vote is premature.

(*Silence.*)

DUKE: There are stringent days ahead. Now that we've chosen to end the war. His Royal Highness might well face a shortage of funds.

CHRISTINA: They don't trust you Karl. Or they think I'm a fool. You've got the betrothal, what more do you want?

AXEL: The marriage.

DUKE: We need the marriage.

CHRISTINA: It's too late for the summer.

AXEL: The autumn, then.

CHRISTINA: We're here to ratify the succession, NOT the date of a wedding. This matter is on the table and I will have it resolved.

(*Silence.*)

Very well, adjourn the council.

(*She turns away.*

The DUKE and COPLEMAN bow and leave.)

AXEL: What do you think you're doing?

CHRISTINA: You know very well what I'm doing.

AXEL: If we ratify the succession will you agree to the autumn?

CHRISTINA: What wouldn't you do to have me staked down…tried Chanut's diet yet, Karl?

KARL: Anything to please, cousin.

CHRISTINA: I doubt if you'd take to it. (*She waves, dismissing him, he goes.*)

AXEL: I don't deny that I shall be relieved. The beauties of both sexes that you see fit to keep about you are costing the privy purse a fortune.

CHRISTINA: Oh come, a few wild oats, surely?

AXEL: So far as I'm concerned, once there's an heir, you can do as you please.

CHRISTINA: I see. Tell me, how many royal confinements do you require before I'm allowed to fornicate? To secure this throne, give or take a miscarriage of so, will take the next twenty years of my life. If it doesn't put me under the ground.

AXEL: The same for all women.

CHRISTINA: All the more reason to stay chaste.

AXEL: Have you been listening to that damned Catholic? Hang him about your neck much longer, you'll have the whole nobility affected. Resign yourself. They will not have the succession without the marriage. And if you continue to prate about choice, freedom, and all the other fashionable rubbish you'll have the church at your throat and I shan't answer for your future, your throne or your personal safety. Have I made myself clear?

CHRISTINA: (*Loud.*) Don't bully me! I grew up with it. Your stinking sweat, bellowing in my ears for as long as I can remember.

AXEL: Fulfilling my duty.

CHRISTINA: Why didn't you leave me in the parlour with the rest of the women, it's what you want!

AXEL: Not at all. Your unique position demands both the manly qualities of a king, and the fecundity of a woman.

CHRISTINA: Well you can't *have* both.

AXEL: Why not? For twenty years I've prepared you for it.

CHRISTINA: And how? By making a man of me. A man, despising women – just like you. You've had your joke, you and nature between you.

AXEL: I have performed a duty to your father, and to Sweden.

CHRISTINA: You've never even liked me.

AXEL: You have more power, more land than any king before you. Thanks to me.

CHRISTINA: You've lived! You've had a full life! Soldier, courtier, lover…you even allowed your own daughters to marry where their desires led them, you've been a fond father.

AXEL: I hope so.

CHRISTINA: You denied me all of it. I don't even engage your lubricity. I must be unique in Sweden for that.

AXEL: Madam, have I your permission to withdraw?

CHRISTINA: No. You never even liked me. I will be more discreet, with the Frenchman. We'll create a new bishop, that should placate the Church.

AXEL: Very good. (*Bows.*)

CHRISTINA: But...

(*He pauses.*)

...you will respect me.

AXEL: Madam?

CHRISTINA: You will respect the man you've created.

AXEL: In what way?

CHRISTINA: Secure the succession. You may as well know, I am not of a mind to marry.

AXEL: What? These perverse practices –

CHRISTINA: Nothing to do with my habits.

AXEL: Another suitor then! A blacksmith if you will but you must choose! Goddammit, woman, you seek to lay the blame at my door – did I make the world? You are a woman, it's your destiny to marry.

CHRISTINA: No! Haven't you humiliated me enough... No! Do you think I haven't been tempted, with half Europe willing to close its eyes and bed me? No. You've done your job too well. I love men! Their company, their talk...the smell of a man's sweat in the saddle! I love them in the bone... in the flesh...the wildness...the pricky insolence. The truth that is in a man takes him where his flesh decides. The flesh chooses! Do you think I'm going to pollute that, the only truth I know? I will not rape a man. Nor will I be the woman for you to despise. Between the two you have put me off. I've dreamed of murdering you for it.

(*Pause.*)

AXEL: What is to be done?

CHRISTINA: Secure the succession. Don't be a fool, man. do it for your own sake.

(*He looks at her for a long moment, turns and goes.*)
By God, I've frightened him. Hah! The Queen of Sweden, a Catholic convert...but no doubt without a country.
(*EBBA enters.*)
(*Cool.*) Hullo, Belle, what can we do for you?

EBBA: You've been so busy since we returned from Paris. I wanted to thank you for paying our debts.

CHRISTINA: Magnus has his army appointment.

EBBA: I came to see you. I'd like to think we were still friends.

CHRISTINA: You're as beautiful as ever.

EBBA: It slips away. The shine goes.

CHRISTINA: What are you trying to do, console me?

EBBA: I hear you don't need it.

CHRISTINA: Ah, the witty Chanut! How was Paris?

EBBA: Everything we dreamed of...poetic, astringent, full of life and charm. And the women...amazing!

CHRISTINA: The women?

EBBA: They call them blue-stockings – it's a fashion, they wear them. Such independence – they read, write, publish...some of the blue-stockings are even refusing to marry!

CHRISTINA: What?!

EBBA: They revere you, Pixie, they couldn't hear enough of you.

CHRISTINA: Indeed? Come here...I've missed you.
(*She pulls EBBA to her. And lets go at once.*)
Get out. I will not have pregnant cows under my roof. Let me look at you. Ugh, how could you?

EBBA: Pixie, it is natural.

CHRISTINA: So's plague.

EBBA: (*Quietly.*) What's the matter?

CHRISTINA: Nothing.

EBBA: Tell me.

CHRISTINA: Can you feel it, does it move?

EBBA: Oh yes...it lives.

CHRISTINA: I may be going to Rome.

EBBA: Rome?

CHRISTINA: To see the Holy Father.

EBBA: Christina, you can't! You mustn't even think of it!

CHRISTINA: I've been toying with Catholicism...the new scepticism...at least it's arguable. I find no answers in this cauldron of ice.

EBBA: You will find the Catholics less accommodating than you think. Christina these are dangerous thoughts, they attack your position.

CHRISTINA: Oh don't worry. If I convert they will throw me out. There is another reason. I don't intend to marry.

EBBA: Not marry? Why not?

CHRISTINA: Your trouble, my girl, is that you're too fond of the men.

EBBA: You like them too, now don't deny it, Pixie.

CHRISTINA: Yes but they don't like me...so I'm out of it. I might as well be a free rover. Let somebody else breed the tribe. I choose not to. Anyway, what are you worried about, you've got what's in your belly. Oh, what do you want me to say – that you look wonderful, that your skin glows like a pearl – (*Approaches EBBA.*) are you in milk?

EBBA: No. That comes later.

CHRISTINA: Well, God be with you. I'm sure you'll do well.

(*EBBA bows and goes.*)

That's his son you've got...or his daughter! And there'll be more, a brood of beauties like the lilies of the field, striding across their lives... She could be dead by Michaelmas. Rome.

(*CHANUT enters.*)

CHANUT: Madame, I must speak with you!

CHRISTINA: You've heard.

CHANUT: You cannot be serious. You will ruin both of us. Please, I beg you to consider...please! (*On his knees.*)

CHRISTINA: Not so unattainable now.

CHANUT: (*Bewildered.*) But what have you not had from me? And all our talk...did you not understand the nature of it? The conversion of Sweden...the bringing of light and life to the north – you agreed! With you as our ally, the whole of Europe to be embraced in the Catholic cloak!

CHRISTINA: A fine design.

CHANUT: But without your throne, what are you?

CHRISTINA: What indeed?

CHANUT: Are you mad? Have you not understood?

CHRISTINA: My poor man. Having to close your eyes and bed me. And all for nought.

CHANUT: Not so, I swear not so. But this is personal. I beg of you to listen, these matters are vital!

(*CHRISTINA makes to go. He follows.*)

CHANUT: You MUST marry Karl!

Scene 6
Abdication

CHRISTINA's silver throne is set. AXEL enters, with cane. He looks older, walks with a limp, his face slightly twisted, as though he has had a stroke. KARL enters. AXEL crosses to KARL, bows.

KARL: There is not a foot of space in the square. People are jammed against the cathedral doors.

AXEL: Trouble?

KARL: None. They are silent, utterly silent. Ah, Bishop.

(*The BISHOP approaches and bows to him.*)

BISHOP: A grievous day, Sire.

KARL: Yes...yes, indeed. We must all hope, even at this late stage...is that not the case, Chancellor?

AXEL: turns away grimly.

(*EBBA enters, supporting the QUEEN MOTHER.*)

MOTHER: You see? They want the Queen, they'll have no-one else! (*To KARL.*) Traitor! Are they going to cut us to pieces?

BISHOP: Most gracious Majesty...

MOTHER: Ah, my Lord Bishop. Tell them all to go home, we can't have this sort of thing. (*Vicious, of AXEL.*) He's no good, what has he done? Make her do as she's told! (*To EBBA.*) Why can't she be like you, your mother's got three sons, is that fair...I ask, is that fair?

EBBA: Please, madam, come away.

(*MAGNUS enters, bows to the QUEEN MOTHER, crosses to KARL, confers in a whisper.*)

MOTHER: What is it, has she changed her mind…there you are. I told you, she's changed her mind! Abdication! What nonsense! There's no ceremony, no dress for such an occasion…give up, Karl! Traitor!

EBBA: Madam, you distress yourself.

MOTHER: (*Rationally.*) Don't worry, my dear. She isn't coming.

(*The music starts.*

CHRISTINA appears quietly. She wears white, as for a wedding, the crown on her head. As she appears the music comes to an end.)

Look at her! She thinks it's a wedding, she thinks it's a wedding, she thinks it's a wedding!

(*She shrieks with hysterical laughter.*

CHRISTINA takes her position.)

KARL: There is still time.

CHRISTINA: My Lord Chancellor?

(*AXEL looks at her, then nods to BISHOP.*

A drumroll.

Plainsong.

The BISHOP moves forward. He can't find his place in the prayer book, sniffs, wipes his nose with a white handkerchief.)

Oh, get on with it, man.

(*The BISHOP mumbles prayers in a cracked wail. A murmur of 'amen'.*

Plainsong.

Hiatus. No-one knows what to do next.

CHRISTINA looks about the assembly, then to the BISHOP.)

Bishop, I think you must now take the crown from my head.

MOTHER: Not at all, not at all.

KARL: Christina, please! Stay on any terms!

CHRISTINA: Bishop…

(*The BISHOP approaches, lifts his hands over her head, then:*)

BISHOP: I cannot do it, Majesty. If it were to cost me my head I could not – (*He gives way.*)

CHRISTINA: But you must.

(He stands before her, head bowed.)

EBBA: No!

KARL: Please!

MAGNUS: Don't go, ma'am!

EBBA: Please...

KARL: Christina, there is still time. Think...think...

MOTHER: She mustn't...don't let her...don't let her...

EBBA: Sweden begs you.

(CHRISTINA gives her a long look.)

CHRISTINA: My Lord Chancellor, will you do it?

AXEL: There is still time. Nothing is irreversible.

CHRISTINA: Come, take your crown. After all, it is fitting – you've been its guardian all your life. Is it too much to ask?

AXEL: You know my heart.

CHRISTINA: Don't tell me I've broken your heart – I never had it. Very well. Retire with honour and breed your fine horses. Karl...Karl, you must do it.

KARL: Not I, Christina.

MOTHER: Make her stay, Karl, she'll listen to you, she likes you – take Karl, marry Karl...he'll do!

(Pause.)

CHRISTINA: Will you take it from me?

(KARL shakes his head.)

Karl...take the crown from me. I order you. Must it fall to the ground?

(She takes off the crown, holds it out, as though to drop it.
KARL takes the crown from her.
The QUEEN MOTHER gives way in MAGNUS' arms.)

(To KARL.) I've treated you badly. But it wouldn't have done, you know.

(She kisses KARL on the cheek.
He bows, thrusts the crown into MAGNUS' hands and leaves. MAGNUS bows briefly to CHRISTINA and follows his new master eagerly. The BISHOP bows low and leaves.
CHRISTINA crosses to EBBA, who is supporting the QUEEN MOTHER. The QUEEN MOTHER grasps CHRISTINA and clings to her fiercely.)

It's all right, it's all right, it's all right.

(*She unpins a large sapphire and diamond brooch, pins it to her MOTHER's breast.*)

MOTHER: But it's your best one! Look...look, she's given me her best one!

(*EBBA begins to lead the QUEEN MOTHER away.*

The QUEEN MOTHER exits as CHRISTINA detains EBBA by the sleeve. She kisses EBBA.)

CHRISTINA: Don't forget me.

(*EBBA goes.*

CHRISTINA and AXEL are left. She makes a slight move towards him but he turns away. At a distance he turns back and they regard each other for a long moment. He goes.

CHRISTINA stands. Then, in a whirl of movement, she rips off her dress to reveal riding clothes underneath, and boots. She throws the dress across the space onto the throne, whirls round, her arms out in ecstasy, and leaves at the run.)

ACT TWO

Scene 1

Tea With a Visitor

A sunlit room. The staging is not naturalistic, but there is a civilised quality, in contrast to the brutal surroundings in Act One. Some upholstery, flowers, and decoration in blue and yellow. The MARQUISE enters. She is plumpish, soft-skinned, soft-voiced. Her grey gown is trimmed with white, simply cut, but ferociously elegant and well-fitting. She is followed by her friend, CATHERINE de Rohant, younger, more severely dressed. She carries a book. Behind them comes a FOOTMAN carrying a large tray set with wine and cakes.

MARQUISE: Here. No – there.

(*The FOOTMAN sets down the tray.*)

CATHERINE: Splendid. And flowers!

MARQUISE: I thought cakes with the claret – I believe she has a sweet tooth.

CATHERINE: The Queen of Sweden. Our most important coup.

MARQUISE: Yes. Here she will see how we live…our work …the looms…the farm…

CATHERINE: And all without men.

(*A bell, off.*)

MARQUISE: She is here!

(*She nods to the FOOTMAN, who exits.*

The WOMEN compose themselves to receive CHRISTINA.

The FOOTMAN enters, and CHRISTINA pushes in behind him, nervous and eager.

She wears battered riding clothes, over which she has draped a skirt in honour of the visit. She doffs her plumed hat in greeting. The TWO WOMEN curtsy, deeply and impeccably.)

CHRISTINA: Oh no ceremony ladies, please…we left all that in Sweden. *Madame la Marquise?*

(*She thrusts out a hand which misses the MARQUISE who is curtsying again.*)

MARQUISE: May I present *Madame de Rohant*?

(*CHRISTINA shakes her hand, then sits.*)

CHRISTINA: Lovely room, I like the blue and yellow… Swedish colours you know.

MARQUISE: Yes, Majesty.

CHRISTINA: What? Oh you mean you did it for me? Good…very nice. (*To CATHERINE.*) What did you say your name was?

CATHERINE: Catherine de Rohant, ma'am.

CHRISTINA: I've read your thoughts on the condition of women!

CATHERINE: *Madame*, your name rings through Europe.

MARQUISE: The Queen of Sweden declines to marry.

(*CHRISTINA grins, cramming her face with cakes.*)

CATHERINE: To refuse to procreate, even at the cost of a throne!

CHRISTINA: Oh, I wasn't kicked out, if that's what they're saying – no, no – decision was mine!

CATHERINE: You have asserted the freedom of all women!

MARQUISE: Meeting you, Majesty, is the high point of our lives!

CHRISTINA: Me too…though I must say, I'm very disappointed… (*She sits back, wiping her hands in her skirts.*) I mean…where are they?

(*The WOMEN are mystified and alarmed…what can have gone wrong?*

CHRISTINA swoops, jerking up the MARQUISE's skirts.

The MARQUISE jumps to her feet with a shriek of alarm.)

The stockings…the blue stockings! Shan't believe a word of it without the blue stockings!

(*She laughs uproariously, and they join in, realising that it is a 'joke'.*)

MARQUISE: (*Waits for CHRISTINA to contain her merriment.*) Highness, a toast.

(*She gestures to the FOOTMAN, who pours drinks.*

CHRISTINA knocks hers straight back, so the MARQUISE takes over, re-pours, the FOOTMAN takes a glass to CATHERINE.)

A toast, Majesty. What shall we drink to?

CATHERINE: Why, to women!

(*They murmur, and drink.*

Hiatus.

The FRENCHWOMEN wait for CHRISTINA to speak first.)

CHRISTINA: (*Pause.*) You married?

CATHERINE: My husband and I are separated, ma'am.

CHRISTINA: Any children?

CATHERINE: Two boys. They are away at school.

CHRISTINA: How old?

CATHERINE: Two and four.

CHRISTINA: Seems a bit young.

MARQUISE: (*Soft.*) *Madame de Rohant* is much concerned with her writing.

CHRISTINA: What about you, your husband's dead, I believe.

MARQUISE: I am, happily, freed from that subjection, ma'am.

CHRISTINA: Didn't you like it?

MARQUISE: My purpose was to provide heirs for my husband's title and property. Women, Majesty, are no more than fields for growing corn.

CHRISTINA: By God, you're right. What about sex though, don't you miss it?

MARQUISE: As Your Majesty well knows, men have not the exclusive rights to our bodies.

CHRISTINA: Oh you mean you're together? Jolly good.

CATHERINE: To submit to men is treachery to our cause. The enemy must be attacked, does Your Majesty not agree?

CHRISTINA: To be honest, the word enemy chills my liver after thirty years at war. I see your point...the need to be extreme. You ain't afraid of being laughed at?

CATHERINE: On the contrary, we are well aware that we are considered highly ridiculous…not the least by other women, who call us traitors to our sex.

MARQUISE: And who will be the first to exploit the benefits we achieve on their behalf.

CATHERINE: We are on the move, Majesty. In the end, all slaves rebel.

CHRISTINA: I'm sure you're right, though to tell the truth I've never much enjoyed the company of women, you can't get any sense out of them.

(*Pause, she realises she has put her foot in it.*)

MARQUISE: *Madame*, is that surprising?

CHRISTINA: No…yes, see what you mean. Stuck in the kitchen, that sort of thing – no, not fair.

CATHERINE: Rumour has it, Majesty, that you have converted.

CHRISTINA: Who told you? Well, since we're among friends – yes, I'm on my way to Rome! I mean to be at the centre of things…to expand, with Messer Copernicus, Signor Galileo…devote myself to research at the feet of the Holy Father.

CATHERINE: The Pope, Majesty, is a man.

MARQUISE: Your Majesty's conversion is devout?

CHRISTINA: Lord, no, I'm a sceptic.

(*The FOOTMAN enters with a letter.*)

MARQUISE: I gave strict instructions that we were not to be disturbed.

(*The FOOTMAN whispers in her ear.*)

Forgive me, Majesty, a crisis it seems.

(*She reads the letter, hands it to CATHERINE.*)

CHRISTINA: Bad news?

MARQUISE: My father. He is failing. The heart.

CHRISTINA: We must be deprived of your company. So sad.

CATHERINE: There is no question of your going. Put it to the test. Would such a visit further our cause, or impede it? I am certain of the answer.

MARQUISE: There *is* pneumonia in the lungs.

CATHERINE: Then I trust he has good nurses.

MARQUISE: I will write a letter.

(*She does so.*)

CATHERINE: You find us harsh.

CHRISTINA: Why yes...yes, a little.

(*The MARQUISE gives the letter to the FOOTMAN, who goes.*)

You hate all men?

CATHERINE: It is necessary.

CHRISTINA: I begin to feel like an impostor.

CATHERINE: You are an inspiration to us all. You have shown us the way!

CHRISTINA: But I only pushed off because I couldn't stand it. I wanted to live!

CATHERINE: Precisely! Why shouldn't we demand the same freedoms as men – more, since the breeding of children confines us more!

MARQUISE: With you at our side, ma'am, there is nothing we cannot accomplish.

CHRISTINA: I honour your courage.

CATHERINE: We may rely on your true support?

CHRISTINA: I will write to you – from Rome. By the way, my French ambassador is in Paris. He's a fine doctor, I recommend him.

(*They curtsy and she goes.*)

CATHERINE: What do you think?

MARQUISE: I think she's slipped us. It was the business of my father.

CATHERINE: She's naive. And a moralist.

MARQUISE: Yes. All this fervour for the Pope.

CATHERINE: The nobility of Rome will soon tire of an ex-Queen at table, then where will she be? We recruit them all as their breasts fall.

MARQUISE: How harsh you are. The Queen of Sweden is an important ally.

CATHERINE: Then we'll pursue her.

MARQUISE: Pity she's so little to look at.

CATHERINE: Yes. Whatever was she wearing?

Scene 2
Papa

The Vatican. The CARDINALS and CHRISTINA, apart, wait for the POPE. The POPE enters, a handsome man in the prime of life.

POPE: Our dear daughter.
(*CHRISTINA rushes at him, tries to throw her arms about his neck, a CARDINAL intervenes. She smothers the POPE's hand with kisses.*)
Beloved daughter. Welcome to Rome. We are beside ourself, our joy is without bounds.

CHRISTINA: Oh Papa, my lovely Papa! We've waited so long!

POPE: No tears, my daughter.

CHRISTINA: They're tears of joy, to see your face at last! So handsome! Much better than the pictures – the coins are a slander on that nose, that profile!

POPE: You are too loving. We accept your love. We welcome such a loving heart to our bosom.

CHRISTINA: (*Draws a chair close.*) We've been so hungry for this moment – what? What's the matter with the man?
(*The POPE lifts a benevolent hand and the CARDINAL draws back.*)
I'm hungry for food...for truth...philosophy. We long for talk.

POPE: A garden has been prepared for you. Fine walks, and much shade. The Palace is not so large, but very fine. You will like the views.

CHRISTINA: Where we'll sit together and talk about the meaning of meaning...of life, light, and the new astronomy – I can't wait, Pope! We flew across Europe – well, with the odd dalliance, you won't begrudge me that after years of toil, very good for the bowels, I recommend it.
(*The CARDINALS hiss displeasure.*)

POPE: (*With a sweet smile.*) We have heard of your adventures, daughter. It has come to our attention.

CHRISTINA: Oh. I've been a real rogue, whored my way across Europe! For which I hope you'll hear my confession – I've a tale or two to relate, I can tell you.

POPE: Confession connotes repentance.

CHRISTINA: Oh I don't repent. Best time I ever had in my life...that's something we're going to have to put right in your religion. Celibacy's no good – not in the Bible, you know. Think again...no need to cut it off, Pope!

(*The CARDINALS react with shock.*

The POPE waves them back.)

The chastity of Jesus – no more than an assumption... and to copy it an arrogant act, since God has fashioned us as coupling creatures. Deny the design of creation? Devilish work, Pope. At least, that's my opinion.

POPE: There is much to be achieved here. Humility, daughter. We commend your thoughts to loving humility.

(*Light change.*

The CARDINALS go.

The POPE and CHRISTINA with her arms round her knees.)

Christina, we are not mere animals, subject to season, to blind instinct. God has given us consciousness. To treat other people as a means to an end is both to deny justice, and the inner life. In matters of the sensual, the carnal, there is always another person to be considered, the possibility of exploitation. (*Slight pause.*) We come to the question of self-disgust.

CHRISTINA: To enjoy a meal together...is that disgusting? To sing in unison? Where's the fault in it?

POPE: This is a false innocence.

CHRISTINA: You mean I buy my loves? There's a reason in that.

POPE: My daughter, what reason can you give me?

CHRISTINA: My face.

(*Light change.*

CHRISTINA and the POPE, now sitting further apart.)

POPE: We are disturbed. We would be reassured that Your Majesty's decision to abdicate was not, as rumour persists, taken for reasons of defiance.

CHRISTINA: Rumours. What rumours now?

POPE: That you reject the marriage bed. That you refuse to procreate.

CHRISTINA: Is that so bad? Where does it put you? Sorry, Pope, free will…I concede.

POPE: You are a woman, with a sacred destiny. Without procreation, mutual love, and loving care, society cannot hold.

CHRISTINA: No copulation without a swelled belly or we're in sin, is that it?

POPE: (*Shakes his head.*) Marriage is for procreation, for the orientation of desire, and thus for harmonious conjugal life.

CHRISTINA: Oh, we're allowed a little fun in the marriage bed? Hah…take my mother. Eighteen pregnancies, stillbirths, premature drop…dead infants in the churchyard, unnamed corpses, flesh of her flesh, torn, cut out…you should see that woman's quarters, she can neither sit nor stand without pain. And don't tell me she's blessed to suffer in the name of the Lord, the woman's banal. She's banal because of it.

POPE: Alas, the need for an heir.

CHRISTINA: So you would sanction the exploitation of the female? What's wrong with intervention, I see you avail yourself of physic.

POPE: Thank you for your good wishes and gifts during my fever.

CHRISTINA: It's still the quinine that's put you on your feet. Intervention, Pope – Intervention.

POPE: We have heard of your views on the bearing of children. If parenthood is excluded from marriage, why then the character of the relation is utterly diminished.

CHRISTINA: What's wrong with pleasure? (*Pause.*) What about sexual need?

POPE: We employ the urge for natural purposes, for which it was created. Where it threatens to degrade, to corrupt, we abjure, we employ continence.

CHRISTINA: Pope, you ignore nature!

POPE: Nature cannot be conquered by violating its laws! We know of these practices! Of the murder of the child in the womb! We are in a state of grief. These are dreadful acts.

CHRISTINA: But women are in need!

POPE: Woman is creation! Would you turn her into an assassin? What of the child, in the womb? What of its sacred life?

CHRISTINA: And what of a woman's flow? A child a month, deceased. And a man's ejaculation? Whole armies, whole populations denied breath. Nature is wasteful, Pope. We must look to ourselves.

POPE: This comes near blasphemy.

CHRISTINA: I don't intend to defy, nor to reject. But you say that you understand...that your pastoral work gives you knowledge, even at second-hand. You do not know. You abstract yourselves. You use yourselves up in dealing with your frustrations, with the ruination of your body selves. And you would condemn those of us who live in the world. You speak of love, and you would destroy us. You're a smart, careful man, and you live by a complexity of rule from a wide gathering, and it gives you conviction. But where are you in your nakedness? I will quieten down my private life...not to embarrass you under your walls. But I cannot close my mouth. I seek guidance. But by brotherly, sisterly discourse. I'm on the move, you see. Don't disaffect me.

(*The POPE rises.*)

POPE: We are not angry. My daughter, if you do not feel yourself drawn to the true God, through His medium, the Church, to the command to love...to charity...why then...I pray for your soul. (*He makes the sign of the cross on her forehead.*) Be at peace. (*He goes.*)

CHRISTINA: (*Bitter.*) The command to love? And what of the command to BE loved...who can command that? You bloody, handsome, arrogant man! What a charmer. What a waste! And what a devil. We won't deny the body. Never mind self-mutilating priests... (*Presses her hands to her body.*) You shall be placated...you shall be loved! If not for desire then for my purse – come on, man...out of the shadows...let's take a look at you.

(*MONALDESCHO moves forward.*)

MONALDESCHO: Madonna...ah, bellissima!

CHRISTINA: Do you know who I am?

MONALDESCHO: I only know, mysterious stranger, that my life is forever changed. Whoever you are, wherever you are, I beg to follow and serve you for the rest of your days...may they be as beautiful as your smile.

(*CHRISTINA laughs heartily.*

Encouraged, MONALDESCHO pursues her.)

If fortune is cruel...if circumstance does not permit... why then I shall sit at your gate, living for the moment when you pass...for your shadow...for the print of your heel on the grass...

(*He kisses her foot, she kicks him away genially.*)

CHRISTINA: Get away, you must know who I am.

MONALDESCHO: Only that you are a wild, eager fawn...a hare, soft, panting... (*Into her ear.*)

CHRISTINA: What's your name?

MONALDESCHO: (*Deep bow.*) I am, cara madonna, your devoted and humble servant, the Marchese di Monaldescho. But we forget rank, adorable stranger – I spit on convention.

CHRISTINA: You know very well I'm the Queen of Sweden.

MONALDESCHO: A queen? But I would not dare –

CHRISTINA: Oh, I think you would.

MONALDESCHO: (*Pause.*) I am dismissed?

CHRISTINA: Not necessarily. Only don't presume too far for your pretty face.

MONALDESCHO: But I love you.

CHRISTINA: (*Harsh.*) What?

MONALDESCHO: You are a queen!

CHRISTINA: Oh, I like it! Honest trade! In a country where nepotism is virtue and a bribe common sense – at least there's human warmth in it. (*She moves away.*)

MONALDESCHO: (*Uncertain.*) Madonna?

CHRISTINA: (*Objective.*) What use are you to me? What can you do?
MONALDESCHO: I ask only to serve.
CHRISTINA: Hah.
MONALDESCHO: Whatever you desire is yours! I will provide. You shall be Queen of Rome – Queen of the world!
CHRISTINA: I want the best.
MONALDESCHO: Already yours.
CHRISTINA: The best painters, the best sculptors, the best dancers…
MONALDESCHO: (*Escorting her off.*) But of course.
CHRISTINA: What did you say your name was?

Scene 3
Forever Roma

CHRISTINA and MONALDESCHO, lying together, chatting quietly.

MONALDESCHO: I'm not ambitious. No more than the next man. All I ask is some responsibility…a piece of land to leave my children.
CHRISTINA: Instead of which, you find yourself a lackey.
MONALDESCHO: Ah, but to a queen.
CHRISTINA: Don't tell me you're a romantic.
MONALDESCHO: I take what the world offers and count myself lucky that I please. You're not complaining, are you?
CHRISTINA: No. Though I wish there could be more honest connection between us.
MONALDESCHO: Who's the romantic now? There's limitation in all things. To be Alexander was to die young…and the Virgin was probably plain.
CHRISTINA: (*Laughs.*) What can I give you to make you happy?
MONALDESCHO: Why should you please me?
CHRISTINA: Why indeed…I hold the purse. A logical man.
MONALDESCHO: I have to be, I have dependants.

CHRISTINA: Yes, we have discovered the wife and children. We are so pleased when you tell us the truth.
MONALDESCHO: As often as I can, that's common sense.
CHRISTINA: How real you are. A survivor. You may even survive me.
MONALDESCHO: Do I need to?
CHRISTINA: Of course not. Have you ordered the centrepiece for the dinner table?
MONALDESCHO: Not yet.
CHRISTINA: Good. I want the Descent from the Cross. In pink sugar.

Scene 4
A New Game

CHRISTINA on stage.

CHRISTINA: (*Calls, in a rage.*) Monaldescho!
MONALDESCHO: (*Off.*) Yes? (*He enters, eating, pulling on his jacket.*) Yes?
CHRISTINA: Mind your manners.
MONALDESCHO: I couldn't come any faster, what do you want?
CHRISTINA: Bend your bloody leg, that's what I want.
MONALDESCHO: You're in a bad mood this morning.
CHRISTINA: And you're getting too quick for your own good.
MONALDESCHO: I have to be pretty smart to keep us out of the bankruptcy court.
CHRISTINA: That's your affair, I pay you enough.
MONALDESCHO: What's the matter with you, anyway?
CHRISTINA: I'm bored!
MONALDESCHO: There's a Cardinal here.
CHRISTINA: Let him wait – I'm bored, I tell you! If something doesn't happen soon, I shall commit murder.
AZZOLINO: (*At the entrance.*) Perhaps Your Majesty needs a new direction.
CHRISTINA: Who let you in?
AZZOLINO: God. And the Pope, of course.

(*CHRISTINA waves MONALDESCHO off.*)

CHRISTINA: What are you here for, to scold me again?

AZZOLINO: No, my daughter. His Holiness sends warm greetings, and his love.

CHRISTINA: He must want something. (*She sits, indicates for him to sit.*)

AZZOLINO: Your Majesty continues to be…happy in Rome?

CHRISTINA: You were listening. I'm bored. I was bred for work. It seems that without the whip one loses direction…even my intuition deserts me. One becomes a sort of shifting fable. I've come to the conclusion that the world lacks meaning.

AZZOLINO: Purpose and meaning are not objective facts. Value exists in ourselves, not in the world. Integration is decided by choice…it is we who decide who we are.

CHRISTINA: I knew who I was in Sweden – why not here?

AZZOLINO: Alas, when we are thrown back on ourselves we perceive only that we do not exist.

CHRISTINA: What sort of conundrum's that? (*Slight pause.*) I exist. Something feels. Perhaps you can tell me why, having left that Lutheran prison in order to enjoy my life, it seems impossible that I should do so. Why must there be interpretation?

AZZOLINO: It may be that you seek a cause.

CHRISTINA: The cause of service is an impertinence which you know full well I've abandoned. Sweden was lucky I was poxed or vicious. At least here my influence is confined to empty ceremony. Which I might enjoy since I've taste enough for the frivolous if it were not for the fact that, having come to the conclusion that life is meaningless, I'm still invaded by the conviction that it ought not to be so.

AZZOLINO: (*Slight pause.*) There is concern for the kingdom of Naples. (*He sighs.*) Alas, the people there cry out to be free.

CHRISTINA: What are you doing, offering me the Crown? You're a handsome man, *Monsieur* Cardinal.

AZZOLINO: Thank you, Majesty.

CHRISTINA: A handsome man, bearing gifts. I must be careful. Spain won't give up Naples, not without a fight. Oh, you want me for a fight? No, not even for your beautiful eyes.

AZZOLINO: Your statecraft is renowned.

CHRISTINA: Nor for your flattery, Cardinal. Tell me, are you chaste?

AZZOLINO: (*Smiles.*) I must ask Your Majesty to forebear.

CHRISTINA: No, no...you must answer.

AZZOLINO: Madam, I cannot.

CHRISTINA: Suppose I order you to?

AZZOLINO: Such – discipline would be hard to resist.

CHRISTINA: Good, you're a naughty man. Naples eh?

AZZOLINO: A cause worthy of wit and intention...the cause of freedom.

CHRISTINA: I doubt the Neapolitans will savour one foreign boot more than another.

AZZOLINO: Madam, they will greet you as a saviour.

CHRISTINA: But will they fight?

AZZOLINO: They are hot for revenge.

CHRISTINA: Hot, are they?

AZZOLINO: Perhaps Your Majesty would care to see papers?

CHRISTINA: (*Peruses the papers.*) Pity about your chastity. We've no need to do anything. Nothing directly carnal.

AZZOLINO: Alas, it is impossible.

CHRISTINA: Come, you're an Italian.

AZZOLINO: A poor emissary. On a failing mission, it seems.

CHRISTINA: I wonder how I might be more...compliant.
(*They regard each other.*)
We will consider your matter. With attention.

AZZOLINO: There speaks the daughter of Gustavus Adolphus.

CHRISTINA: My father? He's dead, man...and so am I, I think.

AZZOLINO: I do not believe it.

CHRISTINA: Well, we will acquaint you of our purpose. Come tomorrow. The motives of the Holy Father –

AZZOLINO: Are towards the alleviation of suffering. He knows your generous heart, and your respect for freedom.

CHRISTINA: We'll talk again.

(*She kisses the ring. The CARDINAL bows and goes.*)

By God, they must want me out of Rome to offer me a country. (*To MONALDESCHO.*) What do you want?

MONALDESCHO: You were going it with the cloth.

CHRISTINA: Tell me about Naples.

MONALDESCHO: Not much revenue.

CHRISTINA: The people?

MONALDESCHO: Mostly thieves and scavengers, present company excepted.

CHRISTINA: Fancy yourself, do you?

MONALDESCHO: Why not, I'm Neapolitan. Good family. We'd be a popular alliance, you and I.

CHRISTINA: We'll see.

MONALDESCHO: He's a good looking fellow.

(*She turns in enquiry.*)

The Cardinal.

(*She turns away, he pursues her.*)

I'm your man. I'm loyal.

CHRISTINA: True. Very well, come if it pleases you.

MONALDESCHO: In command of the army?

CHRISTINA: *I* shall be in command of the army. Oh, don't sulk man, we'll see you get something out of it. Why not play the cards dealt – why not? I was a queen, I'll be a queen again, at least I've the training for it.

MONALDESCHO: And the rest of us get our rewards in heaven, eh?

CHRISTINA: What are you complaining of, you're good-looking!

MONALDESCHO: Plenty of plain women aren't Queen of Sweden.

(*She clouts him.*)

Is *he* coming? The Cardinal?

CHRISTINA: Perhaps. So don't get too ambitious.

(*She goes.*)

MONALDESCHO: Why you, you hump-backed mare? Why you? Why not me?

Scene 5
Action

Enter AZZOLINO, cloaked, followed by a CAPTAIN of the Queen's guard.

CAPTAIN: Welcome back, sir, your presence has been much missed.

AZZOLINO: I wish my news was good. How goes it in the field?

CAPTAIN: Badly. Our formations are too well known. We suspect a traitor.

AZZOLINO: Where is the Marchese?

CAPTAIN: In bed sir. He is not himself.

AZZOLINO: And the Queen? We heard of the sad death of her mother.

CAPTAIN: Alas, yes sir.

(*CHRISTINA enters.*)

CHRISTINA: You're back, why weren't we told?

AZZOLINO: I was on my way to pay my respects to you. I am so distressed to hear of your loss.

CHRISTINA: Eh?

AZZOLINO: Her Majesty, your mother.

CHRISTINA: Oh who cares, she's not important. A foolish woman.

AZZOLINO: Perhaps the simple suffer less.

CHRISTINA: Not her...always in pain or a rage – miserable life.

AZZOLINO: She bred you.

CHRISTINA: I bolted!

AZZOLINO: We all fail our parents.

CHRISTINA: Not at all, you're a Cardinal.

AZZOLINO: But I am not the Pope. Be comforted. I must speak with you privately.

(*The CAPTAIN goes.*)

There is a traitor in the camp.

CHRISTINA: By God there is! We marched east after you left us, they were waiting. When we broke out across the river, the Spaniards were there in force. Our troops tired and we are without reserve.

AZZOLINO: And you have no knowledge of who has betrayed you?

CHRISTINA: None.

AZZOLINO: Then I am the bearer of ill news.

CHRISTINA: Who? His name.

AZZOLINO: The Marchese.

CHRISTINA: No, no, that's impossible, you're mistaken.

AZZOLINO: There can be no error.

CHRISTINA: He's my man! I'm in his interest!

AZZOLINO: My Lady, I have proof. There is a letter. You will recognise the handwriting.

(*He hands her the letter.*)

CHRISTINA: No. I won't believe it. He must be killed at once.

AZZOLINO: No.

CHRISTINA: (*Calls.*) Fetch Monaldescho!

AZZOLINO: You must remain within the law! It is as vital politically that you do nothing in haste as it is vital for your soul that you do nothing in anger.

CHRISTINA: Oh don't codge me, Pope's man. Where is he?

(*The CAPTAIN returns with MONALDESCHO, who throws himself at CHRISTINA's feet.*

A SOLDIER stands by to cut off MONALDESCHO's retreat.)

Why? Why? (*She kicks him.*) What's the matter, lost your tongue – don't worry, you soon will!

MONALDESCHO: Highness...Highness...please...

CHRISTINA: Recognise this? No wonder you've been stinking the place out! Think I don't know your ignorant hand?

AZZOLINO: It must be exposed to the process of law!

CHRISTINA: What was it, money? You've bled us white for your pretty face! Kill him.

AZZOLINO: No! At least confess him first!

CHRISTINA: Do it then.

MONALDESCHO: (*Clinging to the CARDINAL's legs.*) Save me...please...please...please...

AZZOLINO: My son, you must make your confession.

MONALDESCHO: No, I don't want to die…save me, don't let them kill me…father…father…

CHRISTINA: Get on with it!

AZZOLINO: Majesty, he will not confess, he asks me to intercede for him.

CHRISTINA: Oh, do what you please. Take him away.

(*MONALDESCHO breaks free, falls at her feet. He kisses her skirt, clinging to it, and babbling.*)

MONALDESCHO: Madonna, madonna…I love you…

CHRISTINA: What!

MONALDESCHO: I love you…I love you…I love you…

CHRISTINA: Kill him!

(*And she snatches the dagger from the CAPTAIN and strikes MONALDESCHO in the throat.*

He gurgles, gasps, and is silent.

AZZOLINO kneels by the body, praying.)

Not so pretty now. Remove the carcass.

(*The SOLDIERS take the body off.*)

Perhaps now you will take me seriously.

AZZOLINO: But I have always done so.

CHRISTINA: Why do you look like that?

AZZOLINO: I am frightened, madam.

CHRISTINA: Are we all to be like you…hiding from life in a woman's skirts?

AZZOLINO: The act was barbaric.

CHRISTINA: Help me.

(*He bows slightly and goes.*

The CAPTAIN enters.)

CHRISTINA: Has he gone?

CAPTAIN: Ma'am?

CHRISTINA: The Cardinal.

CAPTAIN: Yes, ma'am.

CHRISTINA: Fetch him back. I am ill.

CAPTAIN: Shall I call the leech, ma'am?

CHRISTINA: Fetch him back. No. Give him a bowl of cherries.

CAPTAIN: Ma'am?

CHRISTINA: Who's that? Is someone there? And tell them I won't sign – you can cry your eyes out, just remember that. You know who you're speaking to?

CAPTAIN: Ma'am? (*He approaches.*)

CHRISTINA: No you don't, you don't catch me…oh no, no, no. (*Brisk.*) I'll take a hot bath now. (*Goes, abruptly.*)
(*The CAPTAIN stands, amazed.*)

Scene 6
Dolls

CHRISTINA, in a dressing gown and cap, seated. She is immobile, hands in lap. LUCIA enters.

LUCIA: Majesty?
(*No response. LUCIA sighs.*)
Your favourite bonbons, from the Contessa! No? (*She puts them on CHRISTINA's lap and tidies her, sighing.*) You must eat! If you don't eat you will die and what will become of us?
(*She goes.*
A pause.
ANGELICA, LUCIA's daughter, enters, carrying her dolls. She notices the sweets, and takes one. Then she feeds her dolls the sweets.)

ANGELICA: Say please. Good girl. Please…good girl. Eat up. Be good.
(*She pushes a sweet into CHRISTINA's mouth. Seeing that she does not eat it, she slaps her lightly on the hand.*)
Naughty girl. Eat up…eat up.
(*CHRISTINA starts to cry silently, her face contorting.*)
Very naughty! Stop crying!
(*She slaps CHRISTINA on the hand. Then, tiring of the game, she picks up her dolls to go…pauses, puts another sweet into CHRISTINA's hand.*)
Eat up.
(*She goes.*
CHRISTINA slowly turns her head after the child, then slowly begins to eat.)

Scene 7
A Visitor

LUCIA enters with flowers, returns with wine, followed by ANGELICA, with ribbons in her hair. CHRISTINA is sitting in her chair, but is wearing an overgarment in pink, festively decorated.

CHRISTINA: The paintings…you don't think they might be too –

LUCIA: No, no, madonna…he is a man of the world.

CHRISTINA: Of course. And the *porco alla Romana*?

LUCIA: Will be to perfection.

(*LUCIA bobs and she and the child go.*

CHRISTINA moves about restlessly. She opens a book, puts it down, picks up a glass, picks up a whip from the sidetable and plays with it, puts it down. She sits with the book, arranging her skirt.

LUCIA enters.

CHRISTINA leaps to her feet, dropping the book.)

Majesty, he is here!

(*CHRISTINA nods, then gets on her hands and knees, looking for the book.*

AZZOLINO enters, looks about.)

CHRISTINA: (*From the floor.*) Oh, there you are. Please, be seated.

(*Pause.*)

AZZOLINO: (*Soft.*) You are well?

CHRISTINA: Much better, much better. How long are you in Rome?

AZZOLINO: His Holiness feels that –

CHRISTINA: We had a letter. Perhaps you should read it. As you see, we are allowed to meet. So long as we don't touch the body. Not much chance of that. (*She smiles. Pause.*) You didn't come.

AZZOLINO: It was forbidden.

CHRISTINA: Would you have come?

AZZOLINO: I was so pleased to get your letters. You are, as always, superbly informed.

CHRISTINA: I know how you hate being out of Rome. And now you're here. On Vatican orders. What is your mission?

AZZOLINO: (*Produces papers.*) The suggestion that Your Majesty be offered the throne of Poland –

CHRISTINA: I've refused it.

AZZOLINO: The offer is a secure one.

CHRISTINA: I have no choice. This room is now my whole world. To go as far as that door fills me with terror. I can no more step into the street than fly from the rooftops. It seems I am to be a prisoner for the rest of my life. So, as you see, I need a friend.

AZZOLINO: It will pass.

CHRISTINA: (*Throws herself at his feet.*) Please, I am in torment! How may I be absolved? I took his life for mere temper – not even necessity, conviction.

AZZOLINO: My dear friend.

(*He lifts her.*
She holds on to him.)

CHRISTINA: Say you forgive me…say you forgive me. Don't leave me, say you will stay, they will let you stay…please, please stay…I need you!

AZZOLINO: You must find a way to forgive yourself.

CHRISTINA: No, please. You know what I want.

AZZOLINO: My daughter…pray.

CHRISTINA: I beg you. I've waited. I've been patient.

(*She makes to embrace him.*
He steps back.)

AZZOLINO: (*Gently.*) I think I must now withdraw.

CHRISTINA: Oh. You're afraid. There have been women. Why not me? Oh, what am I but the bag of excrement that St Bernard would have all women? Please.

AZZOLINO: (*Low.*) You must understand. There can be nothing. Nothing at all.

CHRISTINA: I agree. Your presence…that's all I ask –

(*LUCIA enters.*)

LUCIA: Madonna…madonna…quickly…my child…she is choking!

CHRISTINA: (*Howls.*) Angelica!

(She rushes from the room, followed by LUCIA and AZZOLINO.
Pause.
Enter AZZOLINO and CHRISTINA.
She stops short.)
I left the room!

AZZOLINO: Yes.

CHRISTINA: Why are you smiling?

AZZOLINO: You saved the child's life!

CHRISTINA: Nonsense, I gave her a fine blow in the stomach!
(They laugh, stimulated by the success of the rescue.)
How flimsy rank is. In human need it dissolves at once. So warm down there! The smell of ironed clothes… linen…lace – food…baking… And babies. The smell of babies. I like the smell of babies – can that be wrong?

AZZOLINO: Of course not.

CHRISTINA: Does it take so many cooks – I was never in a kitchen before.

AZZOLINO: They are proud and happy to be in your service.

CHRISTINA: Why?

AZZOLINO: You are a queen.

CHRISTINA: A hundred servants, to wait on one woman? Can that be right? Why do we prey on one another – we should all be on the same footing.

AZZOLINO: These thoughts are valuable. And can be fruitfully employed.

CHRISTINA: *(Drily.)* Poland, you mean?

AZZOLINO: Can it be wrong to bring peace and prosperity to an unhappy land?

CHRISTINA: Peace in Poland? You are disingenuous or naive.

AZZOLINO: I do not deny the instability of Poland's borders.

CHRISTINA: No. There'll be no more killing.

AZZOLINO: Even if the cause be just?

CHRISTINA: I have been as a man. I have commanded. I have signed the death warrants, consigned regiments to the sword. All done in my name. I have even committed murder. What more do you want?

AZZOLINO: We live in an imperfect world.

CHRISTINA: Oh, be your own man...for once! I look at you and your eyes are made of lint, and so you can sit there and send me to hell. In the name of our friendship, what sort of man are you?

AZZOLINO: I am ashamed. I know you suffer – have suffered.

CHRISTINA: Must it always be the sword? By God, half the world are women! They've learned subversion, to keep their teeth in their mouths and the rope off their backs. Why not try that?

AZZOLINO: Alas, are women free? I speak to you as to a man who has been a king but who, as a woman, has that compassion not only to save the life of a child but to respond to the poor and needy, those in your own service, who, I may say, are as Croesus compared with the poor devils of Cracow under the yoke.

CHRISTINA: Yet who are the poorest of all? Women, children...the old. Are they the fighters, the creators of war? You say you want me for the fight, and it's true, I was bred as a man, despising the weakness of women. I begin to question the favour. To be invited to join the killing, why, where's the advantage? Half the world rapes and destroys – must the women, the other half, join in?

AZZOLINO: It's a pretty point.

CHRISTINA: Pretty?

AZZOLINO: Peace and human dignity are not to be guarded without cost.

CHRISTINA: Guarded from what? From whom? I speak not only of the battlefield. I have been in the courtroom and sat through the cases of murder, and robbery with violence. Who does this – the women? I begin to see that I have been a traitor to my sex – oh, I believed, when I commanded an army, that I fought for the weak and helpless. We fought for land! And the conscripted men got none of it, poor devils...ripped away from their fields – for I don't condemn every man as a murdering brute, far from it, or we'd not have survived this far. But when I think of it...young men destroyed, infants burned in their cradles...women violated...how wrong, how wrong I have been to condemn women for their weakness...they have kept us alive!

AZZOLINO: No-one denies this. We revere the mother. We depend on her...on her love.

CHRISTINA: But there is no respect. Only power is respected. Who respects slavery, the dispossessed? A women acquiesces in her slavery, and why? For the chains of her own flesh...blood, bone, sinew! We should listen to them! They know how to share rather than take ...by God, they share their very bodies with their own young, with us! They give. And we think nothing of it.

AZZOLINO: Do not the Scriptures tell us...the meek shall inherit the earth?

CHRISTINA: But you still want me for Queen-General of Poland. No. No more killing. I begin to perceive that I am a woman. What that is, heaven knows...the philosophy is yet to be written, there is a world to be explored.

AZZOLINO: A world without action?

CHRISTINA: (*Shows him a plate she has been playing with.*) Beautiful, don't you think? From San Bernardino. So blue. But the dye was poisonous, it killed the potters who used it. Until one day they put down their brushes, all of them. The Count was powerless, he had not the skills himself. The blue is softer now, not so angry. I never saw the nature of it. Women submit, not from weakness, but for love. I have been betrayed. This... (*She slaps her abdomen.*) ...this has been betrayed.

AZZOLINO: You are upset. It is the accident with the child, it has distressed you. Do not distress yourself. Be calm.

CHRISTINA: You are afraid that I shall be hysterical? Yes, I too have despised hysterical women. You want me, all of you, as a man. You will allow me in...as your confederate...to suit your purposes –

AZZOLINO: But you are magnificent! Think what you could not do for Poland! Poland can give you the power to contribute…with meaning…to extend yourself. A new purpose.

CHRISTINA: (*Pause.*) And can Poland give me a child?

AZZOLINO: Christina… (*Helplessly.*) …if you see that as your function –

CHRISTINA: Why not? Why must I make apology, or prove my case? It is my nature. True, in my case an alternative has been offered – I have been offered the choice of an active life. In God's name, why must I choose?

AZZOLINO: You could have married.

CHRISTINA: And been denied my mind.

AZZOLINO: But that is nature.

CHRISTINA: Nature is us! We are nature! It is we who change and create change! If you want my mind, then you must take my body. I see it so clearly now. I have been denied my birthright. I have been denied the very centre of myself. Why is it so warm down there? Why is it so cold here?

(*Silence.*)

AZZOLINO: So your answer to Poland is no.

CHRISTINA: Cannot you give me a child?

AZZOLINO: Christina, please…!

CHRISTINA: Is that so bizarre?

AZZOLINO: I beg you…

CHRISTINA: What would it cost you? I'm a woman, Decio, and I've no-one to weep for.

AZZOLINO: My dear, you have had a whole country. And could have, a second time.

CHRISTINA: They were not my children. Lucia can weep, she has someone to weep for. Look at me, my eyes are dry. I have nothing. You offer me the whole world – for nothing. The privilege of action…at the cost of oneself. What sort of bargain is that?

AZZOLINO: But we must all submit to circumstance –

CHRISTINA: Why? Why should we? What are you, a fool or a liar, I shall beat you up in a minute.

AZZOLINO: Christina...

CHRISTINA: Look at me, what am I? I'm even beginning to grow a beard. I'm to be what I'd have given half my life for once – I'm to be a man!

AZZOLINO: Christina, stop it, you're becoming unreasonable!

(*She picks up the whip and slashes at him spitefully. He grapples for it, then dodges round the table. She chases him, half laughing, half crying.*)

Christina, stop it, you're getting excited.

CHRISTINA: I want my children. Where are they...where are my children?

AZZOLINO: Christina...

CHRISTINA: Where's my daughter, where's my son, you've cheated me, all of you!

AZZOLINO: Now stop it...ow!

CHRISTINA: Don't tell me what I can have if I fight. I won't fight. I won't fight, I tell you, I won't fight! If you want arms and legs to blow up, make them yourself. I want my children, do you hear...I want my children. (*She flops down, and begins to cry.*) I want my children and I won't fight. I won't fight, I tell you – I won't fight!

(*She catches him with a slash as he skirts round the table. He reverses quickly and she strikes at him again.*)

AZZOLINO: Not on the face, Christina, not on the face!

CHRISTINA: I won't fight.

(*They are both breathless.*)

AZZOLINO: Pax...pax – then what will you do? (*He is breathless.*) What can be achieved without it?

CHRISTINA: Oh you fool – everything. (*Ecstatic.*) Everything! Everything, you fools... everything!

(*She approaches him, dropping the whip. She embraces him.*)

(*Mood change.*) Everything...oh please...

(*She reaches up to kiss him. And he flinches away from her. CHRISTINA becomes hysterical.*

LUCIA enters quickly. She and the CARDINAL confer, she shakes a hand, as to indicate not to interfere.)

AZZOLINO: Is she often like this?

CHRISTINA: I can hear you, you know.

(*CHRISTINA recovers.*)

AZZOLINO: You are recovered?

CHRISTINA: I am well. (*She crosses, to exit at a distance.*) You must come and see my new library. Volumes you won't find anywhere else.

AZZOLINO: I look forward to that.

CHRISTINA: Till our next meeting then.

(*She blows her nose loudly on her skirt, and goes.*)

LUCIA: My poor lady.

AZZOLINO: We are indebted to you for your loving care.

LUCIA: Thank you, father.

AZZOLINO: A great, brave woman. Fine intellect.

LUCIA: Learned.

AZZOLINO: And caring.

LUCIA: Indeed. We are all in her debt.

AZZOLINO: I echo that.

LUCIA: (*Sighs.*) Nothing to look at, of course.

(*She pats her hair.*)

They exchange a smile and exit.)

The End.